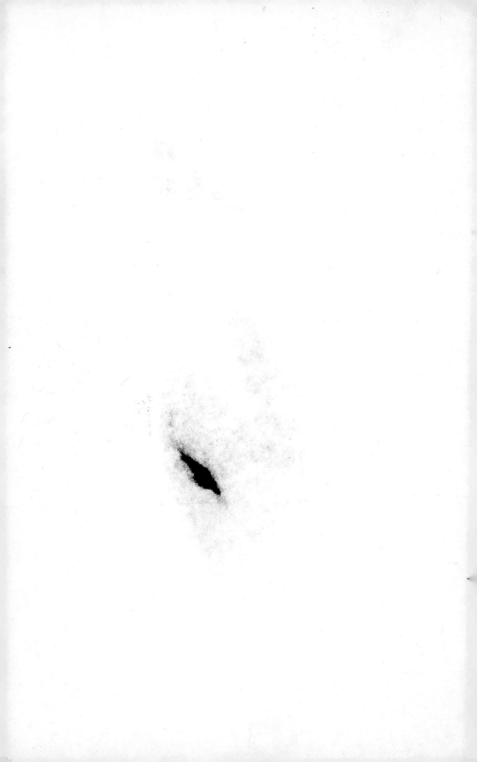

The Great White Lie

JACK GRATUS

The Great White Lie

*Slavery, Emancipation
and Changing Racial Attitudes*

Monthly Review Press
New York and London

Copyright ©1973 by Jack Gratus
All Rights Reserved

Library of Congress Cataloging in Publication Data
Gratus, Jack.
　The great white lie.
　Includes bibliographical references.
　1. Slavery in the British West Indies. 2. Slavery in Great
Britain—Anti-Slavery movements. 3. Slave trade—Africa,
West. I. Title.
HT1091.G69　　301.44'93　　72-84113　　ISBN 0-85345-
268-7

First Printing

Monthly Review Press
116 West 14th Street, New York, N.Y. 10011
33/37 Moreland Street, London, E.C. 1

Manufactured in the United States of America

Contents

Contents

Illustrations

Following page 101

Jamaica negroes cutting cane in their working dresses; an idealised view painted by M. De la Beche. From *Notes on the Present Condition of the Negroes in Jamaica*, 1825, by H. T. De la Beche. (*Reproduced by permission of the Trustees of the British Museum*)

Branding a negress; the frontispiece to Theodore Canot's memoirs, *Twenty Years a Slaver*, 1854. (*Reproduced by permission of the Trustees of the British Museum*)

Mutiny on board a slave ship; from C. D. Wadstrom's *Essay on Colonization*, 1794. (*Reproduced by permission of the Trustees of the British Museum*)

The boycott of West Indian sugar. James Gillray's cartoon of George III and his family, March 1792. (*Reproduced by permission of the Trustees of the British Museum*)

Following page 190

Oroonoko. The death of Imoinda; the frontispiece by Grignion to the 1776 edition of Thomas Southerne's play. (*Reproduced by permission of the Trustees of the British Museum*)

Thomas Clarkson's map of the sources of the anti-slavery movement; from his *History of the Abolition of the Slave Trade*, 1839. (*Reproduced by permission of the Trustees of the British Museum*)

A street map of Clapham Common, circa 1801. (*Reproduced by permission of the Clapham Antiquarian Society*)

The medallion of the anti-slavery movement, donated by Josiah Wedgwood. (*Reproduced by permission of Josiah Wedgwood and Sons Ltd.*)

The entertainer, Charles Mathews, in his two costumes of Agamemnon, the runaway slave, and Jonathan W. Doubikin, his young master. From *The London Mathews*, 1823. (*Reproduced by permission of the Trustees of the British Museum*)

Now do I feel how all men are deceived,
Reading of nations and their works, in faith,
Faith given to vanity and emptiness.

The Prelude—William Wordsworth

Let your honest heart be merry,
British boys will still be right,
Till they prove that black is white;
Black is white; black is white;
Till they prove that black is white.

The Blackamoor—Charles Dibdin and
H. B. Dudley, 1775

Introduction: The Abolition Myth

The Atlantic slave trade, the crux of the British, American and European slave system, was the largest forced transportation of human beings from one part of the globe to another in the world's history, and certainly one of the greatest unnatural disasters of all times. It lasted approximately 250 years and estimates put the total figure of slaves transported as high as forty million.[1]

Contrary to the myth which grew up in the nineteenth century and has now become hallowed by time, slavery was not simply a business conducted by a single and clearly identifiable group of cruel and unscrupulous individuals. It was a complete, all-embracing economic system involving, directly and indirectly, the colonists of the West Indies, the inhabitants of large areas of Africa, and countless numbers of people in Europe, Britain and America.

British West Indian slavery was an integral part of a triangular trade in which manufactured goods for barter, such as textiles, iron, guns and spirits, left Britain for the Guinea coast, there to be exchanged for, among other goods, human cargoes. On reaching the New World these were in turn exchanged for raw materials such as sugar and cotton which were transported to Britain to be turned into manufactured products, thus completing the triangle. In this way the system perpetuated itself for the benefit primarily of those who operated it—the plantation owners, the merchants, manufacturers, ship owners, and the bankers who supplied them with the capital necessary to run their respective businesses. Profits derived from the system found their way through reinvestment into other industries and agriculture, and it is not an exaggeration to say that they contributed substantially to the development of the Industrial Revolution on which Britain's nineteenth-century prosperity was based.[2]

As it was evil in every respect, whoever touched slavery was tainted by it, even many of those who eventually came to oppose it. Both Zachary Macaulay and James Stephen, two of the leading abolitionists, had lived in the West Indies, the first as a plantation manager and the second as a lawyer. As their writings indicate, they were unable to shake off completely the attitudes to blacks which they absorbed during their residence there. The international consequences of the system were so cataclysmic as to defy complete documentation and as to far exceed both the short- and long-term effects of any natural catastrophe. Britain, America and Africa are to this day suffering from that period of their history, and will go on suffering for a long time to come.

Even today most whites seem unable or reluctant to understand that the traumas of the past live on in the present, and that the racial conflicts of today have their origins not in the mists of antiquity but in a specific period of their history. The blacks, however, as the victims have been aware of it all along. Martin Luther King once commented that all too few people realised to what extent slavery had 'scarred the soul and wounded the spirit of the black man'.[3] Some black radicals are even more insistent about going back to slavery to understand the present. According to Leroi Jones the history of Western culture begins for the American black with the importation of slaves.[4] The same can be said of the population of the West Indies. For them their African past can be but 'an emotional abstraction',[5] whereas their slave past is the factual foundation upon which their present has been built.

Whites find it conveniently easy to forget that neither the American blacks nor the West Indians asked to be transported. Politicians who speak of West Indian immigrants in Britain as 'strangers' in our midst, and who count heads with obsessive persistence, are denying the historic fact that the immigrants are the direct descendants of the slaves their forbears removed forcibly from Africa. They, the immigrants and the American blacks, are justified in demanding that the whites remember their history and cease to treat them as unwanted anachronisms. The black man in the West, through the white man's own act, is an integral part of the latter's world.

Understanding and awareness by the whites has not always been made any easier by historians of slavery and, as far as Britain is concerned, of its imperial past, possibly because they were part of what they were trying to describe. There is a mathematical theorem which is apposite: a mathematical system cannot be completely self-descriptive since all the rules necessary for describing the system cannot be stated within it.[6] This theorem can be applied equally well to any political or economic system; thus the operators of slavery and the slave trade and their opponents, as well as those who wrote their history, were not able to stand far enough outside the system to describe it objectively, nor generally to analyse it accurately. What certain historians did was to perpetuate the abolition myth according to which the slave system was not a system at all. Rather it was a large and unsavoury business run by some very nasty characters who treated the poor blacks badly until a handful of white heroes organised the entire country against them, routed them after a long battle, gave liberty to the blacks, and cleansed the nation for ever more of the taint of guilt and racism. Certainly this is still the view the man in the street and his children have of their past.

'The unwary, unostentatious, and inglorious crusade of England against slavery may probably be regarded as among the three or four perfectly virtuous pages comprised in the history of nations', was how the historian W. E. Lecky saw it.[7] Sir Reginald Coupland's classic study *The British Anti-Slavery Movement* is a good example of the way in which historical fact, interpreted by an historian defending rather than examining objectively his nation's past, can be relegated to the realms of mythology. 'It would be hard to overstate what the movement has owed to the character of its leaders,' he concluded, 'but they could not have done what they did if a great body of opinion among the British people had not been resolutely and persistently bent on the destruction of an evil which Britain had once done so much to create and sustain. There are dark and dubious passages enough in British history, but that one at least is clean.'

The cleanliness of this passage of British history has been seriously and successfully challenged by more recent historians. Eric Williams, the Prime Minister of Trinidad and Tobago, who was for many years the Professor of Political and Social Science at Howard University, Washington D.C., published in 1944 a vigorous attack from an economic standpoint on the Coupland version of this period of history. He demonstrated that the success of the anti-slavery movement was largely dependent on the decline of the West Indies as a source of colonial wealth for Great Britain.[8] Since his book there has been continual controversy on the subject, though it seems that now a middle road may have been reached between the 'philanthropic' and 'economic' view of abolition. Both philanthropy and economics helped to bring down the system.

When talking about the history of attitudes it is not possible to be rigid about dates. Unlike wars, changes in social views do not begin and end at precise times. What we think of as 'Victorian' began years before Victoria's reign and was on the decline before her death. Dates do serve one purpose: they help set the scene. The two approximate dates which concern me in this book are 1780 and 1880 because it was during these years that the great propaganda war was fought between the pro- and anti-slavery factions in Britain and America. It was during this period that philanthropy and evangelical Christianity fostered a spirit of responsibility and concern for the welfare of others that became one of the motivating factors in Britain's late nineteenth-century colonial expansion into Africa.

The anti-slavery movement won the victory against the slave owners and their supporters, who were usually known by the generic title of 'West Indian' so that where this phrase is used it should not be confused with the present-day populations of the West Indian islands. The slaves were given a semblance of freedom by the Abolition of Slavery Act of 1833, but the terrible irony is that it was views similar to, if not as extreme as, those of the pro-slavers which won the uneasy peace and which helped destroy the freedom of the blacks for another hundred years and more.

The belief cherished by Britons and Americans alike that

for all their sins they are more humanitarian than anyone else in the world was another view which found considerable favour in the course of the anti-slavery debate. The fact that they operated, supported and benefited from the slave system, that they vigorously opposed every measure to ameliorate it or abolish it, and that in the end they did so only half-heartedly resulted not in critical self-examination but in national self-congratulations. A period which should have been remembered with humility was recalled with triumphant pride as proof of that great humanitarianism of which they boasted. That, in turn, became the British excuse for subjugating blacks whenever and wherever they opposed the advances of white 'civilisa-tion', and is still used by Americans as a justification for their policies of aggression in the Far East.

The intellectual battle between the abolitionists and their opponents was superficially characterised as between, on the one hand, the heroes who believed that all men were created equal and were entitled to liberty, and, on the other, the villains who believed that all blacks were natural slaves because they were pagan and inferior. In fact its range was much wider. It involved people of every class of white society, and it reached down to the very depths of that society's existence. When the philosopher Montesquieu affirmed ironically in 1748 that 'it is impossible to suppose these creatures to be men, because allowing them to be men a suspicion would follow that we ourselves are not Christians',[9] he was posing the crucial existential problem that troubled white society. If slaves were men, not sub-human, then the entire society was unchristian because the system involved everyone so long as it was condoned and permitted to continue. On the other hand, if 'these creatures' were not men, Christ's martyrdom and message were a fraud and a lie.

The abolitionists were first and foremost religious zealots who held equally strong views on the corruption of society in general as on the slave trade and slavery. The fight between them and the West Indians was for them another aspect of the continual war between 'good'—represented by themselves—and 'evil'—represented by the pro-slavers.

Leading churchmen, many of whom supported the latter, by doing so helped bring Christianity into disrepute and made a mockery of its basic tenets. Their biblical 'justifications' for white domination which had their origins in the slavery debate are still heard today in those countries where the white man feels threatened by the black.

It can, I think, be argued that one of the results of the conflict of ideas was to focus doubt on western ideals of morality because it forced the protagonists to examine their beliefs and find them, in terms of national experience, wanting. This continued so long as slavery continued. After the main battle had ended and after the battlefield had been cleared of its aged and exhausted combatants there remained the detritus of racism. Anti-black attitudes had become transformed into economic and political weapons.

The abolitionists in Britain like William Wilberforce, Thomas Clarkson and Thomas Buxton saw their campaign as both 'positive' and 'negative'; the latter policy was the destruction of the slave trade by persuading or coercing participating nations to cease the traffic. The 'positive' policy can be summarised as Christianity, commerce, and colonialism.[10] To destroy slavery once and for all, they argued, it was essential to maintain a legitimate trade with Africa, to make the heathen blacks Christian, and to bestow on them the benefits of white Christian morality. Since the basis of their 'positive' policy was a belief in the inherent superiority of white Christian civilisation, this belief became entrenched and respectable, and in a less obvious but more insidious way than outright racism became the moral and religious *raison d'être* for colonial expansion and imperial arrogance.

By examining what the leaders of the abolition movement —and their opponents—said in parliament, in the press, in essays and tracts, in diaries and letters, I have attempted to trace how the very successes of the movement became distorted into narrow, chauvinistic imperialism, and how the great lie of white supremacy, far from being destroyed, was paradoxically reinforced and strengthened.

The noble savage, the comic 'nigger', the degraded slave, and the system of slavery itself were favourite subjects for poets and comedians alike. Songs, plays and poetry showed sympathy for the plight of the slaves and contempt for the blacks in equal measure, and the importance of the conflict can be seen from the number of satirical sketches devoted to it by leading cartoonists.

Through extracts from documents and contemporary writings, quoted without comment between each chapter, I have tried to expose the whole sordid business of slavery and the slave trade. These extracts form a disconnected but continuous narrative which gives both the background and substance to the intellectual and cultural processes discussed in the text. The extracts take the reader from the capture and purchase of slaves on the African coast, the journey to the New World, the sales, plantation life and plantation death.

A wall of language was built up around the slave system, disguising its horror in bland statistics and shielding its cruelty and inhumanity in legalisms and officialese so that those who looked on but did not directly participate in the system were more easily able to ignore its existence. That some did not, provides the starting point for this book.

PART ONE

Letter from Thomas Starke, Virginia landowner and London merchant, to James Westmore, African trader.

London, Oct. 22, 1700

I have here enclosed an invoice and bill of lading for the cargo of goods shipped on board your ship, African Gally . . . and these are to desire you to make your best way . . . to the Grand Coast of Guinea and there purchase what Guinea grain, Teeth and gold dust you can. . . . I would have you go down to New Callebarr and at every opening where you may with safety anchor and send your boat on shore and trade for Negroes [and] Teeth. . . . I am informed there is plenty of Slaves and Teeth, and if any encouragement you may stay six or seven days. . . .

(*Documents Illustrative of the History of the Slave Trade*— Elizabeth Donnan (ed))

About three miles [further] we halted in a thick wood, and kindled our fires for the night. We were all, by this time, very much fatigued, having, as I judged, travelled this day thirty miles; but no person was heard to complain. . . . When we had finished out supper of kouskous, moistened with some boiling water, and put the slaves in irons, we all lay down to sleep.

The slaves are commonly secured by putting the right leg of one, and the left leg of another into the same pair of fetters. By supporting the fetters with string they can walk though very slowly. Every four slaves are likewise fastened together by the necks with a strong rope of twisted thongs, and in the night an additional pair of fetters is put on their hands, and sometimes a light chain passed round their necks.

They were led out in their fetters every morning to the shade of the tamarind tree where they were encouraged to play at games of hazard and sing diverting songs to keep up their spirits; for though some of them sustained the hardships of their situation with amazing fortitude, the greater part were very much dejected, and would sit all day in a sort of sullen melancholy with their eyes fixed upon the ground.

(*Travels to the Interior Parts of Africa*—
Mungo Park, 1799)

I

Questions of Policy

On the 22nd of May 1787 twelve men met in a room in George Yard in the City of London and came to a decision which one of them recorded in neat handwriting in a ledger. Having taken into consideration the slave trade, the note said, they resolved that it was both impolitic and unjust.[1] Two months later they took a lease on a suite of offices at 18 Old Jewry. They called themselves the Committee for the Abolition of the Slave Trade.

Ten of the twelve were Quakers, members of the Society of Friends, which for a number of years had issued public statements condemning the trade on religious and humanitarian grounds. The other two men, both of them also deeply religious, had virtually committed their lives to the cause they and all the many others who were to join and follow them saw as no less than holy and sacred.

Thomas Clarkson was the prime mover of the Committee, and by unanimous decision Granville Sharp was elected its chairman. Sharp was the elder of the two. He was born in 1735, the product of an unbroken line of theologians; the Archbishop of York was his grandfather. He himself was a scholarly man who devoted his life to the pursuit of knowledge, the main source of his interest and inspiration being the Bible. He was one of fourteen children, and his father's resources were used up in the education of Granville's brothers, so he was apprenticed to a linen draper. But his intellectual curiosity found subjects for study and argument even in a drapery shop. In order to argue with a fellow-apprentice who quoted from the original Greek in one of their frequent discussions about religion Granville learnt Greek in his spare time. He also learnt Hebrew so that he could debate with a Jewish apprentice on the interpretation of the Old Testament. One of his employers, he found out, had a claim to an obscure barony, and as a result of his researches Granville succeeded in sending him to the House of Lords.

Sharp eventually left the drapery business and took a position as a clerk in the Ordnance Office. In 1765 he came face to face with the slave system, not in the far-off West Indies, but in a London street. At the time he occupied apartments in the house of his brother, a surgeon in Wapping, East London. Black people in that area and in all the major ports were not uncommon; many of them were slaves who had been brought to England by their masters and had absconded rather than return to the West Indies.

One day a slave by the name of Jonathan Strong arrived at the surgeon's house. He had been badly treated by his master, a planter from Barbados, who had abandoned him when the slave's ill-health made him no longer useful. Granville Sharp became acquainted with Strong during the time his brother was treating him.

When the slave had recovered sufficiently to be of use again, his master seized him and resold him for £30. Strong sent a desperate message to Granville Sharp, who secured his immediate release. But Strong's troubles were not over. His master made another attempt to capture him, but under the threat of prosecution his would-be purchaser released him.

By now Strong had become a minor *cause célèbre*. Like many slaves before him, he believed that as soon as he touched the soil of England and had been baptised he was a free man, as it was generally understood that slavery and Christianity were mutually incompatible, at least in England. So firmly had this belief been held and acted upon by generations of slaves before Strong that slave owners in England had approached the Solicitor-General and Attorney-General for their opinion. In 1729 these gentlemen pronounced as follows: 'A slave, by coming from the West Indies to Great Britain or Ireland, does not become free and his master's property or right in him is not thereby determined or varied.' They added that 'baptism does not bestow freedom on him nor make any alteration in his temporal conditions in these kingdoms'.[2]

That was how the law stood when Granville Sharp involved himself in Strong's plight, and he was determined to change it. Almost single-handedly he took on the might of the law and the West Indian planters, the most powerful of whom were by this time resident in England. Almost single-handedly he beat them.

Strong's case was his first victory, but it was only a partial success. Strong was finally emancipated, but the law, in the person of the Lord Chief Justice, Lord Mansfield, had not made any pronouncement on the legal standing of West Indian slaves in England, nor on slavery in general, which altered the earlier opinion. At least it meant a curtailment of slave dealing in England, and people who up to then had made a fair profit out of catching runaways and either collecting the advertised reward or selling them were now less willing to involve themselves in the business.

Soon after Strong's case, Hylas, an African slave, successfully prosecuted a dealer for having kidnapped his wife and sending her to the West Indies. The man was forced to bring Hylas's wife back and to pay Hylas one shilling in damages.[3]

Two years later Thomas Lewis, a runaway, was dragged one night by his master to a boat lying in the Thames, where he was gagged, tied up and rowed down the river to a ship bound for Jamaica. His screams attracted the attention of the servants of the botanist Sir Joseph Banks. They told Lady Banks what they had found out about Lewis, and she in turn informed Granville Sharp, offering also to pay any legal expenses involved in freeing the runaway.

This time Sharp, who had earned himself the reputation as the slaves' best friend, engaged a well-known barrister and put all his energy into preparing a case against Lewis's master, who pleaded that he had every right to seize Lewis since he was his property. In a stirring speech Lewis's counsel maintained that 'our laws admit of no such property', and the jury were of the same opinion. The case ended with jurymen crying out: 'No property! No property!',[4] but the

Lord Chief Justice was unhappy. 'I don't know what the
consequences may be if the masters were to lose their
property by accidentally bringing their slaves to England.
I hope it will never be finally discussed; for I would have
all masters think them free, and all negroes think they were
not, because then they would both behave better.'[5]

His wish was not to be granted. Two years later, in 1772,
he was faced with just such a decision. Before him in court
was another runaway, James Somersett. He had come to
England from Jamaica with his master, but just before their
return he had run away. His master had tried to seize him,
a habeas corpus writ had been issued by Granville Sharp, and
the master and the captain of the ship on which Somersett
was due to sail were required to show cause why he should
not be released. The master, Granville Sharp was disturbed
to notice, was represented by the same barrister who had
pleaded so convincingly the slave's cause in Lewis's case,
and who now brought forth all the same skill and conviction
to show the court that the laws of England recognised property in slaves.[6]

Somersett's counsel argued that his client was a Christian,
that, as the previous cases had indicated, in a Christian
nation there could be no slavery, and accordingly he should
be freed. Lord Mansfield was now confronted by the question
he had been so reluctant to face: did the state of slavery
exist in English law? He came to his decision. Apologising
for the inconvenience that might follow, he concluded that
positive law in England neither allowed nor approved of it.
James Somersett, and every slave living in England, from
that moment on was free.[7, 8]

Thomas Clarkson, the younger associate of Sharp's on
the Committee for the Abolition of the Slave Trade, was born
in the market town of Wisbech, Cambridgeshire, in 1760.
A large, rugged man, he was impatient and aggressive in
manner with little sense of humour. He spoke as he wrote,
ploddingly and pedantically, and both his readers and his
acquaintances found he could be boring. His wife, in contrast,
was a brilliant conversationalist and an excellent hostess.
During Clarkson's retirement from public life from 1794 to
1804 they lived in a house in the Lake District where they

were visited by many well-known people, including the Wordsworths.

Thirteen years after Somersett's case Clarkson was an undergraduate at Cambridge. He was set as the subject for his Latin thesis: *Anne liceat invitos in servitutem dare?* Is it right to make slaves of others against their will? Displaying a characteristic persistence and the enthusiasm for collecting details which he later put to the service of the abolition movement with great effect, Clarkson read whatever he could on the African slave trade. He obtained access to some manuscript papers of a friend who had been in the trade, and he was also acquainted with some officers who had served in the West Indies. An advertisement drew his attention to a book by a Quaker in Philadelphia, Anthony Benezet, and in it he found all the facts and inspiration he needed.[9]

He read his essay to an audience at the university, and later was awarded the first prize, but something more important happened to him on the way back to London which, like Sharp's meeting with the slave, Strong, altered the course of his life.

'The subject', he wrote in *The History of the Abolition of the Slave Trade*, 'wholly engrossed my thoughts. I became at times very seriously affected while upon the road. I stopped my horse occasionally and dismounted and walked.' Finally he was so overcome that he sat down by the roadside, and there had what amounted to a minor revelation. 'A thought came into my mind that if the contents of the Essay were true it was time some person should see these calamities to their end.'[10]

He suddenly realised that slavery was not merely an abstract problem of purely theoretical application but that it existed in British colonies which were governed by the laws of England, and that its existence was not only condoned by the British public but also actively encouraged by them. 'I then began to envy those who had seats in parliament, and who had great riches and widely extended connections which would enable them to take up the cause.'[11]

This was a revealing comment on the political structure

of the day. Popular demands for reform which involved
channelling and directing public sentiment were to change
that structure to some extent, but not yet. The men with
connections, the associates with seats in parliament, were
still absolutely essential in any design to influence the legislature. They began to rally round quite soon, for, as Clarkson
found out, there were others willing, like himself, to devote
their energies to fighting slavery. 'I had been thrown
suddenly among these as into a new world of friends.'[12]

He immediately began translating his dissertation and
in 1786 it was published under the title of *An Essay on the
Slavery and Commerce of the Human Species, Particularly the
African*. The people with wealth took notice of this young
man who had been destined for the Church, but had found
another more urgent calling. 'Both Lord and Lady Scarsdale
read my work with attention. Lady Scarsdale lamented that
she might possibly offend near and dear connections who had
interests in the West Indies by doing so; but that conscious
of no intention to offend these, and considering the duties
of religion to be the first to be attended to, she should be
pleased to become useful in so good a cause.'[13]

Though they were different in interests and temperament,
both Sharp and Clarkson were men of great personal
courage. Sharp was the scholar, Clarkson the man of action,
never happier than when on his frequent tours around the
country on behalf of this Committee. On one of these fact-
finding missions to Liverpool, the port whose livelihood
depended on the slave trade and was therefore understandably unfriendly to abolitionists, he found himself on the
pier, gazing at some small boats tossing in the rough seas.
Suddenly he realised that he was surrounded by eight or
nine evil-looking sailors, one of whom he suspected from
his enquiries had murdered another sailor. They closed in
on him and pushed him back to about a yard from the edge.
He ran at them and, being powerfully built, knocked one of
them down to make his escape, but not without receiving a
few bad blows.[14]

Anyone who at that period interested himself in slavery
was bound to come into contact with the one group who
had spoken out against it consistently—the Quakers—and

though both Sharp and Clarkson were members of the Established Church, they met and corresponded with a number of them who were prominent in their Society's agitation against the system. In 1761 the Quakers had agreed to exclude from membership anyone concerned in slave dealing, and in 1783 they brought to parliament a petition against the trade, an action so unprecedented that it was received with stunned respect. 'It does credit to the feelings of the most mild and humane set of Christians in the world,' said the Prime Minister, Lord North, 'but I am afraid it will be found impossible to abolish the trade because it has, in some measure, become necessary to almost every nation in Europe.'[15]

It was only natural that the Quakers should eventually join forces with Thomas Clarkson to form the Abolition Committee, and right and just that Granville Sharp, who had successfully challenged the financial interests of the West Indians, should be the Committee's chairman.

Within two months of its formation it had requested Clarkson to go to Bristol, Liverpool, and any other places he considered necessary to collect material and information on the slave trade. It had been in touch with the President of the Pennsylvania Society for the Abolition of Slavery, and with Brissot de Warville in France, whose activities on behalf of the slaves in the French West Indies had earned him praise and damnation. And it had elected Josiah Wedgwood, the wealthy potter and philanthropist, a member—the first in a long list of famous names recruited to the cause.[16]

The most important event in the Committee's brief existence was the formulation of its tactics. 'Our immediate aim', it wrote to the Pennsylvania Society, 'is, by diffusing a knowledge of the subject . . . to interest men of every description in the abolition of the traffic, but especially those from whom any alteration must proceed—the members of our legislature.'[17] Slavery itself was not its concern, just the slave trade. 'It was of consequence which of the two evils the Committee was to select as the object for their labours,' Clarkson recalled later. 'It appeared soon to be the sense of the Committee that to aim at the removal of both would be to aim at too much, and that by doing this we might lose all.'[18]

Could slavery be divorced from the slave trade? The
Committee thought so. Were they not trying to separate
the inseparable? The Committee thought not. 'Could that
infernal traffic be annihilated, the condition of slavery in
the islands would be meliorated', wrote the Dean of Middleham in one of the first tracts distributed by the Committee.
'The native negroes would be more tractable, more readily
acquire the regard of those among whom they were born,
and be more readily converted to Christianity because they
might be more easily informed. At length, by the mild,
uniform operation of Christian principles slavery itself
might be abolished.'[19]

It sounded in every respect a reasonable policy, one which
would immediately commend itself to every rational
human being. There was nothing dangerous about it;
nothing too revolutionary. Even the planters in the West
Indies would come to realise in time that it would promote
their interests rather than work against them. 'Let us first
for a moment, look upon the unfortunate Africans in the
light of *cattle*', Clarkson suggested in another essay. 'Is it not
in the power of any farmer, who prefers breeding to purchasing, to supply himself with animals of labour from his own
stock?' Considered as men, he continued, the Africans if
treated well would naturally increase because they were
'peculiarly prolific by nature'.[20] Abolition of the slave trade
would mean that the planter would save money which
before he spent in buying slaves, and in twenty years after
the abolition the slaves would be more valuable, both on
the open market and to the planter himself. 'They would
have been inured from their infancy to labour . . . and be
more hardy and capable of the plantation work than any of
their predecessors who, having led perhaps a life of indolence
in their own country, have been but little capable of sus-
taining the fatigue which they have been sentenced to
undergo.' The planter would cease to be the tyrant and
become the shepherd; a golden age would reign in the
colonial plains, 'and a spot that was once the scene of
accumulated persecution and murder be the mansions of
peace, security, happiness and joy'.[21]

It seemed to the Committee so obvious and sane, and

after talking to members of both Houses of Parliament, to Established clergy and Dissenting ministers, to members of the universities and to representatives of the manufacturing districts, they came to the conclusion that they were not alone in this opinion. It seemed that everyone they spoke to loathed the vicious white traders who bought the innocent slaves at their stations on the west coast of Africa; everyone detested the vile captains of the slave ships who packed them in cramped holds to transport them across the Atlantic; and everyone hated the brutal overseers and managers on the plantations who worked them swiftly and painfully to death. The whole weight of public feeling was on the side of abolition.

There is nothing in the minutes of the Committee to suggest that anyone quarrelled with its tactics. All decisions were carried unanimously and Granville's signature appeared on the reports. But Sharp's biographer, Edward Lascelles, suggests that he did not support them wholeheartedly and that he did not take an active share in the Committee's work. 'I told the gentlemen that it would be impossible for me to undertake any additional trouble and they answered that they would only desire the use of my name and signature', Sharp wrote to his brother.[22]

By the end of the 1780s reform was in the air. The Abolition Committee, which in due course became the nucleus of the Abolition Society, was one of a number of reforming groups which had been founded in response to the enthusiasm for progressive measures. To press for wider parliamentary representation the Society for Constitutional Information, suspended since 1784, was revived in 1791, and the Corresponding Society for the encouragement of constitutional discussion was launched in January 1792.[23] The penal system which permitted the death sentence for the theft of more than twelve pence and in ten months of 1785 hanged ninety-six people was beginning to be the subject of fierce criticism.[24] But, of all, the anti-slave trade movement captured much of the attention and interest of the public and of the wealthy philanthropists who had the time and money to devote themselves to good causes.

Energetic, enthusiastic, naive: the Committee for the

Abolition of the Slave Trade and its friends prepared themselves for a bloody but brief battle against the forces of evil for the soul of the nation. 'Never was the heart of man so expanded', Clarkson remembered. 'Never were its sympathies so generally and so perseveringly excited. . . . In private life it had enabled us to distinguish the virtuous from the more vicious part of the community. It has shown the general philanthropist; it has unmasked the vicious in spite of his pretension to virtue. . . . It has shown us who, in the legislative and executive offices of our country, are fit to save, and who to destroy the nation.'[25]

Here, one of the slaves belonging to the coffle (slave train), who had travelled with great difficulty for the last three days, was found unable to proceed any farther; his master proposed therefore to exchange him for a young slave girl belonging to one of the townspeople. The poor girl was ignorant of her fate until the bundles were all tied up in the morning and the coffle ready to depart; when, coming with some other young women to see the coffle set out, her master took her by the hand and delivered her to the [other slave master]. Never was a face of serenity more suddenly changed into one of the deepest distress; the terror she manifested on having the load put upon her head and the rope fastened round her neck, and the sorrow with which she bade adieu to her companions were truly affecting. . . .

They were all very inquisitive; but they viewed me at first with looks of horror, and repeatedly asked if my countrymen were cannibals. They were desirous to know what became of the slaves after they had crossed the salt water. I told them that they were employed in cultivating the land; but they would not believe me; and one of them putting his hand upon the ground said with great simplicity, 'Have you really got such ground as this to set your feet upon?'

(Mungo Park)

The afternoon was the usual time for trade, but sometimes it would last for three days together, which being my proper business I never neglected. If it ended soon, I would sometimes take a trip to the neighbouring towns, and return'd home to supper, after which I amused myself with writing, reading and visiting neighbours.

(Travels into the Inland Parts of Africa—
Francis Moore, 1738)

The Slave System and Some of its Critics

'Now what a glorious and advantageous trade this is, as every European society . . . must be sensible of. It is the hinge on which all the trade of this globe moves, for put a stop to the peopling of the European plantations abroad, which could be done from no other country but this without depopulating Europe—I say, put a stop to the slave trade and all the others cease of course.'[1] This enthusiastic message by one of the surgeons employed on the Guinea coast by the Royal African Company in 1725 echoes accurately the general attitude at the beginning of the eighteenth century towards the entire slave system. This system embraced a good deal more than merely transporting thousands of people every year from Africa to America and the West Indies.

'The most approved judges of the commercial interests of these kingdoms have been of the opinion that our West India and Africa trades are the most nationally beneficial of any we carry on. . . . The great brood of seamen . . . and the daily bread of the most considerable part of our British manufacturers are owing primarily to the labour of negroes . . . the first happy instruments of raising our plantations', was how Malachy Postlethwayt regarded it in 1746.[2] An economist, he was aware of the beneficial balance of payments the trade brought to Britain. 'What renders the negro trade still more estimable and important is that near nine-tenths of those negroes are paid for in Africa with British produce and manufactures only. . . . We send no specie or bullion to pay for the products of Africa.' In summing up the advantages of the slave system he said, 'As the present prosperity and splendour of the British colonies have been owing to negro labour, so not only their future advancement, but even their very being depends upon our pursuing the same measures in this respect as our competitors do.'[3]

By the middle of the century European exploitation of African slave labour had been going on for 240 years. Portugal and Spain were the first nations to engage in it. It was they who rapidly established the procedure whereby slavery and slave trading became systematised. At the end of the fifteenth century and the beginning of the sixteenth they were conquering and exploring the New World. Mineral-rich lands and limitless expanses of arable soil became theirs for the taking—and they took and took. The native Indians were quickly defeated by superior weapons, their societies broken up, and their cultural cohesion destroyed. Subdued, demoralised, and in the main, docile, they provided the labour to work the mines and the new plantations of sugar and tobacco.

The Europeans were greedy and impatient. The home countries were demanding more and more of the colonies' produce and paying higher and higher prices for it, and it did not take long before the new colonists found the Indians insufficient in number and strength to withstand the enormous strain of endless toil on and below the earth. The labour force began to diminish.

In the march of European colonial aggrandisement the cross of Christ was never more than a few steps away from the banner of the soldier. On occasions, as we shall see later, it actually preceded it. The Portuguese and the Spanish priests who accompanied the conquerors of the New World seized what to them was the God-given opportunity to convert and christianise the heathen, but the hearts of some were moved to pity when they saw their potential converts dying off like flies.

Bartolomé de Las Casas, the Bishop of Chiapa, proposed to the Spanish Crown in 1518 that Africans be purchased as slaves to replace the Indians. The proposal, motivated by Christian pity, was rejected by Cardinal Ximenes for the reason that it was unjust to reduce one race to slavery in order to save another. As Clarkson pointed out, this was a lesson to men in government, 'for evil, when once sanctioned by governments, spreads in a tenfold degree, and nay, unless seasonably checked becomes so ramified as to effect the reputation of a country and to render its own removal scarcely possible without detriment to the political concerns of the state'.[4] Which is exactly what happened. After Ximenes's death, Charles V of Spain encouraged the slave trade from Africa. Though he later regretted his decision and issued orders to emancipate the slaves, slavery was revived when he entered a monastery.[5] By 1576, 40,000 African slaves had been exported to Spanish America.[6]

Las Casas was a Dominican, and others of his order, such as Jean-Baptiste Du Tetre in the seventeenth century, considered slavery to be repugnant to Christianity. In 1537 Pope Paul III declared that owners of Indian slaves should be denied the sacraments, and just as the West Indian colonists of the seventeenth and eighteenth centuries objected to any interference in their slave-holding activities by a British parliament, so the Portuguese and Spanish colonists rose up in anger against their respective mother countries when they attempted to ameliorate or emancipate the Indian slaves. And just as the British West Indies in the nineteenth century expelled the Methodists for attempting to help the slaves, so the Brazilians two centuries earlier threw out the Jesuits for aiding the Indian slaves.

In general the doubts expressed by the early critics of slavery concerned the Indians and not the Africans. Bishop Landa of Mexico condemned Indian slavery but was a strong defender of African slavery, and Du Tetre, who idealised the Indians of the French Caribbean, could comfortably declare, 'to beat a negro is to nourish him'. Worse still, because slavery had become institutionalised, the more the Indians were protected through the efforts of prominent churchmen, the greater was the demand for slaves from Africa. In North America the Indian was marginally better off than the African; in Virginia, for example, though most Africans were slaves, practically all the Indians were free. Later abolitionists like Thomas Clarkson, searching for precedents of anti-slavery from the past, tended to overlook this underlying distinction.

There were some early critics who questioned the slave

trade and the whole system of slavery irrespective of race. In Spain in the sixteenth century Thomas de Mercado, though he regarded Africans as barbarians and criminals, objected to the effects the slave trade was having on them, and was horrified by the cruelty of the slaves' journey from Africa to the colonies. Bartolomé de Albornoz was sceptical of the arguments used by colonists to justify slavery by saying that Africans were better off with whites than with their own people. In the seventeenth century the courageous Jesuit, Vieira, claimed that any man who held another in servitude unjustly was in a state of condemnation, and at the end of the eighteenth century a Capuchin friar, José de Bolonha, was thrown out of Bahia, Brazil, for maintaining that the African trade was unlawful.[7] For the most part, however, the Catholic clergy in Spanish America, like their Protestant brethren in the West Indies, were far more concerned for the souls of the black slaves than for their physical sufferings; and like the Protestants they were not above owning slaves themselves.

2 'In order to transport human beings half across the world— even if they were looked upon and treated simply as cargo— required large numbers of men and plenty of equipment. Ships had to be built and fitted out for two long voyages— one from Europe to the west coast of Africa, and the second from Africa to the Americas. Goods were needed in ever-increasing quantities to be used in the commercial transactions with the black traders for slaves; victuals had to be provided for the sailors and for the slaves once they were on board; and when the latter reached their destination their need for food and clothing continued. In other words, the slaves supplied one kind of demand and in turn created another. Supplying them to the colonists became, therefore, inextricably linked to plantation production in the colonies and to manufacturing industries in the home country. A lucrative triangle of trade was thus established.

Apart from men, equipment and expertise, one thing more was needed. Building and fitting out ships, manufacturing cloth, guns and rum for barter, all these required capital, and lots of it. Men who had money and men who wanted to make money—the established bankers and the speculators—

saw the trade in slaves as an attractive investment even though the risks were high. Ships and their cargoes were sometimes lost and sometimes to save his ship in a storm a captain would jettison his entire consignment of slaves, the healthy and the sick alike.

In 1781 Captain Luke Collingwood, of the slave ship *Zong*, finding that many of the slaves were dying from illness, ordered 132 of them to be flung overboard. In the trials which followed on a disputed claim by the ship's owners against the underwriters it was alleged by the former that the supply of water had become insufficient and therefore, in order to save most of the cargo, it was necessary to jettison some of it. In that case the underwriters had to bear the cost according to the terms of their policy, but not if the slaves merely died of sickness. The verdicts of the trials conflicted, but it was clearly laid down in them that the only questions at issue were that of property and liability for payment, and that the case was legally exactly the same as if it had concerned horses and not human beings.[8]

Even though the majority of the slave ships arrived at their destinations, the mortality rate on the journey from Africa, which was known as the Middle Passage, was high. Disease, suicide and mutinies were the three main causes of death. But the profits were high, too: 100 to 300 per cent with good luck.[9]

With such rich yields awaiting the adventurous and un-squeamish it was inevitable that other European nations would join in the trade. In 1564, with Queen Elizabeth's blessings, Sir John Hawkins set out in the flagship *Jesus* with another expedition to Africa for more slaves, his first venture two years before having proved highly successful; and so began Britain's participation. In time it was to bring her vast profits, but at first trading was carried on in a perfunctory manner. With the acquisition of extensive Caribbean territories in the middle of the seventeenth century and again after the Peace of Utrecht in 1713, the demand by British planters for more slaves gave impetus to the British trade.

In 1663 an attempt was made to put the trade on a proper footing with the grant of monopolistic trading rights to the Company of Royal Adventurers Trading in Africa. But this and the Royal Charter to the Company's successor, the Royal African Company, caused more problems than it solved. The battle between monopolists and free traders began, the latter maintaining that it was they who started the business for Britain and who first set up the necessary lines of communication with the African chiefs and dealers Eventually, the Company proving itself less than efficient the trade was opened up once more to all, and remained free until it was abolished.

France, too, became a major trading nation, competing with Britain for the big prize—the Spanish concession to supply all her colonies. This, the *Asiento*, was granted to Britain in 1713 by which she undertook to 'commence the bringing of 144,000 negroes of both sexes at the rate of 4,800 in each of the thirty years' of the *Asiento*'s existence.[10] France had San Domingo, the richest colony of all, which demanded many thousands of slaves each year, and after 1776 when Britain lost her American colonies in the War of Independence, it looked for a short while as if France might overtake Britain. But by 1788, when other factors were shortly to affect France's colonial trading position, Britain still headed the list with 38,000 slaves transported each year. France came second with 20,000, then the Portuguese with 10,000, the Dutch fourth with 4,000, and finally the Danes with a mere 2,000.

These figures given to a British parliamentary committee were at the best approximations.[11] British slave statistics were taken from custom-house returns and therefore reasonably accurate for the later years, but for the earlier years when records were not kept, and for the foreign trade in general, guesses had to do. It is impossible to say how many slaves were exported from Africa during the centuries of European slave trading, the highest suggested figure of one hundred million is regarded by the historian, Basil Davidson, as probably too high.[12] Coupland thought forty million was not unlikely.[13] Whichever is correct, one fact is undeniable: it was a cruel, sordid and merciless way of making money.

Slave trading and slavery were not new to Europe even in the fifteenth century. The ancient civilisations of Greece and

Rome had their large slave populations. In Athens there
was approximately one slave for every three free persons,
and they were employed in a variety of different jobs.
Banks were often run by slaves, and slaves were also used
for police duties with powers to arrest free men. Slavery
existed in northern Europe as well, though it was not an
essential part of the social system.[14]

In western Africa, as it turned out so conveniently for
the Europeans, domestic slavery was recognised by most
tribes. Adults captured in war were made slaves; slavery
was a punishment for various crimes; and children could
be sold into slavery by their parents. By all accounts African,
like Grecian, slavery was not the limited kind which, with
few exceptions, occurred in the Caribbean; African slaves
filled many occupations: a tribe's metal worker entrusted
with producing armaments as well as ornaments might
well be a slave.

Wherever societies recognise property in man, trading
in man must co-exist, and by the time the Europeans came
to exploit the African sources there were trade markets and
routes established with Arab dealers. What the Europeans
brought to the existing situation was an insatiable demand
and a more efficient system.

From the sixteenth century onwards slavery became for
many African tribes not merely one of their social institutions but the very root of their existence. Chieftains wanting
guns from Birmingham or cloth from Manchester, wool
from Exeter or rum from Bristol attacked neighbouring
tribes, burnt their houses to the ground and took off as
many of their people as they could. The smell of smoke
and the red glow on the horizon were the signs that told the
traders and their agents on the coast that a fresh consignment of blacks was on its way. Gangs of kidnappers roamed
the forests, snatching the unwary from the paths where they
walked or the streams where they washed, and securing
them with fetters made in Liverpool, added them to the
slave trains winding their weary way to the trading stations.
Chieftain betrayed chieftain; and it was not uncommon
for one trader to set on another and sell him to a waiting
captain.

By the second half of the eighteenth century large areas of West Africa had been left underpopulated.[15] Many of the young and strong had been shipped away, and continual tribal strife had exhausted those who remained. Potentially fruitful mutual relationships between Africa and Europe had been doomed for centuries, and Europe had created a problem of racial conflict in the Americas which is still a long way from solution. It seems at this distance in time a heavy price to pay for a mercantile system, no matter how profitable; but in the seventeenth and eighteenth centuries Europe took the system for granted. Only when people began to question it did it seem a little less self-evident. By that time it was also a little less profitable.

In the course of the Seven Years War Britain established her colonial domination of the Caribbean. Ten years later, in 1773, an Act was brought in by parliament to encourage the subjects of foreign states to lend money upon security in any of King George's colonies in the West Indies. So great, apparently, was the demand by West Indian proprietors for capital that the Act allowed foreign creditors to reclaim their loans even if they were subjects of a country which was at war with Britain.[16]

'It appears to me that the British slave trade had attained its highest pitch of prosperity a short time before the commencement of the late American war', wrote the West Indian historian Bryan Edwards. According to him in 1771 the number of British ships in the trade was 192 and the number of slaves transported by them was 47,146. This dropped to fifty-eight ships in 1777, but picked up again slightly to eighty-five ships in 1787 and 21,000 slaves.[17]

In 1776 when the owners of some 600,000 slaves in the British North American colonies discarded their allegiance to Britain they ceased to become customers for the British slave trade. In the same year the economist Adam Smith published *The Wealth of Nations*. In this he criticised all institutions and customs which encouraged monopolies and which discouraged individual initiative and self-interest from working for the public good. Slavery and the trade was pre-eminently such a system.

Africans to Smith were 'naked savages', and it was not

his heart but his organised mind that reacted so strongly
against their enslavement. 'The experience of all ages and
nations, I believe, demonstrated that the work done by
slaves, though it appears to cost only their maintenance,
is in the end the dearest of any. A person who can acquire
no property can have no other interest but to eat as much
and to labour as little as possible. Whatever work he does
beyond what is sufficient to purchase his maintenance can
be squeezed out of him by violence only, and not by any
interest of his own.'[18]

The whole notion of slavery being a self-evident fact and
part of the unchanging order of things was abhorrent to
Smith's way of thinking. Man's only basic, unchanging
quality, he maintained, was self-love and the self-interest
resulting from it. Man may love to domineer and, wherever
the law allows it and the nature of the product permits it,
to prefer the service of slaves to that of free men, 'but man
has almost constant occasion for the help of his brethren'.
Neither beatings nor benevolence will extract it. 'He will be
more likely to prevail if he can interest their self-love in
his favour, and show them that it is for their own advantage
to do for him what he requires of them.'[19]

For the percipient reader it was clear that the sceptical
Scotsman was forecasting the eventual end of the West
Indian slave system. He admitted that at the time he
was writing the planting of sugar and tobacco could afford
the expense of slave cultivation, but it was doomed as an
economic system, and so, too, was the slave trade which
depended on it. Already fifty years ago, he pointed out,
the slave-trading companies had ceased to be profitable.[20]

Another prominent man of the 1770s had also given
much thought to the system and had condemned it outright,
not for economic, but for religious reasons. In 1772 John
Wesley, the founder with George Whitefield of Methodism,
wrote *Thoughts Upon Slavery*. Whitefield took a more conventional view of the subject. 'Hot countries cannot be
cultivated without negroes', he stated,[21] but Wesley dis-
agreed. 'It were better that all these islands should remain
uncultivated for ever; yea, it were more desirable that they
were all together sunk in the depth of the sea than that

they should be cultivated at so high a price as the violation of Justice, Mercy and Truth.' He placed the responsibility for creating and continuing the system on the merchants and slave holders. They induced the African to sell his countrymen; their money enabled the English traders to pay the African for doing so. The merchants' money was therefore at the root of the evil, and English merchants, safely enjoying the fruits of the trade, bore a large share of the guilt.[22]

'I must beg leave to stop here for a moment just to pay the Quakers a due tribute of respect for the proper estimation in which they have uniformly held the miserable outcasts of society who have been the subject of these minutes', wrote Thomas Clarkson on his account of the abolition movement.[23] In 1671 George Fox, the founder of the Society of Friends in Britain, delivered a sermon to a meeting in Barbados which for its time sounded very courageous. 'Consider with yourselves if you were in the same condition as the poor Africans are—who came as strangers to you, and were sold to you as slaves. I say, if this should be the condition of you and yours, you would think it a hard measure— yea, a very great bondage and cruelty.' Fox, however, did not go so far as to suggest that the slave holders release their slaves; instead he said: 'Consider seriously this, and do you for them and to them as you would willingly have them or any others do unto you were you in the like slavish condition, and bring them to know the Lord Christ.'[24] In time, the slave holders and their apologists would use Fox's own argument against the abolitionists by declaring that that was all Christianity demanded of them in relation to their slaves.

The American Quakers advised against the continued importation of slaves in 1696 and repeatedly throughout the eighteenth century. William Burling of Long Island, Ralph Sandiford of Philadelphia, and Benjamin Lay all published treatises against slavery, and John Woolman travelled to Long Island, Virginia, North Carolina, and Maryland preaching against the system during the mid-1800s.[25]

In general their objections were aimed more at the slave

trade than at slavery. The Society's resolution of 1758 against the trade is interesting for its vehement attack, not so much on the immorality of owning other human beings but on the commercial aspects of the system. 'We fervently warn all in profession with us that they carefully avoid being any way concerned in reaping the unrighteous profits arising from the iniquitous practice of dealing in negro or other slaves. . . . We, therefore, can do no less than, with the greatest earnestness, impress it upon Friends everywhere that they endeavour to keep their hands clear of this unrighteous gain of oppression.'[26]

In 1783 the Quakers' Committee of Sufferings branded the system 'an oppression which in the injustice of its origins and the inhumanity of its progress, has not, we apprehend, been exceeded or even equalled in the most barbarous ages'. They expressed a fear which came to be repeated in various forms again and again in anti-slave-trade literature—the fear of just retribution. 'We are taught, both by the holy scriptures, and by experience of ages to believe that the Righteous Judge of the whole earth chastises nations for their sins, as well as individuals; and can it be expected that he will suffer this great iniquity to go unpunished?'[27]

This fear, it may be mentioned, did not stop some Quakers from owning and trading in slaves. William Penn owned slaves, and Pennsylvania, the state he founded, had harsh slave laws. The Barclay and the Baring families, the most prominent of the English Quakers, were involved in the Royal African Company, and as these families flourished so their capital was reinvested in banking, textiles and iron, three aspects of commerce vital to the slave trade.[28]

The man whose book so inspired Clarkson when he was preparing his thesis on slavery was also an American Quaker, Anthony Benezet. Benezet was actually born in Picardy in 1713. His father sought asylum in England after the persecutions of Protestants in France following the revocation of the Edict of Nantes. Benezet served an apprenticeship with a mercantile house in London and in 1731 he left with his family for Philadelphia where he joined the Quakers. 'Anthony Benezet may be considered as one of the most zealous, vigilant, and active advocates which the cause of the oppressed African ever had', Clarkson said of him.[29] The Quaker recognised that the slave system involved not only those directly concerned in buying, selling and holding slaves, but 'the revenue of the government, the profits of the merchants, and the luxury of the people have involved the whole nation as *participes criminis*'.[30] Like other Quaker critics of the system he thought the slave trade ought to be abolished before slavery. 'The emancipation of those already in slavery and the means of procuring the supplies of freemen will claim, no doubt, the maturest deliberation of wise and experienced men.' The phrase 'maturest deliberation', which he used in 1784, turned out to be an apt one. It took those 'wise and experienced men' another fifty years in England and nearly eighty years in America to make up their minds to emancipate the slaves.

The American War of Independence was regarded by many religious critics of slavery in Britain as the just retribution which they had warned against for owning slaves.[31] Each mutiny or slave rebellion, each tornado or famine in any of the colonies, was immediately ascribed to God's vengeance for the evils of slavery. In fact, so insistent were these critics on the imminence of God's punishment that it is not clear what was more important to them—the sufferings of the slaves, or the souls of the white Christians engaged in the system.

Thomas Clarkson stated his priorities quite unequivocally: 'Though nature shrinks from pain, and compassion is engendered in us when we see it become the portion of others, yet what is physical suffering compared with moral guilt?' The body dies and returns to dust, but 'when the moral springs of the mind are poisoned we lose the most excellent part of the constitution of our nature, and the divine image is no longer perceptible in us'. Because we are mortal, 'the torments of the oppressor are but temporary; whereas the immortal part of us, when once corrupted, may carry its pollutions with it into another world'.[32]

Slave owning and slave dealing were sinful and corrupting. There being no limitation to the power of one man over another, the slaver was tempted to play the role of God.

The abolitionists often quoted Milton's lines from *Paradise Lost* to reinforce this argument.

> O execrable son, so to aspire
> Above his Brethren, to himself assuming
> Authority usurpt, from God not given.
> He gave us only over Beast, Fish, Fowl
> Dominion absolute; that right we hold
> By his donation: but Man over men
> He made not Lord; such title to himself
> Reserving, human left from human free.[33]

The whip, the cruel tortures and punishments, the harsh working conditions—these were bad enough, but what was regarded with even greater disapproval was the state of moral degradation the planter on his plantation and the slave captain on his ship allowed themselves to sink into. Surrounded by pagans, they cohabited with slave women whom custom decreed could be used by them in whatever way they wished. Owners, overseers and managers took slave mistresses who bore them bastard children, and it was common for male visitors to the estates to be offered a slave girl for the night. This, the religious critics of the system declaimed, was all taking place in supposedly Christian lands under the rule of a Christian king.

'Let the slaveholders be mindful of the approaching consummation of all earthly things', warned Granville Sharp, 'when perhaps they will see thousands of those men who were formerly esteemed mere chattels and private property coming in the clouds with their Heavenly Master to judge tyrants and oppressors, and to call them to account for their want of brotherly love.'[34]

The slave ships generally lie near a mile below the town, in Bonny River, in seven or eight fathoms of water. Soon after they cast anchor, the captains go on shore to make known their arrival, and to inquire into the state of the trade. They likewise invite the kings of Bonny to come on board, to whom . . . they usually make presents which generally consist of pieces of cloth, cotton, chintz, silk handkerchiefs, and other India goods, and sometimes of brandy, wine or beer. . . .

On arrival of the ships . . . it is customary for them to unbend the sails, strike the yards and topmasts, and begin to build what they denominate *a house*. . . . Near the mainmast a partition is constructed of inch deal boards which reaches athwart the ship. . . . It serves to keep the sexes apart; and as there are small holes in it wherein blunderbusses are fixed, and sometimes a cannon, it is found very convenient for quelling the insurrections that now and then happen. . . . The design of this house is to secure those on board from the heat of the sun . . . and from the wind and rain which at particular seasons are likewise extremely violent. It answers these purposes however but very ineffectually. . . .

While I was upon the coast . . . the black traders brought down in different canoes from twelve to fifteen hundred negroes which had been purchased at one fair. They consisted chiefly of men and boys, the women seldom exceeding a third of the whole number. . . .

When the negroes whom the black traders have to dispose of are shown to the European purchasers, they first examine them relative to their age. They then minutely inspect their persons, and inquire into their state of health; if they are afflicted with any infirmity, or are deformed, or have bad eyes or teeth: if they are lame, or weak in the joints, or distorted in the back, or of a slender make, or are narrow in the chest; in short, if they have been or are afflicted in any manner so as to render them incapable of much labour . . . they are rejected. The traders frequently beat those negroes which are objected to by the captains, and use them with great severity. . . . Instances have happened that the traders, when any of their negroes have been objected to, have dropped their canoes under the stem of the vessel, and instantly beheaded them in the sight of the captain.

(An account of the Slave Trade on the Coast of Africa—
Alexander Falconbridge, 1788)

3

The Privy Council Report

In Britain's unreformed parliament of the 1780s addresses
and petitions were the best method by which the unrepre-
sented public could bring their grievances, complaints
and needs to the notice of the legislature. On February the
4th, 1788, the Lord Mayor, Alderman and Commons of
the City of London presented a petition to the House of
Commons in which they stated that the honour of the
British nation called for an impartial and immediate
inquiry into the 'nature and present state of that trade
which appears to the Petitioners to be conducted on principles highly inconsistent with the dictates of justice and
humanity'.[1]

In May the merchants, traders and other inhabitants of
Liverpool also presented a petition, declaring that the
African slave trade formed a very considerable part of the
commerce of Liverpool and was advantageous to the whole
of Great Britain. It was also, they stated, inseparably
connected with the very existence of its West Indian territories.[2] On the first point they knew what they were talking
about. Liverpool had been underselling Bristol and London
since the early days of the trade which brought it on average
£1,117,647 a year. It had five-eighths of the African trade of
Great Britain; three-sevenths of all Europe, according to
a history of the city.[3]

With these two petitions the first shots had been fired
in the long battle which was to follow between those who
wanted the trade to continue and those who wanted it
totally abolished. There were some who were prepared
merely to see it regulated. Sir William Dolben, a member
of the House of Commons, had been down to the Thames to

see a slave ship which was preparing to set sail for Africa. He wanted to see for himself what all the fuss was about, and he was shocked by what he was shown. Though not a reformer, he immediately brought in a Bill for the regulation of the trade by limiting the number of slaves which could be transported on one ship at one time.

'I have been most hospitably entertained at Liverpool', he said, introducing his Bill. 'Indeed, I believe I have eaten more turtle there than I've ever eaten in my life. But I will readily give up their turtle and burgundy for mock turtle and plain port if they will consent to forgo some part of their profits for the sake of accommodating the poor negroes better while on ship-board.'[4]

William Pitt, who had already been Prime Minister for five years though he was only thirty, pointed out to the House that he had cautiously avoided giving any opinion respecting the legality or illegality of the slave trade, or whether it ought to be continued and under what conditions. He did not know that any abuses existed, but he was prepared to concede that it was possible they did.[5] It was generally a very lukewarm start for the man who was to identify so fervently with the abolitionist cause—at least for a time.

The House of Lords, in contrast to the Commons, tackled Sir William's Bill with enthusiasm. There was a long exchange of scientific data on the capacity of the negro to withstand hardship, especially lack of air and space in the cramped holds between the decks. Lord Heathfield came to the conclusion, after a good deal of thought, that the negroes were actually quite well off. 'They are allowed full thirty cubical feet of air to breathe', he said. 'More than our soldiers in tents who only have seventeen cubical feet of air to breathe.'[6]

The merchants did not oppose the Bill with much vigour, and it duly became law.[7] It limited the number of slaves to five for every three tons of shipping; it specified the minimum space between decks which had to be provided for the slave cargo, and it established a registry of slave ships. It also tried to give ships' captains and surgeons an incentive to keep their cargoes alive by offering a reward of £100 for the captain and £50 for the surgeon if they succeeded in ensuring that not more than two slaves for every hundred died during the voyage. Only one member of the Commons pointed out that by 'regulating' the slave trade, the House was, for the first time, actually sanctioning it.[8]

Parliament, however, was anxious not to commit itself finally on the question of the continued existence of the trade, so on the 11th February 1788 a committee of the Privy Council was appointed to consider 'all matters relating to . . . the trade in slaves and the effects and consequences of this on Africa and the West Indies'.

The Council sat in committee for a year collecting evidence, and its Report was published in April 1789.[9] In a number of ways it was the most important document published on the subject up to that time, both for what it contained and for what it left out. On the question of the morality or otherwise of slavery itself it was silent, but its hundreds of pages of evidence gave it its unique value. Thomas Clarkson and the Committee had been busy arranging for witnesses to appear before the committee of the Privy Council, and so, too, had the West Indian interests which had their own organisation. Matters which had been the subject of speculation only were now documented and available to all concerned. For years to come the evidence would be quoted again and again in parliament, in tracts, newspaper articles and books.

The Report was in six parts: the first dealt with Africa; the second with the Middle Passage; the third with the treatment of slaves in the West Indies; the fourth with the extent of the trade; the fifth with that problem which was a constant source of irritation to the British Government— just how and why were the French colonies supposedly more successful than theirs; and finally, another source of concern, the extent of the trade of other nations with Africa.

The evidence about the Africans in their own country tended to be accepted as the final word on the nature of the black man. 'The common people have all sorts of superstitions; in general they worship trees', said one witness. Another, an officer in the African Corps, said, 'They have no idols, nor any form of worship. Their principal tenet is that they are to be happy in this world, and they endeavour to make themselves so by every species of licentious enjoyment which they even pursue under affliction.' One who had been on the coast of Africa for twelve years raised a point the abolitionists were to use frequently in arguing their case for ending the trade. 'They enjoy civil rights and privileges that are of more ancient date than our settlement among them. I do not believe that the natives are much improved in their morals by their intercourse with Europeans; on the contrary I think the worst blacks are those who have been most concerned with the whites.'

In answer to the question: 'Are the people a moral people, and do they have a due sense of right and wrong?' Richard Miles, the late Governor of the Cape Coast Castle, replied: 'In their intercourse and dealings with each other they are very exact and strict; they are punished with the loss of liberty for the smallest theft.' This remark confirmed two of the slave traders' arguments: firstly, the trade was simply a continuation of an existing situation because all slaves bought by them were already enslaved by their own people for crimes they had committed, and, secondly, that it was, in fact, a humane system since it saved the poor black slaves from the terrors of domestic slavery by shipping them to the Christian paradise of the West Indian colonies. It was also used by the colonists to justify their harsh laws; they argued that as the majority of slaves imported to the West Indies were criminals in their own country it was no more than natural that the colonists should protect themselves and their families from the potential danger of such people.[10]

From Africa the Privy Council turned its attention to the notorious Middle Passage into which was compressed the real horror of the slave trade. When the evidence came to be sifted and organised by the abolitionists for the furtherance of their campaign, they tended to concentrate on the Middle Passage to excite pity for the slaves with stories like that told by Mr Wadstrom to the Privy Council committee. According to him the French captains usually carried with them a certain amount of mercury so that when their ships were becalmed and their provisions began to fail they would put some of it into the food given to the slaves who would die in great numbers and then be thrown overboard. This, he pointed out, was considered as an act of humanity in contrast to the English captains who treated the slaves with less ceremony and threw them overboard alive.[11]

The opinion of most witnesses was that the trade was vital to Britain's well-being, and that if it stopped it would fall into other hands. Mr Norris, a well-known Guinea trader, confirmed the close link between the trade, the banking establishment and the manufacturing interests. 'The cause why the English have the largest share of this trade is to be imputed to the credit which the British merchant has with the manufacturers.' This was something no other nation in Europe enjoyed, nor did they have the spirit of enterprise 'which is peculiar to the British merchant'.

The nearest the Privy Council came to considering slavery itself was the review of the slave laws in the colonies which was prepared with great thoroughness by the law clerk to the committee.[12] According to the review, the basis on which all these laws were made was 'that negroes were *property*, and a species of property that needed a rigorous and vigilant regulation'.

The effect of the laws was to deprive the slaves of even the smallest and least consequential of freedoms, and, moreover, to restrict the owners themselves to grant, out of the kindness of their hearts, the slightest concession. Slaves were not allowed to buy or sell anything without their owner's permission, nor without that permission were they allowed to leave the plantation. Ownership of mules and horses was denied them, and in some of the islands, Bermuda for example, slaves were even denied the right to wear bright clothes or ornaments. Even at this distance in time, and in a world which has seen tyrannies of every kind, the laws enacted in the British West Indies in the 1700s make chilling reading, expressed, as they were, in the formal, legalistic language of a nation which prided itself on its advanced enlightenment and humanity:

'Whereas notwithstanding several good and wholesome laws for regulating negroes and other slaves have been enacted', read the preamble to the Bermudan law of 1730, 'yet frequently complaints are made by the inhabitants of these islands of their insolency and daily theft . . . which we conceive is chiefly occasioned by the great liberty given to many of them by their masters to buy for themselves and wear fine clothes or other ornaments; . . . it is thereby enacted that . . . no master shall upon any pretence whatsoever give liberty or suffer them to wear any silk, lace, ribbons, rings, bracelets, buckles . . . nor any sticks (except them that are decrepit or lame)'.

'And whereas the indulgence given by their owners to negroes and other slaves to propagate and reap cotton on their plantations and to expose same to sale within these islands having proved prejudicial to the interest of white persons desirous of cultivating small plantations,' read an Act of the Virgin Islands of 1783, 'it is enacted that if any person shall suffer or allow any slave to plant cotton in his estate, he shall forfeit one hundred pounds for the first transgression, two for the second, and so on'.

'If any slave shall impudently strike or oppose any white person, any justice shall order a constable to cause such slave to be publicly whipped at his discretion, and if resistance, such offending slave shall have his nose slit, or any member cut off', was another clause in the Virgin Island act.

The Jamaican Assembly in 1761 decided to end the practice of owners leaving property to favourite slaves. 'Such bequests tend greatly to destroy the distinction requisite and absolutely necessary to be kept up in this island between white persons and negroes and may in time be the means of decreasing the number of white inhabitants in this island; and whereas it is the policy of every good government to restrain individuals from disposing of property to the prejudice of their heirs and relations and to the injury and damage of the community in general . . . it is enacted that no lands, etc. be given or granted by any white person to any negro whatever.'

The catalogue of punishments and the number and variety of crimes for which punishments could be exacted was shocking even to a nation whose penal code was one of the severest in Europe; and shocking too, was the fact that came to be realised that these cruel and vicious statutes enacted by British colonies were theoretically British laws. An old Act of Monserrat of 1693 permitted any white man to kill any negro seen stealing his provisions, and another stated that 'when any negro shall have any theft proved against him, and the value not amounting to twelve pence, then such negro shall only suffer a severe whipping and have both ears cut off'. These statutes, the colonists said, had fallen into disuse, but the Bahama Islands' current penal code still included twenty lashes on the bare back for selling spiritous liquors; twenty lashes for selling eggs, fruit and vegetables; death for assault on a white person; whipping for gambling. Slaves producing fraudulent certificates of manumission were punished with gaol and fifty lashes; however, whites fraudulently claiming property in them were only fined £30.

By the time the Privy Council's Report was published, the abolitionists had formed themselves into the Abolition Society with the original Committee for the Abolition of the Slave Trade as its guiding executive. The Committee had already put into motion the techniques for rousing and organising public indignation which was to serve it throughout the campaign against the trade and subsequently against slavery, and, incidentally, to serve also as the model on which reforming societies of one kind or another were to base their campaigns throughout the nineteenth century and right up to the present day. Committees had been set up in every city and every county, and through these were disseminated its annual reports, tracts, and copies of parliamentary speeches and debates which favoured the abolitionist view. The Privy Council Report had provided the Abolition Society with a great deal of useful ammunition in the battle to come; but in the same year—1789—it had acquired something far more valuable—a parliamentary champion.

With our ships, the great object is to be full.

The ship in which I was a mate on board, left the coast with two hundred and eighteen slaves on board, and though we were not much affected by epidemical disorders, I find, by my journal of that voyage, that we buried sixty-two on our passage to South Carolina, exclusive of those which died before we left the coast.

(*Thoughts Upon the African Slave Trade—*
John Newton, 1788 (2nd Edition))

In each of the apartments are placed three or four large buckets of a conical form . . . to which, when necessary, the negroes have recourse. It often happens that those who are placed at a distance from the buckets, in endeavouring to get to them, tumble over their companions in consequence of their being shackled. These accidents, although unavoidable, are productive of continual quarrels in which some of them are always bruised. In this distressed situation, unable to proceed, and prevented from getting to the tubs, they desist from the attempt; and, as the necessities of nature are not to be repelled, ease themselves as they lie.

(Falconbridge)

Extract from: Memorandum of Slaves consigned to and sold by Alexander Lindo—January to August 1788

Dates	Vessels	Owners	Registered Tonnage	When Sold	Slaves Imported	Slaves Sold	Sold for Island Use
1786 Feb 12	Ship Brooks	Jos. Brooks & co.	300	9 Jan	620	608	180
Apr 14	Snow John	Camden & Calvert	120	22 Feb	155	154	13
Apr 14	President	Gill Slater & Co.	300	2 Mar	370	328	105

Males	Females	Above 4' 4"	Under 4' 4"	From Whence	Sold for Exportation
431	177	525	83	Anamaboe	425
106	48	93	61	Gabon	141
175	153	230	92	Calabar	223

(Report of the Lords Committee of Council, 1789)

4

The Zealous and the Lukewarm

'The abolition of the slave trade was, under God, and when the time was come, the work of a *woman*', claimed a certain Mr C. Ignatius Latrobe, an associate of the abolitionists, in a letter he wrote to William Wilberforce's sons when they were preparing their father's biography. It was Lady Middleton, Latrobe said, 'who was the honoured instrument of bringing the monster within the range of the artillery of the executive justice of the kingdom'.

Lady Middleton was the wife of a Member of Parliament. They were both friends to the cause of abolition and she had urged her husband to bring the subject before parliament. He declined on the grounds that it was far too serious a matter for a man like himself who had never spoken in the House, and it was suggested to her that the person for the task was young William Wilberforce. He had 'not only displayed very superior talents of great eloquence, but was a decided and powerful advocate of the cause of truth and virtue, and a friend of the minister'.[1]

A letter was sent to Wilberforce and he replied: 'I feel the great importance of the subject and I think myself unequal to the task allotted to me, but yet I will not positively decline it.'[2] He met and spoke to the Middletons, who introduced him to other abolitionists, and from then on, according to Latrobe, he became committed to the cause. 'God Almighty', he declared, 'has set before me two great objects, the suppression of the slave trade, and the reformation of manners.'[3]

Throughout his active parliamentary career Wilberforce was true to his word. He was always engaged on one or the other of his two great objects. He was born in Hull,

Yorkshire, in 1759. 'His frame from infancy was feeble, his stature small, his eyes weak', his sons wrote of him. 'It was one amongst the many expressions of his gratitude in after-life "that I was not born in less civilized times, when it would have been thought impossible to rear so delicate a child". '4 His father died when he was young, and his mother, for all her virtues, did not possess 'those views of the spiritual nature of religion which she adopted in later life'. Young William was brought up mainly by an uncle and aunt, the latter a great admirer of the Methodist George Whitefield. His mother became alarmed at the 'dangerous influence' the aunt might have on her son, and took him back to Hull where he led an idle, gay life for which he never ceased to reproach himself in later years. At seventeen he entered St John's College, Cambridge.

'I was introduced on the very first night of my arrival to as licentious a set of men as can well be conceived. They drank hard, and their conversation was even worse than their lives.'5 He never became really close friends with these dissolute young men and by the time he left university he had determined on a life of politics. At the age of twenty he was elected for Hull, his opponent being Lord Rockingham, the most powerful nobleman in the country. The election cost him between £8,000 and £9,000, but he had an ample fortune. 'I belonged at this time to five clubs.' He still gambled as he had at university and on one occasion won £600 at a faro-table.6

One of his university acquaintances had been William Pitt, who became Prime Minister of Britain at the age of twenty-four. The acquaintanceship ripened into a firm friendship which lasted throughout most of Pitt's life and gave Wilberforce a unique position of authority in the abolitionist movement. When he advised his colleagues on the direction of their campaign he was listened to as the close friend of the Prime Minister, and his advice was frequently acted on—to the detriment, as we shall see, of the movement.

Pitt began urging Wilberforce to take up the question of abolition in 1787. Why he should suddenly have become so concerned for the Africans has been the matter of some speculation. After all, he had been in the House of Commons for six years and a Prime Minister for three, and never once had he mentioned the subject. Possibly, like so many others, he had been moved by the strong wave of pity flowing out from England towards the inhabitants of Africa. Possibly he had read the figures for the importation of slaves into the British West Indies and had realised that nearly a third of the imported slaves were re-exported to the French colonies, in particular to the much-coveted island of San Domingo. In 1787, of 21,023 slaves imported into the West Indies from Africa, 5,366 were exported to foreign colonies.[7] The trade, it seemed, though profitable to British merchants was, in the long run, detrimental to Britain's interests, and its abolition would mean a slowing down of the French colonial sugar production and consequently a blow to the economy of France.[8]

'Do not lose time', he told Wilberforce, 'or the ground may be occupied by another.'[9] Wilberforce agreed. He arranged to move a resolution in parliament on the slave trade, but then he fell seriously ill. 'As to the slave question,' he wrote, 'I do not like to touch on it; it is so big a one it frightens me in my present weak state. Pitt . . . has taken on himself the management of the business.'

Pitt, in fact, had gone straight to Granville Sharp on hearing of his friend's condition and had told him that he would move the resolution himself. This he did, but it added up to no more than getting parliament to agree to consider the slave trade in the following year.

Wilberforce, in the meantime, soon recovered 'in great measure', say his sons in their biography, 'to the affect of the proper use of opium'. He was a frail and sickly man, and though he lived into his seventies, he was constantly troubled by various ailments. The one which had struck him low at such a crucial time was described by his sons as 'an entire decay of all vital functions' and it looked to everyone that he would not live. But, incredibly enough, within a month he was well enough to travel to Cambridge and to tour the Lake District. After a 'perpetual round of dissipation . . . little suitable to me considered as an invalid, as it is becoming my character and profession as a Christian', he returned to London.[10] With the help of Sharp, Clarkson and the Abolition Society's documented evidence on the slave traffic, he was ready to do battle on behalf of 'my clients', as he liked to call the slaves.

On May the 12th, 1789, he rose in the House of Commons to make the first of many speeches he was to make against the slave trade in the next thirty years.[11] With the recent publication of the Privy Council Report still fresh in everyone's mind it was natural that he should start with a reference to it. 'The nature and all the circumstances of this trade are now laid open to us; we can no longer plead ignorance.' He then dealt with the effect of the trade on Africa. He did not try to contradict the vicious statements made by biased witnesses about the alleged barbarism of the blacks. Instead he accepted them and tried to explain them away. 'With a country vast in its extent, not utterly barbarous, but civilised in a very small degree, does anyone suppose a slave trade would help their civilisation?' he asked. 'Is it not plain that she must suffer from it; that her civilisation must be checked; her barbarous manners made more barbarous.'

In every civilised country, he went on, the rights of property were protected by the legislature; but in Africa, whose only sort of property were slaves, there was no such protection. 'We see them in the nature of things, how easily the practices of Africa are to be accounted for. Her kings were never compelled to war by public principles, by national principles, by national glory, still less by the love of their people. In Europe it is the extension of commerce, the maintenance of national honour, or some great public object that is ever the motive to war with every monarch; but in Africa it is the personal avarice and sensuality of their kings. . . . These two vices of avarice and sensuality,' he said, warming to the subject, 'the most powerful and predominant in natures thus corrupt, we tempt, we stimulate in all these African princes, and we depend upon these vices for the very maintenance of the slave trade. Does the king of Berbessin want brandy? He has only to send his troops in the night time to burn and desolate a village, the captives will serve as commodities that may be bartered with the British trader.'

Finally, before moving his resolutions, Wilberforce introduced his last point—the one which was to become so important in the abolitionists' later campaigns. 'Let us make a reparation to Africa so far as we can by establishing a trade upon true commercial principles, and we shall soon find the rectitude of our conduct rewarded by the benefits of a regular and growing commerce.'

Wilberforce spoke late into the night. The Abolition Society in its report of July called it 'one of the most liberal and argumentative speeches perhaps ever delivered in the British senate, though that assembly be justly character-ised among the surrounding nations by the splendour of its eloquence, and its sacred regard to the rights of mankind.'[12]

In order to understand better why a group of people like the members of the Society and their new champion should be moved to change a system that had lasted virtually unassailed since the sixteenth century, it is necessary to know something about their religious and social attitudes, the first being for them inextricably linked with the second. A useful point to start with is the curious story of a strange gentleman—the Reverend John Newton.

John Newton was a key figure in the early stages of the abolition movement, and the events of his life paralleled the historical events through which he lived and which in turn he helped in some small degree to influence. He was born in 1725 and in his youth he was unsettled and indisciplined. He went to sea and, like so many young men with no money, but with dissolute habits, he joined the Atlantic slave trade. By the age of twenty-five he was already a captain of his own slave ship, but not before he had had many adventures resulting from his wild and reckless behaviour which were remarkable even for the time and the circumstances. On one occasion he found himself virtually a slave to a white trader who sold provisions to the slave ships on the African coast. The white man's black mistress hated him and treated him abominably. After being rescued from the trader Newton was nearly shipwrecked, and it was then, for the first time, that he prayed to God. He thought of Jesus, read his Bible, and he was aware of some hope for himself, the sinner and blasphemer. The conversion was a brief one, and by the time he was on another ship and back in Africa he was almost as bad as before. At length, however, 'the Lord interposed on my behalf', and this time the conversion was total.[13] Now, instead of drinking and swearing, he used his leisure time on ship to good effect: he learnt Latin and read the classics.

'I never knew sweeter or more frequent hours of divine communion than in my last two voyages of Guinea, when I was either almost secluded from society on shipboard, or when on shore amongst the natives.'[14] It was on one of these journeys he wrote the hymn 'How Sweet the Name of Jesus Sounds'. Remembering the hell that the slave ships were with their overcrowding, their stench, the casual and deliberate cruelty, and the complete hopelessness of the slaves' plight, one cannot help feeling when reading the words of the hymn that Newton's powers of disassociation must have been considerable.

> How sweet the name of Jesus sounds,
> In a believer's ear.
> It soothes his sorrows, heals his wounds,
> And drives away his fear.

Newton confirmed this in his autobiographical *Authentic Narrative*. 'During the time I was engaged in the slave trade I never had the least scruple as to its unlawfulness. I was upon the whole satisfied with it, as the appointment Providence had marked out for me; yet it was, in many respects, far from eligible. It is indeed accounted a genteel employment, and is usually very profitable, though to me it did not prove so, the Lord feeling that a large increase of wealth would not be good for me.'[15]

Few slave captains left the trade to become clergymen, and none became as famous as Newton. In 1763 he was brought to the notice of Lord Dartmouth, a young, fervently religious nobleman, who gave him the curacy at Olney, in Buckinghamshire. It was there that Newton wrote his well-known hymns, alone and in collaboration with the poet William Cowper. In 1780 he accepted the offer of the wealthy merchant John Thornton of the benefice of St

Mary Woolnoth, in the City of London. His sermons were long and usually improvised, and though, according to contemporaries, he spoke indistinctly and gestured wildly he drew large congregations who came to look on 'the old African blasphemer'[16] as much as to hear him. They all knew of his sordid past, his conversion, and his fierce conviction of sin, and he became one of the best-known preachers in England. In the nineteenth century his life was frequently used as a model for little Christians to follow. 'I hope that you will not forget that I am telling the story of John Newton, not only to amuse you, but to show you how bad and miserable John Newton was, and all sinners are until they have learned to love the Saviour of sinners', was how a children's history of him put it.[17]

In 1785 Newton met Wilberforce. Wilberforce wrote: 'I called upon old Newton—was much affected in conversing with him—something very pleasing and unaffected in him.'[18] The meeting was crucial for Wilberforce and for the subsequent history of the abolition movement. Newton had by then completed his conversion from sinner to saint by reacting strongly against his slave-trading past. He had become an abolitionist, and later wrote a tract on the subject which was required reading for all those against the trade.[19] Wilberforce was a young politician in the process of converting to Evangelicalism to the consternation of his more worldly friends who saw the end of his political future in such a step. Newton inspired Wilberforce in his religious convictions and was one of the first to draw his attention to the slave trade. 'He told me he always had entertained hopes and confidence that God would some time bring me to him', Wilberforce recalled.[20]

Newton, who died in the same year as the trade was abolished, believed, as did all evangelical Christians, in the direct intervention of God in the individual history of each man; he saw the sins he had committed in the past come to aid in the prevention of future sins by his timely meeting with Wilberforce. He was very much admired by all the members of that group who turned evangelicalism into a social movement and who, in time, were also to give 'Victorianism' its distinctive stamp. They saw the world in dire

need of reform; and thus strongly activated by an over-
whelming sense of sin and retribution, they turned their
attention to the manners of the society and were repelled
by what they saw. Change in morals had to come quickly
before they were all to be consumed by the fires of
Hell.

During most of the eighteenth century the aristocracy, the
first and final arbiters in all matters pertaining to taste and
judgment, paid lip-service to the tenets of Christianity and
performed their religious duties as duties and not out of
any deeply held convictions. The rising and ambitious in
the middle classes followed where they led. Out-and-out
agnostics were few, but so too were the extravagantly devout.
Extremism was looked down upon; reasonableness and
moderation in everything were more desirable. Science and
rational thought, rather than the Bible and the Gospel,
were the proper source of knowledge for the enlightened
who believed that man was basically good though subject
to evil temptations.

When the reaction came it started lower down in the
social scale. Wesley and Whitefield, amongst others, addressed their message of the return to fundamental Christianity
to the farm and factory labourers, to the artisans and to the
small tradesmen, not to the gentry or the mighty merchants.
What they had to say was diametrically opposed to the
comfortable views of the Church of England. Systematic
self-denial, stern discipline, the rejection of the pursuit of
money for its own sake of power and pleasure, were among
their beliefs; but most important was the strong conviction
of the evil side of man's nature, of sin and corruption,
and of the all-seeing, all knowing God who punished the
wicked and rewarded the good. Truth to them was a
matter of dogma, not argument, and it was found through
belief, not through the debates of sceptical philosophers
whom they despised with as much virulence as they in turn
were held in contempt.[21]

By the end of the eighteenth century the heat of religious
fervour had reached and touched the middle classes. It
was never strong enough to consume the Established Church
and destroy it, but it was strong enough to create a separate

movement within it. John Newton had imbibed the spirit of the evangelical movement when he was at Olney and brought it with him to London; Isaac Milner in Cambridge, another important convert to Evangelicalism, was the tutor of young William Wilberforce. Wilberforce, himself the son of a wealthy merchant, met Newton and soon after formed with some of his rich friends a self-conscious 'sect' which derived its name from the suburb of London in which most of them at one stage lived: Clapham.

'When one thinks of a circle of Christians united by mutual affection, animated by the same motives, pressing towards the same object, servants of the same Lord, children of the same Father, we can scarce force from our minds the idea of the most intimate and endearing communion among them, with perfect openness and confidence', wrote Thomas Bowdler of the Clapham Sect in a letter to Wilberforce in 1808.[22] (He was to edit out all the morally dubious parts of Shakespeare and Gibbon and earn himself immortality by having his name added to the English language.)

The Evangelicals, and the Clapham Sect in particular, were never radically to alter the religious life of the country, but because of their place in society they came in time to wield an influence in social and political spheres far in excess of their numbers. They were, behind the new industrialists, in the vanguard of the rising middle class and beginning to win more and more power through seats in a parliament of aristocrats which had been all but closed to them. This development was fully in accord with their religious beliefs since it meant that by having power they could change the morals and manners of society. They were men and women of action, and religion to them was not static. The good things of the earth and of heaven were not the natural rewards of a passive virtue. They had to be won by constant effort and vigilance.

The Evangelicals, however, were never to so antagonise the Established Church as to be forced to break away from it completely. In this way they formed a useful link between Anglicanism on the one hand and Nonconformism on the other. Politically, this meant between the governors and the governed; economically, between the rich and the poor.

As government grew more complex and the demand for administrators increased beyond the capacity of the aristocracy to fill it, the sons and grandsons of the Clapham group and its adherents, with their wealth, education and strong sense of dedication were in the perfect position to assume the responsibilities of service to the nation.

The Clapham Sect was very much a family affair. Wilberforce and his friends were linked by close ties of marriage. Among the founding members were Henry Thornton, the banker, Hannah More, the authoress who gave up a brilliant career to help start village schools for the poor, John Venn, the rector of Clapham and his brother Henry, Charles Grant, Zachary Macaulay, Thomas Babington, William Smith, Dr Stephen Lushington and James Stephen. Thornton, Wilberforce and the six men last mentioned were all members of the House of Commons. In addition, Thornton was Wilberforce's first cousin; Babington and Macaulay were brothers-in-law, and so, too, were Stephen and Wilberforce.[23] This intermarriage continued into the second, third and subsequent generations with the result that their influence spread into every branch of government and civil service, and their domination of the intellectual life of Britain was secured right through till this century.

Josiah Wedgwood, the Sect's very good friend, was connected to the Darwins, who, in turn, were connected to the Huxleys. Zachary Macaulay's one son was the famous historian and he was linked by marriage to the Trevelyans and the Arnolds. His other son, Charles, married the daughter of the founder of the *Manchester Guardian*. The interconnecting family trees reveal name after famous name: Florence Nightingale was the grand-daughter of William Smith; Virginia Woolf was a Stephen, and Henry Thornton's great-grandson was the novelist E. M. Forster.[24]

The colonial service in particular attracted the descendants. James Stephen's third son, another James, became Under-Secretary of State for the Colonies in 1836.[25] His brother, Sir George Stephen, distinguished himself in Australia; one of Charles Grant's sons was to become Governor of Bombay, and the other, Lord Glenelg, Colonial

Secretary. The prominence they achieved in this sphere was
no accident. The attitudes to the world which their forbears held virtually dictated it. 'Consider well the superior
light and advantages which we enjoy, and then appreciate
the superior obligations which are imposed on us', wrote
Wilberforce in *A Practical View of the Prevailing Religious
System of Professed Christians in the Middle and Higher Classes in
this Country contrasted with Real Christianity*, the book he
liked to call 'my religious manifesto'. It was written by
him in 1797 when he was resting from his anti-slave trading
labours. John Newton said it was a book no family should
be without, but its publisher was reluctant to print a first
edition of more than 500 copies. It quickly became a
best-seller; within six months 7,500 copies had been sold.
Within the next thirty years it went into fifteen editions in
Britain, twenty-five in America, and was translated into
five languages.

'True Christian benevolence', wrote Wilberforce, 'is
always occupied in producing happiness to the utmost
of its powers and according to the extent of its sphere.'
The message is repeated frequently: the true Christian is
the man who, not only believes in Christ and adheres
to his Gospel, but who also practises it in every sphere,
public and private. 'The opposite to selfishness is public
spirit, which may be termed, not unjustly, the grand principal of political vitality, the very *life's breath* of states, which
tends to keep them active and vigorous and to carry them
to greatness and glory.'

The kingdom of God and the kingdom of Satan were both
set up in the world; to one or the other everyone had to
belong. In his mind there was not much doubt that the bulk
of the British nation tended towards the latter. 'Sensual
gratification and illicit affections have debased our nobler
powers and indisposed our hearts to the discovery of God.'
His list of transgressions was lengthy: idolatry, lasciviousness,
sensuality, excessive dissipation, general irreligion, swearing,
drinking, fornication, pride, malice, revenge; but of all the
greatest was sabbath-breaking.[26]

The people most guilty of committing these and every
sin which placed the nation in danger of God's vengeance

were the 'nominal' or 'lukewarm' Christians, members of his own class and more so of the upper classes who created the patterns others followed, who pretended to be Christians, but were nothing of the kind. 'Lukewarmness', he fumed, 'is stated to be the object of God's disgust and aversion.' Nominal Christians, both in principles and conduct, had only a very inadequate idea of 'the guilt and evil of sin'; they forgot not only to contend with their own depravity, but also to combat 'the Evil Spirit . . . whose dominion we learn from the Scriptures to be so general as to entitle him to the denomination of "The Prince of the World".'

The soul of the nation was in danger as a result of the ascendancy of nominal and lukewarm Christians. The progress of 'irreligion and the decay of morals at home is such as to claim every considerate mind, and to forebode the worst consequences unless some remedy can be applied to the growing evil.' Not only its soul, but its political power too was endangered. 'We bear upon us but too plainly the marks of a declining empire.' But help was at hand. 'The warm, zealous and affectionate', as he characterised true Christians, could still save the nation. 'Who can say but that the Governor of the Universe . . . may in answer to their intercessions for a while avert our ruin and continue to us the fulness of those temporal blessings which in such abundant measure we have hitherto enjoyed.'

Concerted attacks had to be launched on the bad by the good; on the lukewarm by the zealous; on immorality by strict discipline; on indifference by philanthropy. 'I know that by regulating external conduct', Wilberforce wrote to a friend 'we do not change the hearts of men, but even they are ultimately wrought upon by these means.'[27] Trading in slaves, like breaking the sabbath, was to him and his like-minded friends the kind of external conduct that called out loudest for regulation and abolition. This could only be achieved by public action inspired by a genuine desire to exorcise sin and 'the Evil Spirit'. When they spoke of their abolition cause as 'sacred' and 'holy' they were not using the words loosely.

Extravagant though it may sound today, John Newton meant exactly what he said when he wrote with fervour to

Wilberforce in July 1796: 'You are not only a representative for Yorkshire; you have the far greater honour of being a representative for the Lord in a place where many know him not, and an opportunity of showing them what are the genuine fruits of that religion which you are known to profess.'[28]

Extract from the Evidence of Dr Thomas Trotter, a surgeon in the Royal Navy

Question: Do the slaves appear dejected when they first come on board?

Trotter: Most of them, at coming on board, show signs of extreme distress, and some of them even looks of despair; this I attributed to a feeling for their situation, and regret at being torn from their friends and connections. The slaves in the night were often heard making a howling melancholy noise, something expressive of extreme anguish. I found that it was occasioned by finding themselves in a slave room, after dreaming that they had been in their own country amongst their friends and relatives.

Question: Were the slaves much crowded in your ship in the Middle Passage?

Trotter: Yes; so much so that it was not possible to walk amongst them without treading on them.

Question: Had they room to turn themselves, or in any sort to lie at ease?

Trotter: By no means; the slaves that are out of irons are locked spoonways, according to the technical phrase, and closely locked to one another.

Question: Did the slaves appear to suffer from want of air?

Trotter: Yes; I have seen their breasts heaving and observed them draw their breath with all those laborious and anxious efforts for life which we observe in expiring animals subjected by experiment to foul air of different kinds. I have also seen them, when the tarpaulins were, through ignorance, or inadvertently thrown over the gratings, attempting to heave them up, and crying out 'Kickeraboo! Kickeraboo!' which signifies, 'We are dying!'. On removing the tarpaulins and gratings, I have seen them fly to the hatchways with all the signs of terror and dread of suffocation.

(Minutes of Evidence taken before a committee of the House of Commons, 1790)

A Five Days' Fit of Philanthropy

> Hail to my honour'd country, whose mild laws,
> To burst the wretched captive's knotted chain,
> Spite of the artful plea of lawless gain,
> Nobly have dared! O may the just applause,
> Which on itself the virtuous action draws,
> Await thee . . .

'Britannicus' in his *Ode on the Glorious Attempts of the British Nation to abolish the Slave Trade* captured something of the fervour which had gripped England in the late 1780s.[1] Thomas Clarkson records that in May 1787 the only public notice taken of the abolition movement was by his Committee, but within a year it had arrested the attention of the nation, producing 'a kind of holy flame, or enthusiasm, and this to a degree and to an extent never before witnessed'.[2]

Others saw it differently. A member in the House of Commons exclaimed: 'When I see the infatuation almost bordering on frenzy which has taken possession of the public mind outside the House, and see it also extending to some men of the most enlightened understanding within doors, I tremble for the consequences.'[3] Lord Thurlow, the Lord Chancellor, called it, peevishly. 'a five days' fit of philanthropy', and suggested that as it had lain asleep for so long, it should return to that state for another summer.[4]

But nothing could keep it down. 'The poor African', 'that miserable race of beings', had drawn to them the compassion of the people, and the Abolition Society, with its well-oiled machinery, stirred this compassion to eruption point. In the course of thirteen months the Abolition Society's Committee had no less than fifty-one meetings, each lasting at least five hours. It had printed and distributed 26,526 reports and other short accounts, and nearly twice that many pamphlets and books: Clarkson's *Essay*—3,000; Newton's *Thoughts*—3,000; 5,000 of another of Clarkson's tracts—*A Summary View of the Slave Trade*; 3,000 of the Dean of Middleham's *Letter*; and 3,000 lists of subscribers to the Society. It was in close touch with the Quakers, the Baptists, with societies in America, France and Germany. Robert Barclay of the Quaker banking family had been added to the Committee, and Thomas Clarkson continued to tour the country, collecting information and advising the Society's branches. He also toured the London docks at Deptford, Woolwich and Chatham to see that the slave ships were adhering to the requirements of Sir William Dolben's Regulation Act.

Though tracts and books were their main means of communicating to the public, the Society found two visual aids which proved nearly as effective as all the millions of words written and spoken in furtherance of their cause. The first was a drawing of a slave ship, *Brookes*, which a captain of the Royal Navy had made after examining it lying in Liverpool docks. The drawing showed how 450 slaves were packed, lying down, into every available inch of the space between the decks—six feet by one foot four inches for every man; five feet by one foot four for women; five feet by one foot two for boys; and four feet by one foot for girls. 'No one saw it but he was impressed. It spoke to him in a language which was at once intelligible and irresistible. It brought forth the tear of sympathy in behalf of the sufferers, and fixed their sufferings in his heart', Clarkson said.[5]

The second was the Abolition Society's seal which showed a black slave in chains, kneeling, his hands lifted up to the heaven. Its motto read: 'Am I Not a Man and a Brother?' Josiah Wedgwood reproduced the design in a cameo with the black figure against a white background and donated hundreds of these to the Society for distribution. 'They were soon in different parts of the kingdom', Thomas Clarkson recalled. 'Some had them inlaid in gold on the lid of their snuff boxes. Of the ladies, several wore them in bracelets, and others had them fitted up in an ornamental manner as pins for their hair. At length the taste for wearing them became general, and thus fashion, which usually confines itself to worthless things, was seen for once in the honourable office of promoting the cause of justice, humanity and freedom.'[6]

John Newton's good friend and Olney companion, William Cowper, 'the only true Christian poet', as Wilberforce called him, was responsible for some of the best lines on the subject of the slave trade and slavery. His 'The Negro's Complaint' was written in 1788.

> Deem our nation brutes no longer,
> Till some reason ye shall find
> Worthier of regard, and stronger
> Than the colour of our kind.
> Slaves of gold, whose sordid dealings,
> Tarnish all your boasted powers,
> Prove that you have human feelings
> Ere you proudly question ours.

The poem aroused a great deal of admiration, and the Abolition Society ordered thousands of copies to be printed on the finest paper. It was then folded into book form and given the title *A Subject for Conversation at the Tea-Table*. The poem proved an instant success, and became even more popular with the general public when it was set to music. Sung as a ballad it was heard everywhere, on the streets and in the public houses.[7]

Another popular subject for conversation at the tea table was 'anti-saccharism', the name invented for sanctions against West Indian slave-grown sugar. In an *Address to the People of Great Britain* the merchant philanthropist William Fox set out the reasons for taking what at that time was a new step in direct political action. 'If we purchase the commodity we participate in the crime. The slave dealer, the slave holder, and the slave driver are virtually the agents of the consumer, and may be considered as employed and hired by him to procure the commodity.'[8]

On one of his tours Clarkson reported that 'there was no

town through which I passed in which there was not some one individual who had left off the use of sugar. In the smaller towns there were from ten to fifty by estimation, and in the larger two to five hundred who made this sacrifice to virtue.' His obsession with quantifying everything may have got the better of him, and it is likely that people told him they had given up sugar knowing that this is what he wanted to hear, but 'anti-saccharism' had definitely caught on. 'Rich and poor, churchmen and dissenters, had opted the measure. Even grocers had left off trading in the article in some places. In gentlemen's families where the master had set the example, the servants had often voluntarily followed it; and even children, who were capable of understanding the history of the sufferings of the Africans, excluded with the most virtuous resolution the sweets to which they had been accustomed from their lips. By the best computation I was able to make from notes taken down in my journey no fewer than three hundred thousand persons had abandoned the use of sugar.'[9]

The cartoonist Gillray pictured King George, his Queen, and the six Princesses seated around a bare tea-table. The Queen, trying to tempt the young girls into tasting the tea without sugar, says: 'O my dear creatures, do but taste it! You can't think how nice it is without sugar; and then consider how much work you'll save the poor blackeemoors by leaving off the use of it! And, above all, remember how much expense it will save poor Papa!' The last comment was a reference to the economic groundswell beneath the philanthropic wave of enthusiasm. At the beginning of the 1790s the price of West India sugar had gone up, causing a great deal of dissatisfaction in Britain. East India sugar, which was not slave produced, was cheaper, but not readily available because of monopolistic concessions to the West Indian interests. Economics and philanthropy, therefore, both favoured the sugar sanction, but it was regarded by some abolitionists as far too radical. John Newton thought it might alienate more moderate opinion, and William Wilberforce declared it should be suspended until 'if necessary, it might be adopted with effect by general concurrence'.[10] This hope was, of course, a futile one as he surely must have realised and, in fact, sugar imports from the British West Indies increased steadily, despite the ban, reaching a peak in 1802.

Clarkson wrote that in general the national enthusiasm for abolition was so great that it was possible to distinguish the good from the bad by their disposition to the movement. He echoed Wilberforce's 'the kingdom of God and the kingdom of Satan' when he characterised the population as being divided 'as we may suppose the sheep to be from the goats on the day of judgment'.[11] In parliament all the best men appeared to be on the side of the good. Mr Pitt, in a major debate in 1791 on Wilberforce's motion to abolish the trade, said that it was founded on injustice and that it was opposite to expediency as it was to the dictates of mercy and of religion.[12] The eminent Charles Fox spoke even more strongly against it and against the arrogance of the notion that all inhabitants of Africa had inferior minds. How did we know that such was the case? he asked. 'Why might there not be men in Africa of as fine feelings as ourselves, of as enlarged understandings, and as manly in their minds as any of us?'[13] The brilliant orator Edmund Burke admitted to a full House of Commons that ten years before he had prepared some measures for the abolition of the trade, 'but', he said, nodding towards Wilberforce, 'I have burnt my papers and I make an offering of them in honour of the proposition of the hon. gentleman'.[14]

Wilberforce himself had spoken at great length in support of his proposal to abolish the trade. As in his first major speech on the subject he went into great detail about the supposed inferior nature of the black man. He agreed with Mr Fox that 'the negroes are creatures like ourselves', but, he added, 'their minds are uninformed and their moral characters are debased. In general their state of civilisation is very imperfect, their notions of morality extremely rude and the powers of their governments ill-defined.' It was no good thinking about giving slaves liberty—this was not what he was asking for. To give them a power of appealing to the laws would be to awaken in them a sense of dignity of their nature. Drawing the analogy of a man recovering from a fainting fit, Wilberforce said that the first effect was commonly a convulsion, dangerous to the man himself and to all around him. Such, he thought, might be the consequence to the slaves in the West Indies 'of sudden communication of the consciousness of civil rights'. About the slave trade, however, 'Never, never will we desist till we have wiped away this scandal from the Christian name, released ourselves from the load of guilt under which we at present labour, and extinguished every trace of this bloody traffic.'[15]

One member who had listened to the entire debate in silence pointed out that though the leaders in the House of Commons were for abolition, he hoped that the 'minor orators, the dwarfs, the pigmies' would carry the vote against the proposal.[16] As it turned out, he was right. Wilberforce's motion was defeated by seventy-five votes, but he was not unduly worried. 'In my exertions', he said later, 'I have found happiness, though not hitherto success. It enlivens my waking and soothes my evening hours. I carry this topic with me to my repose, and often have the bliss of remembering that I have demanded justice for millions who cannot ask it for themselves.'[17]

I was greatly struck and indeed affected by the appearance of two little sloops which were fitting out for Africa, the one of only 25 tons, which was said to be destined to carry seventy, and the other of only eleven which was said to be destined to carry thirty slaves. . . . When I looked again at the least of the two—for any person who was tall, standing upon the dry ground by the sides of her, might have overlooked everything upon her deck. I knew also that she had been built as a pleasure boat for the accommodation of only six persons upon the Severn. . . . The length of the room for the thirty slaves was twenty-two feet. The greatest breadth of the floor was eight, and the least four. The whole height from the keel to the beam was but five feet eight inches, three feet of which was occupied by ballast, cargo, and provisions, so that two feet eight inches remained only as the height between the decks. Hence, each slave would have only four square feet to sit in, and, when in this posture, his head if he were a full-grown person, would touch the ceiling or upper deck.

(*History of the Abolition of the Slave Trade*—
Thomas Clarkson, 1839 (2nd Edition))

There is a great peculiarity in the negro constitution: that it is particularly conducive to the health of the negro to be close shut up in foul air. This is death to us white men as we know by the experiment of the Black-hole, and other tropical instances; but for your negro, it is the reverse. Keep him hot enough, he will always do well; and the better, the more you try to stifle him . . .

(The Bishop of Rochester, House of Lords, 1799)

6

The Benevolent Planters

In 1789 a play called *The Benevolent Planters*, written by
Thomas Bellamy, was presented at the Theatre Royal,
Haymarket. Its plot was little more than a framework in
which to present an elaborate spectacle with songs and
dances. The scene was set in the West Indies. Heartfree, a
planter, owned Oran, a black saved by whites from death
and 'happily brought to our mart'. He pined for his beloved,
Selima, who was owned by another planter, Goodwin.
Having been separated from each other in Africa, neither
Oran nor Selima realised that they were living on neighbouring plantations. When the play opens, Goodwin and
Heartfree are planning 'diversions' to be presented by the
'jetty tribes' of slaves on their plantations. Says Heartfree:
'The grateful Africans have hearts as large as ours, and
shame on the degrading lash when it can be spared. Reasonable obedience is what we expect, and let those who look
for more feel, and severely feel, the sting of disappointment.'
   The final scene takes place on the open stage filled with
singing, dancing slaves, and watched by the two planters and
a friend. 'Now,' says Heartfree to the slaves, 'let the air echo
to the sound of enlivening instruments, and beat the grounds
to their tuneful melody; while myself and my two worthy
friends, who since our last festival have reaped the benefits of
your honest labours, in full goblets drink to your happiness.'
   In the midst of the festivities Oran addresses another
slave. 'O my friend! When thy poor Oran is no more, if
chance that Selima yet lives, if blessed Providence *should*
lead her to these happy shores, if she should escape the
cruel enemy and be brought hither with honour unsullied;
tell her how much she owes to these generous men; comfort

her affected spirit and teach her to adore the God of truth and mercy.' His friend replies: 'The same Providence which has turned the terrors of slavery into willing bondage may yet restore thy Selima.'

Providence obliges. Oran and Selima are brought together by the planters. Her owner says: 'You receive her pure as when you parted, with a mind released from the errors of darkness and refined by its afflictions.' To the strains of soft music, Selima comes down the stage attended by six virgins who present her to Oran. There is a flourish of music and a shout of joy goes up. Oran declares: 'You have proved yourselves *The Benevolent Planters*, and that under subjection like yours, *slavery is but a name!*'

Bellamy's idealised vision of plantation life with its kind planters and loyal slaves was exactly the view the West Indians liked to have of themselves, and the picture they tried to project on to the British public. The underlying assumption was that the West Indies were preferable to Africa and that slavery under a white Christian was better than freedom under a black pagan. Moreover, slavery, an ancient system, was in itself not wrong, especially if the slave had the consolation of Christianity, and so long as he remained devoted and uncomplaining he could expect to be treated with fairness and mercy. Every planter was a Heartfree, every slave an Oran; and if the interfering philanthropists would only mind their own business, everyone would be happy.

'The planters of this island have been very unjustly stigmatised with an accusation of treating their negroes with barbarity', said Edward Long in *The History of Jamaica*, published in 1774. 'The planter in reply to these bitter invectives will think it sufficient to urge in the first place that he did not make them slaves, but succeeded to the inheritance of their services in the same manner as an English squire succeeds to the estates of his ancestors; and that, as to his Africans, he buys their services from those who have all along pretended a very good right to sell; that it cannot be for his interest to treat his negroes in the manner reported; but that it is so to use them well, and preserve their vigour and existence as long as he is able.'[1]

Long, who was born in Cornwall, was the son of a plantation owner. After studying law, he went to Jamaica and became in time a judge, but ill-health forced him to return to England where he died in 1813. His *History* was a large work in three volumes, and though he later changed some of his more extreme views, it accurately reflects the educated West Indian attitude to slavery and the slave trade. It became one of those basic sources from which the protagonists in the abolition debate drew their material, and it influenced a better writer and more prominent West Indian advocate, Bryan Edwards, who also wrote a history of the West Indies. So often were Long's volumes quoted that Wilberforce called them 'a sort of West Indian gospel'.

'I will assert', Long wrote, 'that there are no men, nor orders of men in Great Britain possessed of more disinterested charity, philanthropy, and clemency than the Creole [white] gentlemen of this island. I have never known and rarely heard of any cruelty either practised or tolerated by them over their negroes. If cruelties are practised, they happen without their knowledge or consent.'[2] Like Heartfree or Goodwin in the play, Long's planter was loved and respected by his slaves who addressed him with freedom and confidence, 'not with the abject prostration of real slaves, but as their common friend and father. His authority over them is like that of an ancient patriarch; conciliating affection by the mildness of its exertion and claiming respect by the justice and propriety of its decisions and discipline, it attracts the love of the honest and good, while it awes the worthless into reformation.'[3]

Bryan Edwards repeated the idea of the much-maligned plantation owner. 'Much the greatest part of the present inhabitants of the British West Indies came into possession of their plantations by inheritance or accident. Many persons there are in Great Britain itself who . . . find themselves possessed of estates in the West Indies which they have never seen, and invested with powers over their fellow-creatures there which, however extremely odious, they have never abused.'[4]

It is easy to understand the reason why the West Indians and their supporters insisted on their innocence and humanity. What is not so easy to understand is why their opponents, the leading abolitionists, agreed with them so wholeheartedly. Whenever possible, the latter sought to distinguish between the system of slavery and its operators. In his preface to an essay written in 1823 Thomas Clarkson said: 'It is against the *system* then, and not against the West Indians as a body that I am warm. . . . I know that there are many estimable men among them living in England who deserve every desirable praise for having sent over instructions to their agents in the West Indies from time to time in behalf of their wretched slaves.'[5] Wilberforce, in his first major parliamentary speech on the slave trade, refused to accuse the Liverpool slave merchants. 'I will allow them, nay, I will believe them to be men of humanity.'[6] On another occasion he said that 'many of our non-resident West Indian proprietors are as full as ignorant of the real condition of the bulk of the negro population as other men. Often indeed the most humane of the number (many of them are men whose humanity is unquestionable) are least of all aware of it.'[7] Even the Abolition Society in one of its annual reports recorded for all to read that their 'endeavours have not been aimed against any man or set of men, but against the slave trade itself'.[8] Thomas Buxton, Wilberforce's parliamentary successor, called his opponents 'unfortunate . . . rather than culpable'.[9] and Wilberforce himself recommended that they should be treated with 'candour and tenderness'.[10]

One cannot help feeling when reading these recommendations and indemnifications which the leading abolitionists repeated like a liturgy right up until emancipation that they were cowed by the wealth and power of the West Indians. Certainly some West Indians were both rich and powerful, but the fact is that their strength, as a body, had declined by the end of the eighteenth century, having been taken over by the East Indian interests.[11] Yet they continued to dazzle those who should have been least affected by their glamour. One of the more radical abolitionists criticised the leadership on this very point. 'The interests and the prejudices of the West Indian planters have occupied too prominent a place in the discussion of this great question. The

abolitionists have shown a great deal too much politeness
and accommodation towards these gentlemen . . . too
much delicacy and tenderness. They are culprits . . . and
as such they ought to be regarded notwithstanding their
rank and consequence.'[12]

One of the reasons for accommodating and placating the
West Indians was the similarity, social and economic,
between the leading abolitionists and their opponents.
Except for their battle over slavery, they had many things
in common. They lived similar lives, read the same newspapers and books, frequented the same parks and watering-
places. 'The whole surface of society here at home is studded
with men and women who have spent a great part of their
lives in our West Indian colonies', wrote a contributor
in *Blackwood's Magazine*. 'Whole cities here in the midst of
us are occupied by people who have done so, or who are
connected by the closest ties of blood and friendship with
such as have done so. Look, for example, at Liverpool,
look at Glasgow, look at the City of London. Are not these
places crammed with West Indians? . . . The fact is indisputable—the people are here—we see them every day—we
must all have more or less associated with them and their
families. . . . If we are Christians, we sit in the same churches
with them; if we are magistrates, we sit on the same bench
with them.'[13]

Wilberforce once received an anxious letter from a certain
M. G. Lewis who wrote to him in despair. 'On the 1st of
next May I shall have 600 if not 700 negroes at my absolute disposal. Now were you in my situation what would
you do with those negroes at your decease?'[14] Unfortunately,
Wilberforce's reply is not known, but he probably saw
nothing ironic or incongruous in being asked his advice
in such a matter.

Not everyone saw the planters as humane and benevolent.

> The bloated vampire of a living man;
> His frame—a fungus form of dunghill birth,
> That taints the air and rots the earth . . .

was how James Montgomery characterised the typical

slave owner in his long poem on the West Indies.[15] But planters in the West Indies and plantation owners living in England were different breeds of the same species, and while it was easy to attack the ones who lived thousands of miles away and could only return invective with invective, it required considerable daring and fortutude to criticise the others who might, indeed, be friends of yours or friends of friends. Granville Sharp had such courage, but unfortunately for the cause of abolition his colleagues were not all so well endowed. Had they been the campaign to emancipate the slaves may not have taken quite as long as fifty years to succeed. It was only when the younger and more radical supporters of the cause grew tired of their elders' politeness to the non-resident planters and proprietors that political action began to speed up.

The West Indians, of course, were as well organised as the abolitionists to meet the attack. They, too, had their Society—of West India Planters and Merchants—and they met their expenses from a fighting fund which was raised by adding an additional tax on each hogshead of sugar, punchen of rum, and bag of cotton handled by the members. Everyone directly or indirectly connected with the West Indies, mortgagees, annuitants and creditors, were asked for contributions, and books, tracts and other publications were published in support of their cause.[16]

Unless forced by a sharp, telling blow from the abolitionists into angry insult, the tone the planters in Britain tried to maintain in their propaganda was one of reasonableness. Like the abolitionists they adopted the courtly manners of parliamentary debate, acknowledging the respectability of their opponents before attacking them, but they never went as far as the abolitionists in separating the individuals from the views they held. The West Indians thought their opponents wrong, and a dangerous threat to their livelihood. They were over-zealous; as Christians too enthusiastic and as philanthropists too idealistic.

'We were to examine the subject of the African commerce as an advocate for the cause of humanity, and for the natural rights of human kind, without regard to the condition of rival states,' wrote one of the West Indian supporters to the *Gentleman's Magazine*, 'we might be induced to mingle with the general voice and exclaim against the inhumanity of such a traffic. But when the subject is considered in a political view . . . we are inclined to frame our judgment on the maxims of political prudence and on the views of national expediency. . . . Self-preservation is the primary law of nations and in the present state of things the rigid maxims of morality may sometimes be sacrificed to the claims of national policy.'[17]

'The purchase of Africans by the Europeans preserves their lives and adds to their ease and comfort,' an anonymous country gentleman said in his tract, *Reasons for Voting against Mr Wilberforce's Motion*. 'On plantations negroes generally have very comfortable houses . . . and no person would employ a manager of cruel character.' Even plantation slaves approved of the slave trade because 'buying new negroes makes the slaves happy as easing them and affording them wives'.[18]

The West Indian saw himself as the victim not the perpetrator of crime: he did not create the slave system, but when he tried to keep it going for the benefit of the colonies and the home country he was held in contempt by all. He played mercilessly on the fears of men with property: slavery was property—end slavery and you end property of all kind, everywhere. He played mercilessly on the fears of the patriot: end the slave trade and France or the other European Powers will benefit; they will strengthen themselves at Britain's expense. He appealed to the conservative in everyone: the Caribbean islands, for all their economic ups and downs, were the backbone of the British Empire; they were the *eldorado* which had given generations of Englishmen wealth and power; they were richer than India and their claims on the British public were of longer-standing. End the slave trade or emancipate the slaves or do anything to disrupt the stability of the West Indies and they will be lost for ever to Britain as were the American colonies. In fact, when the pressure got too bad, it was even hinted that they might have to seek the protection of the American Government.[19]

'I ever have been and shall be a firm friend to our present

colonial system', declared Lord Nelson to a Jamaican planter in 1805. 'I was bred in the good old school and taught to appreciate the value of our West Indian possessions, and neither in the field nor in the Senate shall their just rights be infringed whilst I have an arm to fight in their defence or a tongue to launch my voice against the damnable, cruel doctrine of Wilberforce and his hypocritical allies; and I hope my berth in heaven will be as exalted as his who would certainly cause the murder of all our friends and fellow-subjects in the Colonies.'[20]

Against an uncertain, over-respectful opposition the West Indian proprietors and merchants employed all their powerful weapons, and when these failed, the abolition leaders in their timidity usually provided them with more. Events in the rest of the world helped. At the beginning of the 1790s, just when it seemed that public indignation against the slave system might bring about radical changes, the French king lost his head and reform in Britain lost its nerve. The five days' fit of philanthropy was over.

A black trader invited a negro who resided a little way up the country to come and see him. After the entertainment was over the trader proposed to his guest to treat him with a sight of one of the ships lying in the river. The unsuspicious countryman readily consented and accompanied the trader in a canoe to the side of the ship which he viewed with pleasure and astonishment. While he was thus employed, some black traders on board who appeared to be in the secret leaped into the canoe, seized the unfortunate man, and dragging him to the ship, immediately sold him.

(Falconbridge)

May 8, 1795: The men slaves were brought on deck. They seemed extremely dispirited, and drooped very much. The captain and the officers seemed to think that they had mischief in their minds.

May 23, 1795: I observe the slaves reject their food. The officer on duty threatened them with the 'cat', and then they made a show of eating by putting a little rice into their mouths; but whenever the officer's back was turned they threw it into the sea.

May 24, 1795: The captain again wanted the slaves to dance, but they showed no inclination till the 'cat' was called for. A few indeed were content to have the 'cat' smartly applied several times before they would so much belie their feelings as to make merry when their heart was sad. Some of the women sang very sweetly and in a plaintive tone.

(The Diary of Zachary Macaulay. *Life and Letters of Zachary Macaulay*—Viscountess Knutsford, 1900)

7

Revolution and Reaction

'How much the greatest event it is that ever happened in the world, and how much the best!' declared Charles Fox at the news of the fall of the Bastille in July 1789.[1]

The Abolition Committee resolved, on Wilberforce's recommendation, to send Thomas Clarkson to France immediately. 'Mr Wilberforce was of opinion that, as commotion had taken place [there] which then aimed at political reforms,' Clarkson recalled, 'it was possible that the leading persons concerned in them might, if an application were made to them judiciously, be induced to take the slave trade into consideration, and incorporate it among the abuses to be done away.'[2]

Clarkson heard bold words spoken in the new National Assembly; Louis XVI expressed a desire to meet him and requested to read his essay on the slave trade; and he met black deputies from San Domingo. But the French planters, like their British counterparts, were well entrenched in the political structure, feeble though it was, and they quickly mounted a campaign against Clarkson, accusing him of fomenting rebellion in San Domingo. He returned to England disappointed.

The abolitionists were not the only liberal-minded Englishmen who saw the Revolution as a signal for reform in England. Throughout the country reform societies of various kinds were formed with members aping the French and calling each other 'citizen'. Tom Paine's revolutionary work, *The Rights of Man*, took the place of the Bible in hundreds of thousands of homes. Demand for wider parliamentary representation grew, sections of the middle class seeing in the general enthusiasm of the time the chance to seize the kind of power, on both national and local levels, to which they felt their wealth and education entitled them. For the educated artisans and workers this was the chance to organise themselves into unions. Within three years of the storming of the Bastille radical ferment in Britain had reached fever pitch.[3]

Events in France, however, outpaced the machinery in England to absorb the sudden impact of reform, and direct it into controllable paths. It started to move into reverse, and as Revolution became Terror in France, with the overthrow of the monarchy, the French Government openly offering to aid the peoples of Europe in their own revolutions, and the king's death, so repressive measures followed in Britain. In 1793 France declared war on Britain, and Britain's flirtation with revolution ended.[4] The abolitionists found that their association with the French at the height of the fervour was just the weapon their enemies had been looking for. The epithet *Jacobin*, which was flung about in the 1790s with the same careless disregard for meaning as was *Communist* 150 years later, was pinned on to everyone who expressed abolitionist views.

'Our opponents represented the Committee as a nest of Jacobins, and they held the cause, sacred as it was, as affording an opportunity of meeting for the purpose of overthrowing the state', wrote Thomas Clarkson;[5] and Hannah More was horrified to find herself branded a revolutionary. To the Bishop of Bath and Wells she complained, 'It has been broadly intimated that I have laboured to spread French principles; and one of my schools is specifically charged with having prayed for the success of the French. . . . I am accused of being the abettor, not only of fanaticism and sedition, but of thieving and prostitution.'[6]

The Jacobins of England were named by *Vindex* in a pamphlet in 1792 as 'the Wilberforces, the Coopers, the Paines, and the Clarksons, the dupes who are flattered into mischief, and those of a far different description who direct their motions'. 'It may be asked', he continued, 'by what motives the promoters of the abolition have been actuated? The answer is plain: fanaticism and false philosophy had exalted their imagination and obscured their reason, and in what they affected to call a reform in the constitution, they saw the means of establishing such a government as best suited their wild ephemeral theory. . . . In France their fellow reformers put arms into the hands of the mob, and dictated the measures of the National Assembly. It was here thought that petitions might have an equal effect. . . . They fondly imagined a few more petitions, no matter by whom signed or how obtained, would reduce this country to the situation of France, *so long their envy, their boast, and their model*.'[7]

Lord Abingdon accused the abolition movement of meaning 'neither more nor less than Liberty and Equality. It has Tom Paine's Rights of Man for its chief and best support,' he told the House of Lords, 'and from such principles flow insubordination, anarchy, confusion, murder, havoc, devastation and ruin. Shall this House, the dernier resort of justice, sanctify an act of injustice?'[8]

It was one thing to be attacked by West Indian supporters for wanting to end the slave trade; it was another to be accused of desiring to overthrow the sacred principles of property and the constitution. To be charged with loving the blacks was welcomed; but to be charged with loving Tom Paine, a republican atheist, was more than William Wilberforce or any of the abolition leaders could take. They, like so many others, rejected their former associates who might be tainted with Jacobinism, and joined in the cry for repression.

'Not only are French politics being imported,' said Wilberforce in a debate on a bill to prohibit seditious meetings, 'but French philosophy also. In the numerous publications by which their opinions are disseminated there is a marked contempt for everything sacred, and avowed opposition to the religion as well as to the constitution of Great Britain. Various means have been taken to put a stop to these proceedings, but in vain. These bad men seem to redouble their efforts, and to press forward with increased audaciousness. In voting for this measure . . . I shall be invigorating the British constitution.'[9]

In 1794 habeas corpus was suspended; in 1795 all large public meetings were forbidden without a special licence; in

1799 and 1800 Acts were brought in to outlaw 'combinations' such as workers' unions. The fast pace of repression kept up with the reaction again liberalism and reform, but no matter how reactionary the abolitionists showed themselves to be, no matter how frequently they disassociated their aims from those of the revolutionaries, they and their cause suffered badly. Then one event which, from their point of view, was the most significant of all those swift, violent events of the 1790s took place: the slave uprising in San Domingo.

The slave war with its wholesale destruction of white people and property perpetually haunted the guilty imaginations of the colonists, and the theme of vengeance is repeated again and again in prose and poetry. Even Bryan Edwards, in a youthful poetic fancy, expressed what many planters like him feared above all.

> The thunder, hark! 'tis Africk's god,
> He wakes, he lifts the avenging rod,
> Now, Christian, now, in wild dismay,
> Of Africk's proud revenge the prey . . .[10]

All the terrifying tortures which the whites could imagine inflicting on anyone who might try to enslave them were projected onto and anticipated from the blacks if they were ever given the chance to revolt. That small uprisings did occur frequently only helped to stimulate their fears despite the fact that the revolts were usually quelled with little trouble and no loss of lives except to the slaves whose leaders when captured were usually rounded up and summarily butchered.

In 1791 the West Indian nightmare became a reality; not in some isolated little island, but in the richest in the whole Caribbean. Up to 1789 San Domingo had supplied France with two-thirds of its overseas trade. With a slave population of half a million it was the largest importer of Africans, and one of the British slave trade's best customers. Between 1789 and 1791 the British West Indies imported approximately 75,000 slaves from Africa; 45,000 went to British colonies, and the bulk of the 30,000 exported by them to

foreign colonies went to San Domingo, a possible reason, as
has been mentioned, for Pitt's sudden conversion to abolition.[11] After two years of the French Revolution and its
colonial repercussions, the French prize exploded. Under
the leadership of Toussaint L'Ouverture the slaves of San
Domingo revolted and defeated the local whites and French
soldiers in a succession of fierce and bloody battles. The
stories of terrible atrocities committed by the slaves quickly
reached the rest of the West Indies and England: wives
had been raped over the dead bodies of their husbands;
children were speared and carried as banners in front of
marching slaves; houses were burnt and plantations destroyed. Everything the West Indians had been warning
the public would happen if the abolitionists were allowed to
continue their agitation against the slave trade and slavery
was happening in San Domingo.[12]

An opportunity like that could not be missed, and the
planters and merchants grabbed it firmly. San Domingo
became their answer to every measure proposed by the
abolitionists, much like the Congo in the 1950s was the cry
of the whites in Africa when their security was threatened
by outside interference. 'Look what happened in San
Domingo', the planters said. 'Do you want another San
Domingo in Jamaica or Barbados or St Christopher? Well,
that's what you'll get if you suggest we end the slave trade,
or treat our slaves better, or—God forbid!—emancipate
them.'

The abolitionists replied that what had happened in San
Domingo was precisely what would happen in every West
Indian colony if the planters continued to treat their
slaves like cattle and continued to import more and more
of them. Thomas Clarkson quickly wrote an open letter
explaining the reasons for the San Domingo revolt and the
Abolition Society had a thousand copies distributed,[13] but
the West Indians drowned out the voices of reason with the
cries of black savagery, death and ruin. Even some abolitionists began to have second thoughts about the wisdom
of their ambitions. Henry Brougham, later Lord Brougham
and Vaux, one of the best known names recruited to the
cause, wrote an early work on colonial policy which in-

cluded a picture of the supposedly murderous San Domingo slaves which would have done the most fervent slave owner proud. He saw 'hordes of bloodthirsty savages, intimately acquainted with every corner of the planter's house, every retreat into which his family may be driven, every crevice in the whole country, mad with unnatural rage against all that deviates from the sable hue of their own ferocious brethren, pouring over every spot where European life exists . . . and enacting deeds of such complicated horror that it is not permitted to the pen of a European to describe or to name them.'[14]

With the cries of Jacobin and San Domingo ringing in their ears, the abolitionists felt the need to retrench. William Wilberforce noted in his diary in 1798: 'Stephen frankly and kindly reproving me for not pleading the cause of the slaves watchfully enough'.[15] The Abolition Society's activities went into decline. In January 1792 they issued a public statement emphasising once again lest it had been forgotten that emancipation was not one of their objects, that it was a misrepresentation to suggest it was, and that the abolition of the slave trade was all that they were concerned with.[16] In April of that year they reported that their funds were nearly exhausted. A year later the Society's Committee resolved 'that all proceedings respecting the expediency of recommending the disuse of West Indian sugar and rum be suspended for the present', and declared in its report that 'we must endeavour to reconcile ourselves to the slow proceedings of the legislature'.[17]

In May 1794 notice was given to the landlord of the Committee's meeting-place in Old Jewry that they no longer required the premises.[18] The Committee met only occasionally in 1795 and 1796. In March 1797 it met again to compose a public statement refuting Bryan Edwards's charges in his *History of San Domingo* of their complicity in the slave rebellion.[19] Thereafter, it did not meet again for seven years.

Once a week the ship's barber scrapes their chins without assistance from soap; and on the same day their nails are closely pared to ensure security from harm in those nightly battles that occur when the slave contests with his neighbour every inch of plank to which he is glued. . . .

The strict discipline of nightly stowage is, of course, of the greatest importance in slavers, else every negro would accommodate himself as if he were a passenger. . . . In order to ensure perfect silence and regularity during the night, a slave is chosen as constable from every ten, and furnished with a 'cat' to enforce commands during his appointed watch. In remuneration for his services which it may be believed are admirably performed whenever the whip is required, he is adorned with an old shirt or tarry trousers.

(Revelations of a Slave Trader—Captain Canot, 1854)

Extract from the evidence of Thomas Trotter, M.D.

Question: Are the slaves during the Middle Passage obliged to take exercise and by what name is this commonly called?

Trotter: I believe the practice of dancing them is very general in the trade, and in all the ships; but in ours it was not practised till their health made it absolutely necessary that they should be allowed some exercise. The men, who were confined in irons, were ordered to stand up, and make what motion they could. Some of them who did not seem to relish the exercise were compelled to it by a lash of the 'cat', but many of them refused to do it even with this mode of punishment in a severe degree.

(Minutes of evidence taken before a committee of the
House of Commons, 1790)

8

The Triumph of Gradualism

In a cartoon by Cruickshank, *The gradual abolition of the slave trade, or leaving off sugar by degrees*, Princess Elizabeth says to her father, George III: 'Indeed, Papa, I can't leave off a good thing so soon. I am sure of late I have been very moderate, but I must have my bit now and then.' Her sister replies: 'For my part I'd rather want altogether than have a small piece.' The combination of indignation, apathy, and indetermination which characterised the period between 1792 and 1804 was summed up neatly in a poem by Cowper.

> He blam'd and protested, but join'd in the plan;
> He shar'd in the plunder, but pitied the man.[1]

The politician who seemed to be doing much of the pitying and protesting was the Prime Minister. In a famous speech delivered to the House of Commons in April 1792 almost when dawn was breaking, Pitt declared himself wholly on the side of immediate abolition. He attacked his fellow-members for their tardiness in coming to a decision on ending the slave trade. 'Where the evil in question is a moral evil which a man can scrutinise and where that moral evil has its origins with ourselves, let us not imagine that we can clear our consciences by this general, not to say, irreligious and impious way of laying aside the question.'[2]

These were brave words, but when it came to doing something positive, Pitt held back and let others take control. In his cabinet he had men who were positively against abolition; Lord Thurlow, for example, the Lord Chancellor, helped persuade the House of Lords in 1792 to vote to hear

the evidence regarding the trade all over again, despite
the voluminous Privy Council Report, in order to create
further delay.[3] But the key man in West Indian affairs in
the cabinet was the Home Secretary under whose control
fell colonial policy. During this period the Home Secretary
was Henry Dundas, later Lord Melville. A close friend
of Pitt's, Dundas was satirised in a verse which echoed
Cowper's:

> For true to public virtue's patriot plan,
> He loves the Minister, and not the Man.[4]

In that same debate in which Pitt declared his hatred of
the slave trade, Dundas also spoke. There were no histri-
onics in his speech. He agreed the trade was immoral and
impolitic; he also agreed that immediate abolition would
cause hardship to those invested in the West Indies. To
solve the dilemma he suggested 'a moderate and middling
way of proceeding . . . measures which should not invade
the property of individuals nor shock too suddenly the
prejudices of our West Indian islands'. He moved, therefore,
to insert the word 'gradually' in Wilberforce's original motion
to abolish the slave trade. It was a small word, seemingly an
innocuous word, but it had the effect of slowing down
almost to a halt the attempts by parliament to end the trade.[5]

Fox called the motion 'delusive and deceptive'[6], but
when a member following Dundas declared that the suggestion 'has relieved me from the utmost anxiety',[7] he was
echoing the feelings of the majority of the members—as
the final voting confirmed: *Yeas* in favour of gradual abolition, 230; *Noes*, 85; majority 145. So great was the relief
of the members that when 1796 was suggested as the year
when abolition should take place, the majority voted for it,
presumably in the belief that when that date arrived,
nothing would be done. They were right. 1796 came and
went; the slave trade continued unabated.

In Cowper's words Pitt was not only protesting, he was
also sharing in the plunder. The history of San Domingo
did not come to an end in 1791 with the slave revolt. It
was too valuable a prize to be lost to slaves. In 1793, even

though a French invasion threatened England, Pitt and Dundas gave their blessing to a military expedition to the island. In September 900 men left Jamaica and landed at Jeremie in San Domingo, where they were welcomed as liberators by the white planters. They quickly succeeded in capturing most of the island. Another expedition of 7,000 men set out from Barbados and captured the sugar islands of Martinique, St Lucia, and Guadeloupe. Being dependent on slaves, it was commercial madness to deprive them of fresh imports from Africa, so that while Wilberforce moved annually in parliament to end the trade, it was actually growing at an enormous pace, financed mainly by British money.[8] It was later computed that under Pitt's administration the British slave trade increased by over double, from an average of about 25,000 slaves exported annually from Africa to 57,000.[9] In the course of the war with Napoleon which was soon to follow more islands and richer colonies were to become British: Berbice, Demerara, Trinidad, Tobago from the French and Spanish; Surinam and the Cape of Good Hope from the Dutch. With each new acquisition the numbers of slaves subject to British law or owned by British merchants and planters increased.

Years later Zachary Macaulay reported in a letter to his wife a conversation he had had with a French count in Paris. 'In England you have many rich and idle people who have nothing to do but amuse themselves with projects of benevolence. . . . If you were in earnest, if you were really sincere in your principles, why do you not abolish slavery? . . . So far are you from being enemies to slavery that you rapaciously stripped France of one of her best possessions . . . to swell the number of your slave islands.'[10] Macaulay's answer was not recorded.

Apart from making his annual motion against the slave trade in parliament, what was Wilberforce doing during this period? His journal records 'seasons of fasting' and 'hours of prayer at large, for God's mercy through Christ; for all Christian graces; for all my schemes; for the poor slaves'.[11] After the capture of Trinidad in 1797 a plan was put forward to move by force slaves from the older islands to clear new lands. This was a good opportunity for Wilberforce to draw the country's attention to the apparent inconsistency of its Prime Minister who attacked the trade, but did everything in his very considerable power to ensure its continuance. Other abolitionists anxiously awaited Wilberforce's denunciation. It did not come. In parliament he firmly rejected the insinuation that he had watched with unconcern the importation of slaves to the conquered lands. 'I bewail the circumstances with the utmost bitterness', he said.[12]

'I still clearly think that you have been improperly silent', James Stephen wrote to him in disgust, on one of the few occasions when that tight little group of 'saints' showed themselves to be in disagreement. 'When you see the government loading the bloody altars of commerce, the idol of this Carthage, with an increase of human victims . . . you are bound by the situation wherein you have placed yourself to cry aloud against it. You are even the rather bound to do so because those high-priests of Moloch, Lord Liverpool and Mr Dundas, are your political, and Mr Pitt also your private friends.'[13]

In 1794, the black army of L'Ouverture, with help from the French, drove the British out of most of San Domingo, but the Prime Minister and his Home Secretary did not lose hope of recapturing the island. Spending nearly a million pounds in 1795 and over £2,000,000 in 1796,[14] they pursued their policy of conquest which Dundas explained to parliament was 'not a war for riches or local aggrandisement, but a war for security'.[15] During this time Wilberforce raised no objections to the unlawful presence of his country's troops in a land which was now in the control of slaves whose advocate he professed himself to be.

Eventually, however, even parliament tired of the wastage of money in San Domingo and a motion was put to withdraw the troops. The mover declared that 'in no place had the war been so badly conducted'.[16] Dundas's reply is interesting. He reminded the House that they were fighting blacks, and that if they were allowed to win, Jamaica and the rest of the British West Indies would go the same way. Then he added, almost as an afterthought, that San Domingo alone produced one-third more than all the British islands, Jamaica included.[17] Wilberforce rose to speak: 'I must dissent from the motion to withdraw the troops,' he said. 'I cannot see any reason for relinquishing what we are now possessed of in the island, though I think the attempt to subdue it is unwise.'[18]

Agitation against the slave trade was not entirely in abeyance. Another Bill regulating the trade was passed and became law in August 1799. As Sir William Dolben's Act of ten years earlier it provided for the registration of slave ships, and laid down how slaves were to be transported. Every ship had to have painted on her in white and yellow letters on a black ground the words—*Allowed to Carry Slaves*—followed by the number of slaves for which a licence had been granted. The space between the decks had to be not less than five feet high, and each slave had to have eight square feet of room around him. The maximum number of slaves which could be transported in a ship was 400.[19]

Another bill attempted to limit the area in Africa where slaves could be purchased. This was thrown out by the Lords. The Duke of Clarence, later William IV, who had once served in the West Indies fleet, came to the aid of his planter friends and attacked the abolitionists. 'On the ill-founded plea of humanity they desire you to relinquish your colonial wealth, the sinews of our commercial existence, and sink into insignificance and contempt in the eyes of Europe and the world by the adoption of their new system of philosophy and humanity. They call upon you to disfranchise the West India merchants and planters, to depopulate Liverpool and to deprive some thousands of industrious and respectable men of the birth-right as British subjects.' Referring to the Regulation Act which was just about to come into force he said, 'Let foreign nations make no regulations for their own vessels . . . We, thank God, are actuated by other considerations than mere gain. We are actuated by principles of humanity. Out of 15,508 negroes shipped in 1796, 559 died, being about 3½ per cent. According to the new carrying Bill the above 15,508 negroes will be reduced to 10,252 which is a reduction of one third.'[20]

In 1799, twelve years after the first meeting of the Abolition Committee and ten years after the first flood of petitions to parliament condemning the trade and calling for its abolition, the fortunes of the abolitionists were at their lowest point. Wilberforce admitted to the Commons when moving once again the motion to abolish the trade that he could not expect the entertain great hopes of success. Even the West Indians had lost interest in the parliamentary battle; only one gentleman was roused to object to Wilberforce's assertion that Africans in the interior of the continent 'were advanced two or three hundred years in knowledge and civilisation beyond those who were in habits of intercourse with British merchants'.[21] 'Books! Books!' the gentleman cried in indignation. 'The blackamoors have books! and this hon. mover gives this as a reason for not exporting them as slaves! I think if the hon. mover had recollected all the mischief that books have done, especially of late years, in the world, he may have spared this argument at least. What produced the French Revolution? Books! The House will not be induced to put a stop to the slave trade in order that the inhabitants of Africa might stay at home to be corrupted by reading books.'[22]

There was little to do after 1799 but to abandon the effort, and for another four years Wilberforce ceased to move for abolition. One point about this low period of inactivity which remains curious is that parliamentary success was never very far away. In 1796 Wilberforce's motion was lost by only four votes with the Home Secretary, Dundas, voting with Pitt, Fox and Wilberforce in favour of immediate abolition. In 1797 the majority against abolition was greater, but in the following year it was again only four. These narrow margins prompted one impatient abolitionist into an angry attack on Pitt. He accused him of not being 'in earnest and bona fide', an accusation which Dundas was quick to point out was unparliamentary.[23] But the point was taken. Most abolitionists came to believe that Pitt could have turned the scales in their favour had he so wished, and that by not doing so he gave implicit encouragement to the opposition. James Stephen said in later years: 'An impartial judgment must now regard the death of Mr Pitt as the necessary precursor of the liberation of Africa.'[24]

In March 1803 Wilberforce wrote in despair to Lord

Muncaster. 'Then our poor black clients,' he sighed. 'O, my dear Muncaster, my heart bleeds to think of their wrongs.'[25] A few years earlier the Abolition Society reported that they could at least console 'ourselves with the reflection that we have earnesly laboured to avert these evils by endeavouring to effect the abolition of the slave trade by just and temperate measures'.[26] Yet, despite their bleeding hearts and their earnest endeavours, the slaves' friends had temporarily abandoned them. 'We do not think the present juncture favourable for any further public measure', the Society told its members in the same report before bringing its activities virtually to a halt.

Jamaica negroes cutting cane in their working dresses. An idealised view of West Indian slavery painted by M. De la Beche. From *Notes on the Present Condition of the Negroes in Jamaica*, 1825 by H. T. De la Beche, the proprietor of Halse Hall, a Jamaican plantation. (*Trustees of the British Museum*)

Branding a negress. Frontispiece to Theodore Canot's memoirs, *Twenty Years a Slaver*, 1854. (*Trustees of the British Museum*)

REPRESENTATION of an INSURRECTION
on board
A SLAVE-SHIP.

Shewing how the crew fire upon the unhappy Slaves from behind the
BARRICADO, *erected on board all Slave ships, as a security whenever such commotions may happen.*

See the privy council's report part I. Art: SLAVES.
Minutes of evidence before the House of Commons.
Wadstrom's Essay on Colonization §. 471.

Mutiny on board a slave ship; from C. D. Wadstrom's *Essay on Colonization*, 1794.
(Trustees of the British Museum)

The boycott of West Indian sugar. James Gillray's cartoon of George III and his family, March 27, 1792. (See page 75) *(Trustees of the British Museum)*

PART TWO

It frequently happens that the negroes, on being purchased by the Europeans, become raving mad, and many of them die in that state. In a former voyage, on board a ship to which I belonged, we were obliged to confine a female negro of about twenty-three years of age on her becoming a lunatic. She was afterwards sold during one of her lucid intervals. . . .

Most of the sailors were treated with brutal severity; but one in particular, a man advanced in years, experienced it in an uncommon degree. Having made some complaint relative to his allowance for water, and this being construed as an insult, one of the officers seized him, and with the blows he bestowed upon him, beat out several of his teeth. Not content with this, while the poor man was yet bleeding, one of the iron pump-bolts was fixed in his mouth, and kept there by a piece of rope-yarn tied round his head. Being unable to spit out the blood which flowed from the wound, the man was almost choked, and obliged to swallow it. He was then tied to the rail of the quarter-deck having declared, upon being gagged, that he would jump overboard and drown himself. About two hours after, he was taken from the quarter-deck rail and fastened to the grating companion of the steerage under the half-deck where he remained all night with a sentinel placed over him.

(Falconbridge)

At the appointed day [in March 1827], 'La Fortuna' sailed with 220 human beings packed in her hold. Three months afterwards I received advices that she safely landed 217 in the Bay of Matanzas and that their sale yielded a clear profit on the voyage of forty-one thousand four hundred and thirty eight dollars.

		Dollars	
	1. Expenses Out		
	(Including cost of ship, fitting out, provisions,		
	wages, cargo and hush-money)	20,742	00
Add	*2. Expenses Home*		
	(Including provisions, wages, etc)	6,430	46
		27,172	46
Add	*3. Expenses in Havana*		
	(Including commissions, 217 slave dresses at		
	2 dollars each)	12,808	00
		39,980	46
	4. Returns		
	Value of vessel at auction	3,950	00
	Proceeds of 217 slaves	77,469	00
		81,419	00
	Résumé		
	Total Returns	81,419	00
	Total Expenses	39,980	46
	Nett profit . . .	41,438	54

(Canot)

9

Tender Hearts and Closed Minds

For five years a young French botanist, Michel Adanson, toured the west coast of Africa to observe the flora and fauna of that little-known continent. He returned to France to write an account of his travels, and in 1759 a translation appeared for the first time in England. The French forts on the coast had recently been taken over by the British, and interest in Africa was very keen. The book was a great success.[1]

'Which way soever I turned my eyes on the pleasant spot', Adanson wrote, 'I beheld a perfect image of pure nature: an agreeable solitude, bounded on every side by a charming landscape; the rural situation of cottages in the midst of trees; the ease and indolence of the negroes, reclined under the shade of the spreading foliage; the simplicity of their dress and manners; the whole revived in my mind the idea of our first parents, and I seemed to contemplate the world in its primeval state.'[2]

In that passage and others like it in the book Adanson was not only describing what he saw, he was also expressing the longing which was part of European culture: the longing to return to the condition of Adam and Eve. European man boasted of his large cities, his fine clothes, his manners, his books and libraries, and his religion: but he also felt shackled by them. Roaming free, naked, untutored, in the wilds, hunting for food and enjoying the lusts of the flesh without guilt, was by comparison, an ideal state in which to live.

The European conquests in America and the opening up of trade on the African coast brought the ideal within the bounds of reality. That happy state of innocence seemed not to be merely a dream-world in which to escape. It actually existed. There were people living such lives: strong, brave men and soft sensuous women casually loving and idling their days away without a single thought for a wrathful god or a retributive deity.

'They are generally above middle sized, well shaped, and well limbed', said Adanson of the Senegalese. 'There is no such thing ever known among them as cripples.' The women were perfect beauties with 'skin surprisingly delicate and soft; their mouths and lips are small, and their features regular. . . . Being generally well made they have a very good air in this deshabille, especially when a person is used to their colour.'[3]

Another traveller who for several years was an agent for the Royal African Company also found strong evidence to support the idea that the societies he visited on the coasts of north-west Africa were, by European standards, ideal. Francis Moore in his *Travels into the Inland Parts of Africa* published in 1738 described the Pholeys as having such a plenitude of food that 'they never suffer any of their own nation to want, but support the old, the blind, and lame, equally with the other. . . . They are very rarely angry, and I never heard them abuse each other; yet this mildness does not proceed from want of courage for they are as brave as any people of Africa.'

These accounts were not simply pleasant escapist literature; they were written for other travellers, for merchants, and for the scientists of the day; but they were also popular with the general reading public. They helped to expose a dilemma in European thinking: the happy societies they described were being systematically destroyed in order to keep up the supply of slaves, and the innocent people who lived in such simple splendour were those who were being bought, transported and forced into brutal slavery. The dilemma was partially resolved by the conjuring up of another stereotype which was at least as old as that of the noble savage: the evil and depraved black. If the Africans were not beautiful creatures who roamed pleasant plains, but wild, vicious beings who skulked in the dark forests, capturing and murdering each other, then it did not matter nearly so much if they were shipped off to that 'constellation of Elysian isles',[4] the West Indies, where their excess energy could be put to some use and their savage tempers cured by the lash.

Sometimes in the same account both ideas of the noble and the degenerate savage appear almost side by side. Adanson complained of the poor roads and blamed them on the 'laziness and indolence of the negroes'.[5] Yet Mungo Park, perhaps the most celebrated of African travellers of the late eighteenth century, found the Africans energetic. Surely, he said, 'a people whose wants are supplied, not by the spontaneous productions of nature, but by their own exertions' could not be described as lazy.[6] Yet, a few pages later he lamented that 'a country so abundantly gifted and favoured by nature should remain in its present savage and neglected state', or that its people should be 'immersed in the gross and uncomfortable blindness of pagan superstition.'[7]

When reading these travellers' tales one cannot help feeling that they themselves were often inclined to see the African as bearing a closer resemblance to the noble ideal, but that they inserted the uncomplimentary passages in order to pander to the tastes of their European readers and particularly their patrons who were, like the Royal African Company, actively engaged in slave trading. Though he denied it, Bryan Edwards was said to have 'edited' Mungo Park's journals; as secretary of the African Association which sponsored Park, Edwards certainly had the opportunity.

Not every traveller found the African noble. Dr Houston of the Royal African Company dismissed the whole country as producing 'nothing fit for exportation but slaves', and he thought all Africans were 'barbarously cruel, selfish, and deceitful. . . . Vice being left unchecked becomes a virtue. As for their customs they exactly resemble their fellow creatures and natives, the monkeys.'[8] For apologists of slavery, like Houston, it was important to emphasise the stereotype of the degenerate black to the exclusion of everything else. Edward Long expressed the kind of racist sentiments which became in their time a permanent feature of the white man's view of the black wherever they confronted each other in situations of the ruler and the ruled. 'In general they are void of genius, and seem almost incapable of making any progress in civility or science. . . . They have no moral sensations; no taste but for women, gormandising, and drinking to excess; no wish but to be idle.'⁹ Africa was no Garden of Eden, but 'that parent of everything that is monstrous in nature; where the passions rage without any control, and the retired wilderness presents opportunity to gratify them without fear of detection'. The Africans were not warm and friendly and generous as Adanson and Park claimed; rather 'their hospitality is the result of self-love; they entertain strangers only in hopes of extracting some service or profit from them'.¹⁰

Yet, no matter how hard Long and writers like him tried to pervert it, no matter how radically the fact of African culture contradicted it, and no matter how deeply the slave trade and West Indian slavery undermined it, the ideal of the noble savage persisted. If the noble savage was the thesis of a Hegelian dialectic and the degraded black its antithesis, pity was the synthesis. Not any kind of pity, but the all-embracing love of mankind and forgiveness of its sins which comes through the knowledge of Christ.

Poets and dramatists found in the task of creating this synthesis a perfect subject. Pity at once satisfied the more sensitive European feelings about the exploitation of the Africans, preserved the idea of the nobility of the savage, and yet managed to keep it from threatening the underlying notion of white superiority.

> In these romantic regions man grows wild;
> Here dwells the negro, Nature's outcast child.
> Is he not *Man*, though knowledge never shed
> Her quickening beams on his neglected head?
> Is *he* not man, by sin and suffering tried?
> Is he not man for whom the Saviour died?¹¹

James Montgomery in his poem *Christian Negroes* tells of how the slave is delivered from his degradation in slavery by the sudden 'sweet tones of pity' which touched his ears. By the Grace of Christ,

Arise! his fetters fall, his slumbers flee;
He wakes to life; he springs to liberty.
He pray'd for blessings to descend on those
That dealt to him the cup of many woes. . .[12]

Pity at its most sentimental found expression in a number of favourite themes: for example there was the slave mother's lament as in Hannah More's poem *The Sorrows of Yamba*:[13]

With the baby at my breast,
(Other two were sleeping by)
In my hut I sat at rest,
With no thought of danger nigh.

Then:

Driven like cattle to a fair,
See, they sell us, young and old;
Child from mother too they tear,
All for the love of filthy gold.

The most popular theme of all was that of the dying negro. Here it was possible to bring in all three elements: the black man's nobility in his natural state, his degradation as a slave, and lastly the Christ-like pity of the white man which had the two-fold effect of unifying the contradictory stereotypes of the black man and relieving to some extent a heavy sense of guilt. The poem usually followed this pattern: the opening verse described the slaves 'stretch'd on the ground', 'wither'd and feeble was each toil-worn limb'. With his dying breath he welcomes death. 'With joy I view the lifted hand of death.' He recalls how 'the tyrants snatch'd me for ever from my much lov'd shore', how they pushed away his wife and parents, and dragged him towards where 'the sick and dying strew'd the infected ground'. He tells of the trials and tribulations of the plantation, and castigates the planter for living the good life while he suffered.

Think, think amid your heaps of needless food,
How much is tainted with your brother's blood.

He cries out for some 'nobler son of feeling' to plead the slave's cause. 'Our constant blessings shall his steps attend'. With a last glance back to his happy past, 'my friends, my sports, my hours of calm content', he dies.

> His pulse no longer beat! his spirit fled![14]

Of all the dying negro poems, the best known was that of Thomas Day which first appeared in 1773. As it was one of the first and best of its kind, the abolitionists used it quite openly as propaganda for their cause. The edition of 1793 was dedicated to those men who had brought the sufferings of the slaves into the open. 'Since the period has arrived for a more general discussion, their grievances have excited universal pity in Europe, and this most unfortunate part of the human race will have cause to bestow everlasting thanks and praises on Great Britain for her late humane and disinterested exertions.'[15]

The poem was based on a reported incident. A black slave was engaged to the white servant of his master, the captain of a slave ship. To marry her he has himself baptised, but his master hears of this and the slave is sent on board ship for transportation to America. Rather than go, he stabs himself.

> A slow consuming death let others wait,
> I snatch destruction from unwilling fate.

The poem is in the form of an epistle to his love and it is interesting in that it contains long passages which are lifted almost directly out of Michel Adanson's *Voyage to Senegal*. Day, like other poets, depended on the travellers' accounts for their details of the African countryside. The poem ends with another favourite device— the curse on the white Christians, and the threat of vengeance to come.

> Thanks, righteous God! Revenge shall yet be mine.

The dying slave promises 'the stern genius of my native land' will pour 'the plagues of Hell on your devoted shore', and everyone, blacks as well as whites, shall die.

> One common ruin, one promiscuous grave.

It was on the stage that the divergent elements of the white man's view of the black man were most effectively synthesised. The results, judging them as literature, were almost as bad as the poetry. Noble savages, degraded blacks evil planters and Christian slave owners were popular characters, particularly in the late eighteenth century and the early nineteenth century when the theatre, thanks to a strong evangelical distaste for the place, was shunned unless its drama had an ennobling theme and an improving moral. Slave kings, slave revolts, slave trades, slave hunts, faithful slaves, and slaves who, by practising the Christian virtues of patience, endurance and forgiveness, set examples for the whites, were acceptable subjects for drama since they conformed to the contemporary standards of good theatre.

The most enduring of all the slave plays—*Oroonoko*— had its first performance at the end of the seventeenth century, and was based on an even earlier novel by that curious lady Aphra Behn, the first professional woman writer in English.[16] In the novel Oroonoko was a 'Moor', and Mrs Behn took great care to italicise the point that not only did he act but that he also looked different from other blacks— the ordinary ones who did not have his nobility. 'He had nothing of barbarity in his nature, but in all points address'd himself as if his education had been in some *European* court. . . . His face was not of that brown, rusty black which most of that nation are, but of perfect ebony, or polished jet. . . . His nose was rising and *Roman*, instead of African and flat. His mouth the finest shaped that could be seen; far from those great turn'd lips which are so natural to the rest of the negroes.'

The story, simplified, is as follows: Oroonoko, the prince, loves Imoinda, but so, too, does his father, the king. The latter sells Imoinda into slavery as a punishment for being caught with Oroonoko, and he is tricked into slavery by a white trader to whom he has sold slaves in the past. Both Oroonoko and Imoinda are shipped to the Dutch colony of Surinam, and given different names. When Oroonoko learns that Imoinda is carrying his child, he decides to rebel. With the other slaves they make their escape, but he is tricked into giving himself up. He is cruelly tortured, and when he and Imoinda are alone together, with her consent, he kills her. Noble savages usually had good masters and Oroonoko's was no exception, but while he was away and could not protect his slave, the other whites arrange for his execution. Oroonoko is gradually hacked to pieces, and when both arms are chopped off 'he gave up the ghost without a groan of a reproach'. Mrs Behn concludes: 'Thus died this great man, worthy of a better fate.'

These words could perhaps have been applied to her novel as well. The dramatist Thomas Southerne, when he adapted the story, obviously felt that the audience of well-to-do London theatre-goers for which he was writing, and which must have contained a fair sprinkling of those with interests in the West Indies, would not have taken the tragedy of Oroonoko in its undiluted form, so he added a complicated sub-plot of marital intrigue. Like the novel, though, the play was set in Surinam.[17] It opens with the arrival of the slave ship transporting Oroonoko. A young onlooker bewails their fate and Blandford, soon to become Imoinda's master, answers: 'Most of 'em know no better. They were born so, and only changed their masters. But a Prince, born only to command, betray'd and sold! My heart drops blood for him.' The prince, of course, is Oroonoko. He has a conversation with the captain who has betrayed him into slavery in which the subject of the true meaning of Christianity in relationship to slavery is raised.

Oroonoko: So, sir, you have kept your word with me.

Captain: I am a better Christian, I thank you, than to keep it with a Heathen.

Oroonoko: You are a Christian; be a Christian still:
       If you have any God that teaches you
       to break your word, I need not curse you more.

Oroonoko is bought by the governor of the colony; Imoinda by Blandford; their plantations are attacked by Indians, and Oroonoko nobly employs his military skill to drive them off. He sees and recognises Imoinda, and he is perfectly happy to remain a slave as long as she is near him. The other slaves are plotting rebellion and ask him to lead them. He will have none of it. 'Murder the innocent!' he exclaims in horror. 'Innocent?' his friend Aboan replies in astonishment.

> *Oroonoko:* These men are so, whom you wou'd rise against:
> If we are slaves, they did not make us slaves;
> But bought us in an honest way of trade
> As we have done before them . . .
> They paid our price for us, and we are now
> Their property, a part of their estate,
> To manage as they please.

When Aboan reminds the prince how cruelly slaves are treated he sighs, 'I pity 'em, and wish I could with honesty do more.' But when Imoinda tells him that she is carrying his child he realises that his offspring will be born a slave, and he agrees to lead the rebellion. Aboan fears that one of the slaves is a traitor, and wants to kill him. Oroonoko refuses. 'His murder will make 'em suspect us of barbarity.'

As in the novel, the rebellion is betrayed and Oroonoko turns angrily on his fellow-slaves who have let him down. To their masters he shouts:

> Whip, whip 'em to the knowledge of your gods,
> Your Christian gods, who suffer you to be
> Unjust, dishonest, cowardly, and base,
> And give 'em your excuse for being so.

Against the desires of the good planters, Oroonoko is tortured. One of them reassured him that:

> We are not guilty of your injuries,
> No way consenting to 'em, but abhor
> Abominate, and loath this cruelty.

In the end Oroonoko is executed after killing Imoinda.

The curtain comes down on the dead noble savage, and the white audience have been duly castigated and purged of their guilt. They have suffered pity for him and for his fellow-slaves. As to any real, useful suggestions as to how the

degraded may be restored to their nobility—or even humanity—there are none; not even the hint of a remark that the
Africans should be left in Africa and the slave trade ended,
and certainly no hint that the present race of slaves in the
West Indies should be emancipated. Just pity—and some
reinforcement of the *status quo* since the audience have heard
their hero actively supporting the institution when he
refuses to rebel and gives as his reason that the planters
'bought us in an honest way of trade'.

Finally, just in case the audience may have taken the
whole thing too seriously, an actor comes out to speak the
epilogue—written by William Congreve—in which everything is put in its proper perspective. Light-hearted and full
of verbal witticisms it reminds the audience how much
safer it is to be a 'London wife' because she won't be killed
by her husband.

> She might have learn'd to cuckold, jilt, and sham,
> Had Covent Garden been in Surinam.

Oroonoko is interesting not only for the views and attitudes
it expressed but also for the changes which took place
in the original version over the 150 years of its repeated
appearance in London and provincial repertory. The
changes reflected current attitudes to slavery as well as to
the theatre itself. In the latter half of the 1700s Southerne's
sub-plot of the young ladies in search of husbands in Surinam
had been dropped, and the planters who in the original
version had little to say were now given substantial scenes of
their own from which they emerge as cruel and heartless.
Their lines were heavily underscored with irony. 'The poor
industrious planter loses the money they cost him,' complains
one planter, 'and his ground runs to ruin for want of their
labour.' 'Aye, in truth,' replies his friend, 'a Christian
colony has a hard time of it that is forced to deal in this
cursed Heathen commodity. Here every time a ship comes
in my money goes for a great rawboned negro fellow that
has the impudence to think he is my fellow-creature with
as much right to liberty as I have and so grows sullen and
refuses to work; or for a young wench who will howl night

and day after a brat or a lover forsooth which nothing can drive out of her head but a cat-o'-nine-tails; and if recourse is had to that remedy, 'tis ten to one but she takes the next opportunity to pick my pocket by hanging herself.'

The character of the slaves altered, too. Originally, Imoinda was not even black, but the daughter of a white commander of Oroonoko's father's army. Later both she and Oroonoko became full-blooded Africans from Angola. Oroonoko still held back from rebellion, but his compatriots were much more eager, and when he was betrayed, his bitter lines against those who ran to their owners for protection were cut. Congreve's epilogue virtually disappeared after 1775, and festive songs which were featured as an interlude underwent considerable revision to reflect the growing concern for the immorality of the institution. In 1696 the slaves sang of:

> A lass there lives upon the green,
> Cou'd I her picture draw . . .

But in 1775:

> Thy voice thy anxious heart belies
> I read thy bondage in thy eyes . . .
> Love and Joy must both be free
> Must both be free, for both disdain
> The founding scourge and galley chain.

A correspondent of the *Gentleman's Magazine* complained in 1788 that 'Poetry and Romance are racked to torture the tender feelings of John [Bull] in behalf of his tawny kindred'.[18] The educated eighteenth-century reader or playgoer brought up on the wit of Congreve, Dryden or Pope, was justified in thinking that the heavy sentimentality of much of the poetry and drama written for the purpose of 'humanising' the black man was bad art in a good cause. Very little, if any, of the work has lasted; most of it is self-indulgent, clumsy, patronising and maudlin. The black man, for all the noble things said about him, never really emerged as a real person. If he had done so, real problems demanding real solutions would have had to be faced; instead the caricature drawn of him produced a warm glow of sympathy which soothed the white man's uneasy conscience.

Yet to underestimate the total effect of this huge outpouring of sentiment on behalf of the slave would be wrong. The poetry of Cowper, Montgomery, More and others; *Oroonoko* and all the many slave plays which appeared regularly in the theatre repertoires between 1750 and 1850 were like continuous background music played to the drama of parliamentary debates, petitions and public meetings. They stirred jaded consciences, disturbed apathy and nudged indifference. They helped promote the atmosphere of active benevolence and purposeful philanthropy which was essential to the eventual accomplishment of progressive legislation against the slave trade and slavery.

Fetterwell: A pretty decent show.

Marrowbone: Yes, the women are tricked out as gay as a pork-shop on Saturday night; and the men seem tolerably strong.

(*The Africans*—George Colman, 1808)

I was witness to a sale by scramble where about 250 negroes were sold. Upon this occasion all the negroes scrambled for bear an equal price; which is agreed upon between the captains and the purchasers before the sale begins. On a day appointed the negroes were landed and placed together in a large yard belonging to the merchants to whom the ship was consigned. As soon as the hour was agreed on arrival, the doors of the yard were suddenly thrown open, and in rushed a considerable number of purchasers, with all the ferocity of brutes. Some instantly seized such of the negroes as they could conveniently lay hold of with their hands. Others, being prepared with several handkerchiefs tied together, encircled with these as many as they were able. While others, by means of a rope, effected the same purpose. It is scarcely possible to describe the confusion of which this mode of selling is productive. It likewise causes much animosity among the purchasers who, not infrequently upon these occasions, fall out and quarrel with each other. The poor astonished negroes were so much terrified by these proceedings that several of them, through fear, climbed over the walls of the courtyard and ran wild about the town, but were soon hunted down and retaken.

(Falconbridge)

The End of the (Legal) British Slave Trade

In 1804 the Committee for the Abolition of the Slave Trade met again for the first time in seven years. It elected James Stephen and Zachary Macaulay as new members.[1] The one thing these two men shared in common and distinguished them from the other leading abolitionists was the fact that both had had direct experience with slavery in the West Indies.

Stephen was born in 1758 and when he was in his twenties an uncle in the West Indies sent for him. At St Christopher's he practised at the bar, but he developed very quickly a disgust and hatred for the slave system. He visited England in 1788 and became friendly with Wilberforce whose sister he married twelve years later. He returned permanently to England and became one of the most ardent abolitionists. A good public speaker and a man of fierce temper, Stephen tended to be more radical and less patient than Wilberforce. To his son George, Macaulay said of him: 'In anger, your father is terrific!'[2]

Macaulay's early reaction to slavery was a much slower one than Stephen's. In an autobiographical memoir written in 1797 and quoted at length in his grand-daughter's biography he told of how, in 1784, as a callow youth of sixteen, he resolved to get rid of any squeamishness when witnessing the daily cruelty to slaves on the plantation where he worked as a manager. In this he achieved 'a success beyond my expectations'. In 1785 he wrote to a friend: 'You would hardly know your friend ... were you to view me in a field of canes, amidst perhaps a hundred of the sable race, cursing and bawling while the noise of the whip resounding on their shoulders and the cries of the poor wretches would make you imagine that some unlucky accident had carried you to the doleful shades.'

Macaulay returned to England in 1789 and there met Thomas Babington, the young Leicestershire country gentleman who, at his family home at Rothley Temple, created a centre of evangelical Christianity similar to that at Clapham. Macaulay 'now found himself living in intimate association with men [who were] voluntarily renouncing that ease and enjoyment to which their wealth and position entitled them in order to labour unceasingly for the welfare of their fellow-creatures'.[3] Babington married Macaulay's sister, and Zachary's own son, later Lord Macaulay, was christened Thomas Babington.

George Stephen described Macaulay's appearance as 'not striking; his sight was very defective and partially lost; his tongue was not fluent and his pen was not attractive'. However, 'he was blessed with a good constitution. . . . Like Atlas he was useless except to carry a world. Blue books and state papers were child's play to him, however dull or voluminous. . . . His memory was retentive . . . but his habit of extreme accuracy obtained for Zachary Macaulay the reputation of being cold and insincere.'[4] As the editor of the *Anti-Slavery Reporter* Macaulay kept the subject of slavery alive in the minds of the British public, especially during the first years of the nineteenth century.

In May 1804 William Wilberforce again moved in the House of Commons for the abolition of the trade. He expressed concern because some advocates engaged in the cause had hurt the interests of his 'clients' by representing them as superior to the whites in the acuteness of their feelings. Hurriedly redressing the balance he said, 'We must not forget what share we have had in fixing the uniformity of their character. We must not forget what share we have had in converting them into an ignorant, low, peevish, a bloody, and a thievish race.'[5]

The opposition from the merchants and planters to the motion was strangely muted. A speaker following Wilberforce said, 'I do not oppose abolition now. At this time the colonists are less disposed to enter on such a trade. Their profits are not one-third what they used to be, and their temptations to speculation are consequently curtailed.'[6] Some of their bumptious self-confidence had gone, declining perhaps with the sudden and devasting decline in sugar exports to Britain as a result of the increased cost of the commodity. People were reminded of Adam Smith's warning that slave production, though it seemed cheaper, proved to be more expensive in the long run.

Britain had also started to move with a vengeance into the industrial nineteenth century. New technological processes were changing, slowly at first but inexorably, the face and fortunes of the nation. The number of patents taken out in the last decade of the previous century was up from an average of 41 since 1770 to 65½. The output in pig-iron in Great Britain in 1788 was 68,000 tons. In less than twenty years it increased to 258,000 tons thanks to Abraham Darby's coke-smelting process and Henry Cort's 'puddling' process, and to the latter's invention of the rolling-mill. From 1750 to 1790 coal output had grown by 40 per cent; in 1804 it had increased by more than a further 30 per cent. New inventions in production, bleaching, dyeing, printing and packing had revolutionised the cotton industry, and the single most important agent of innovation had already made its first appearance—the railways.[7] In 1801 the Surrey Iron Railway Company obtained an Act of Parliament for building a railway line between Croydon, on the outskirts of London, and Wandsworth in south-west London. As part of a proposed London to Portsmouth line, it was officially opened in 1804.[8]

Compared to all that was taking place in Britain, the slave labour of the colonies, of which not a great deal was known in detail by the ordinary member of the public, and the more notorious slave trade would both soon seem almost anachronistic and out of place in the modern world.

Wilberforce's Bill to end the trade went through to a third reading in parliament with little difficulty, and it was approved by the House of Commons in June 1804. 'I think it is better to pass the bill immediately,' said the Attorney-General, Spencer Percival, 'so that the blacks will see that "Massa Wilbee" has every wish and desire to alleviate and better their situation, but that he has no intention of eman-

cipating them.'⁹ But the parliamentary session was nearing
its conclusion; the House of Lords seized on this as an excuse
to delay consideration of the Bill until the next session,
knowing that the passage of the Bill would have to start
from the beginning again.[10] Thus, once more, despite lack
of active opposition, the abolitionists lost the initiative.

When Wilberforce came to reintroduce the Bill in February
of the next year the climate of opinion in the House had
changed against him.[11] The opposition now was far more
vociferous. Britain was at war with the most dangerous
enemy it had had to face in centuries—Napoleon. This
was no time to enter into such discussions, the merchants
maintained. If Britain gave up the trade would not Napoleon
seize the advantage of it being thrown into his hands?
They also touched on the abolitionists' most sensitive spot—
abolition meant emancipation. In this some planters were
genuinely confused by their opponent's speeches since the
abolitionists themselves were confused by their efforts to
separate slavery from the slave trade.

In speaking in support of the second reading of his Bill
Wilberforce, objecting to the fact that he had been accused
of trying to bring about emancipation immediately, said
that had that been his object or his hope, the word 'mad'
should deservedly been used to describe it. 'I feel that the
immediate emancipation of the negroes in the West Indies
cannot be expected; before they can be fit to receive freedom
it will be madness to attempt to give it to them.' But he
looked forward to the time when they 'shall have the full
enjoyment of a free, moral, industrious and happy peasantry'
in the West Indies.[12] In other words, abolition of the trade
now; emancipation in the far distant future. But to slave
owners emancipation meant emancipation no matter when,
and this had to be avoided at all cost. Wilberforce's Bill was
thrown out, but by a majority of only seven.

Refusing to accept defeat with victory so close, the
abolitionists continued the fight outside parliament. The
Committee, which now numbered forty, having just added
the Prime Minister to its illustrious list of members, was as
usual in the forefront of all the activity. Clarkson was asked
by Wilberforce to collect more evidence for submission to

the House of Lords; funds were raised; pamphlets distributed; sub-committees in the provinces contacted. 'The
ardour of all the former friends of the abolition remains
unabated', Clarkson wrote to Wilberforce.[13] Ireland, since the
Act of Union in 1800, was recognised as an important new
source of support, and sub-committees were set up there,
too.

In the meantime Wilberforce was busy trying to bring the
various parliamentary factions together on his side. Whig
and Tory, though the names denominated basic differences
in outlook, were not yet consolidated into political parties in
the modern sense of the word. On questions such as the
slave trade, supporters and opponents could be found
on both sides of the House. Throughout his career in parliament Wilberforce remained an independent with Whig
and Tory friends; he also supported the king's government
whenever he was able though it, the king, and the Royal
family were hostile to abolition.[14] His task, therefore, was
to bring the abolitionists and the ruling clique closer
together, though how to do this is without betraying his
cause was always a problem. 'I cannot but entertain some
hopes that the wish to mollify and even conciliate and gain
over a number of strange, impracticable, and otherwise
uncomeatable fellows . . . may have its weight—at least it
will tend to counteract the fear of offending the West
Indians', he wrote to a colleague about one such attempt.[15]

The political scene changed with Pitt's death in 1806.
As we have seen, many abolitionists regarded this as a
deliverance. He had been, in their eyes, the secret traitor,
pretending support but inhibiting the progress of any
proposed legislation by failing to use his influence and power
in its favour. Certainly the speed with which the long-
awaited legislation was enacted after his death, and by a
government under Lord Grenville which was much weaker
than Pitt's, affords some proof of the accusations made
against him. Within a few months a Slave Importation
Restriction Bill was passed. From the beginning of 1807
it was unlawful for any British subject to transport slaves
into islands or colonies belonging to any foreign powers;
no foreign slave ship could clear out of any British port;

and slaves could not be exported from one British colony to another without special licence.[16] The slave trade had not been abolished, but a start had at last been made.

In January 1807 a Bill for the abolition of the trade was brought into the House of Lords,[17] and by February the 5th had been passed despite vigorous opposition from the Duke of Clarence and other West Indian diehards.[18] On February the 10th a message from the upper House was received by the Commons of the passing of the Bill and Lord Howick rose to move a first reading of it.[19]

On the eve of the debate Wilberforce received a letter from an old friend and fellow-member of the Clapham Sect, Thomas Babington, which reflects the exaggerated esteem in which Wilberforce was held. 'May God bless you and your cause! Do not be too anxious, for events are in His hands, and He may see fit that you should not be victorious at present. . . . Remember how many years elapsed when Moses was marked out as a deliverer of his nation, and left the court of Pharoah, and his final success in the work assigned to him.' If comparison with Moses was not enough, Babington went on to say that if Wilberforce did not wholly succeed, 'you will be in the very situation of our Saviour who tells his disciples that they would reap what others had sown'.[20]

In fact Wilberforce said very little in the final debates except to praise the younger members 'whose lofty and liberal sentiments . . . show to the people that their legislators, and especially the higher order of their youth, are forward to assert the rights of the weak against the strong'.[21] The House divided on the second reading with 283 in favour of the Bill, and only sixteen against it.[22]

The Abolition Act was finally passed on March the 16th, 1807.[23] The African slave trade and all manner 'of dealing and trading in the purchase or transfer of slaves, or of persons intended to be sold . . . in, at, or from any part of the coast or countries of Africa' was abolished, prohibited and declared unlawful. All vessels carrying slaves were liable to be seized and forfeited, and those responsible would be fined £100 for every slave found on board. Slaves taken from ships were regarded as prize of war and were forfeited to the king who was entitled to enlist them as soldiers or seamen for ten to fourteen years, whether of full age or not. The Act added, however, that 'any rules or regulations for the granting of any pensions or allowances to any soldiers discharged after certain periods of service shall not extend to any negroes enlisting or serving in any of His Majesty's Forces'.

The Act also provided for payment to captors of ships or slaves a bounty of £13 for a man, £10 for a woman, and £3 for a child.

After nearly twenty years of battle both in and outside parliament the British slave trade was declared illegal. The joy and relief of the abolitionists and of the public in general was immense. Sir George Stephen recalled that though he was only a child at the time, 'the expression of triumph was so general and so strong that it left an indelible impression on my mind, greatly assisted perhaps by a week's holiday given to our school to commemorate it'.[24]

The nation indulged itself in a feast of self-congratulations. One Member of Parliament called it a measure which 'washes out this foul stain from the pure ermine of the national character'.[25] The Bishop of London called it 'a great and signal act of humanity . . . a great legislative measure of relief to an oppressed and degraded population' which would 'immortalise the British senate and display to an admiring world the striking contrast between this country, the great stay and hope of the civilised world, and the conduct of that arch enemy of human happiness', meaning, of course, France.[26] Zachary Macaulay wrote years later to his famous son, Thomas: 'I had received a still richer reward in being permitted to participate in the counsels of the great names associated in one of the noblest designs which the world has ever witnessed, delivering half the world from bondage and blood, and pouring upon it light, liberty, and civilisation.'[27] And Lord Grenville wrote to William Wilberforce: 'I trust we may all of us who have in any degree contributed to this great work of mercy each in proportion to our exertions in it look to a reward far beyond those of this world from that Being who has declared to us that inasmuch as we have done it to our fellow-creatures

He will accept it (such is His immeasurable goodness) as done even to Himself.'[28]

William Wordsworth wrote a poem in honour of Thomas Clarkson:

> The blood-stained Writing is forever torn;
> And thou henceforth will have a good man's calm;
> A great man's happiness; thy zeal shall find
> Repose at length, firm friend of human kind!

and Clarkson himself declared that 'the stain of the blood of Africa is no longer upon us. . . . We have been freed (alas, if it be not too late) from a load of guilt which has hung like a mill-stone about our necks, ready to sink us to perdition.'[29]

In all this wallowing in sentimental self-satisfaction it seemed that the nation's leaders and the abolitionists themselves had forgotten that for nearly a million blacks in the West Indies nothing had changed. Directly after the Act was passed Wilberforce left parliament and went with his friends to Clapham to celebrate. There at one of their houses he permitted himself a rare moment of frivolity. He turned to the banker, Henry Thornton, and said, 'Well, Henry, what shall we abolish next?' As serious as always Thornton replied, 'The Lottery, I think.'[30]

But some of those young abolitionists whom Wilberforce had earlier praised had different ideas. In the Commons on the following day Earl Percy rose and moved for leave to bring in a Bill for the gradual abolition of slavery in the West Indies.[31] It was left to the slaves' friend, 'Massa King Wilbee' himself, to reply.[32] 'I and those who think with me', he said, 'not only abstain from proposing such a bill, but are ready to reject such a proposition when made by others. . . . I and those who act with me are satisfied with having gained an object which is safely attainable.' He did, he said, 'look forward with anxious expectation to the period when negroes might with safety be liberated', but because of the effect 'which long continuance of abject slavery produces on the human mind . . . I look to the improvement of their minds, and to the diffusion among them of those domestic charities which will render them more fit, than I fear they now are, to bear emancipation.'[33]

As the House numbered only thirty-five members, there was no vote on Earl Percy's motion. Emancipation was shelved without the West Indian representatives having to lift a finger. It was not they who said the slaves were not 'fit for freedom'. That was Wilberforce's statement, and it turned out to be the heavy hammer with which they struck down him, his colleagues, and the people they were supposed to represent for another thirty years.

By the law of the United States, the importation of slaves ceased on the first of January, 1808; but the free republicans of Charlestown took such pains to provide a sufficient number of slaves before the proscribed time (no less than fifteen thousand, six hundred and seventy six being imported into that city in the year 1807) that the markets were glutted with them. The slave merchants could find no sale for them; but they resolved to keep them on board a ship until an opportunity for disposing of them should occur—in consequence of which upwards of seven hundred of them died in less than three months.

(*The Anti-Jacobin Review,* 1814)

Immediately on our coming to anchor in Carlisle Bay, a woman appeared alongside the ship in a small boat with some bad fruit, tobacco, salt fish, and other articles of traffic. She was rowed by two negroes who were her slaves. Two such objects of human form and human misery had never before met our eyes! They were feeble, meagre, and dejected—half-starved, half-naked, and, in figure, too accurately resembling hungry and distempered greyhounds! They crouched upon their heels and haunches in the boat; their bones almost pierced their filthy and eruptive skins; hollow eyes and famished countenances rendered them ghastly images of horror, their whole appearance shocked humanity and appalled the sight! Are these, we exclaimed, what are called slaves?

(*Notes on the West Indies*—George Pinckard, M.D., 1806)

The Saints and the Heathen

Four months after the Abolition of the Slave Trade Act was passed, a meeting was held at the Freemason's Hall, Lincoln's Inn Fields, London, which was attended by all the leaders of the abolition movement. It was presided over by the only member of the royal family to come on to their side, William Frederick, Duke of Gloucester, nephew of George III, and cousin of the future king and present Duke of Clarence. A sweet, simple man whose intellectual powers were said not to be of a very high order, he spent much of his large income on charity. Though he was without any real power, the Duke's presence on the platform of an abolition meeting was proof of the movement's growing importance, its progress in public esteem, and its untarnished respectability. The cry of *Jacobin*, though it was still to be heard in muted fashion in the years to come, no longer rang with much effect in the arena of public debate.

The Evangelical movement which had fostered abolitionism was also increasing in popularity in the middle class. Religious zeal was not scoffed at by those *soi-disant philosophes* of the past; it was they who were now held in contempt. Belief, rigorous and dogmatic, discipline, virtue, responsibility—these were the watchwords of the new age. The morality expounded by the Evangelicals was becoming the morality of the nation. 'Ours in the only free country which has ever existed', Wilberforce complained when one of his pet societies—The Society for the Suppression of Vice—brought a prosecution against Mary Carlile for publishing Paine's book, and was criticised in parliament, 'in which there is no special tribunal for the protection of religion and morals. A small select body of men employed in suppressing an act of this nature . . . is a great benefit to the nation.'[1]

With the Abolition Act behind him, Wilberforce had reached the pinnacle of his career. At the age of fifty he was regarded by the general public as one of the most saintly men of the age. Though he was never a member of a cabinet he wielded great power over public opinion, and his pronouncements on matters of politics and morals were heeded by many as almost pontifical. He was in demand on the committees of many societies and at the dinner tables of many hostesses.[2] The essayist William Hazlitt tells the story which was current at the time when Richard Sheridan collapsed drunk in the gutter late one night and was picked up by the watch, who asked him roughly who he was. 'Mr William Wilberforce,' Sheridan announced, drawing himself up with dignity. The watch reverently offered Sheridan his arm and conducted him home 'with all the honours due to Grace and Nature'.[3]

Among the many 'benevolent designs'[4] which occupied his time were the missionary societies, the growth of which was encouraged by the same spirit that directed the abolition movement—evangelicalism. Within a dozen years four major societies had been founded: the Baptist Society in 1792, the London Missionary Society in 1795, the Church Missionary Society in 1799, and the British and Foreign Bible Society in 1804. Wilberforce was one of the founders of the last two, and he took an active interest in the work of the London Missionary Society whose most distinguished African missionary of the century was David Livingstone.

The reformation of his own country's manners, in particular the observance of the sabbath, was almost dominated by his obsessional interest in the manners and morals of Africans and Indians in their own countries; and it was through the missionary societies that he and his friends endeavoured to effect a change in these. To a clergyman Wilberforce wrote in 1807: 'To me . . . our suffering our East India subjects . . . to remain, without an effort to the contrary, under the most depraved and cruel system of superstition which ever enslaved a people is . . . the greatest by far, now that the slave trade has ceased, of all national crimes by which we are provoking the vengeance and suffering the chastisement of Heaven.'[5]

He took with his usual seriousness Hannah More's wish 'to be the grand agent of Providence to consummate the glorious work to which He has, in his mercy, been pleased to call you—that of being the instrument of giving that liberty . . . to the souls of our black brethren which you have in measure obtained for their bodies'.[6] When the charter of the East India Company came up for renewal by parliament he was ready to attack those nominal Christians whom he chastised so vehemently who permitted so many millions to live without Christ's Gospel.[7] Immense regions under British control were deeply sunk by their religious superstitions 'in the lowest depths of moral and social wretchedness and degradation', he said. Mohammedanism and Hinduism were not religions as far as he was concerned, but diseases for which there was only one remedy— Christianity, which took on her true character when she protected 'those poor, degraded beings on whom philosophy looks down with disdain'.

If the heathen was inferior, it followed that the Christian was superior; but not all Christians. 'Surely it cannot be necessary for me to attempt in this place to prove that though much of the large mass of comforts which we in this country enjoy . . . is owing to our invaluable constitution, yet that it is in no small degree, also, to be ascribed to our religious and moral superiority; for it is with gratitude alike and with pleasure that I declare my firm persuasion that the influence of Christianity is greater in this country than in any other upon earth.' It was because he wished to raise the heathen 'out of their present degraded state to the just level of their nature' that he was presenting to parliament their real character and that of their gods which were 'absolute monsters of lust, injustice, wickedness and cruelty. In short, their religious system is one grand abomination.' 'Am I not', he asked his fellow-members, 'therefore acting the part of the real friend?'

Between 1818 and 1820 he had another opportunity to act 'the real friend', this time to Henry Christophe, King of Haiti, with whom Wilberforce conducted an extraordinary correspondence. The San Domingo of the eighteenth century had become the independent black state of Haiti after the final defeat by the ex-slaves of Napoleon's expedition to the island in 1803. The first leader, Toussaint L'Ouverture, had died in a French gaol and his successor had proclaimed himself its king. Needing advice on certain matters relating to the education of his people, Christophe wrote to the man who was now universally acknowledged as the black man's best friend.

Wilberforce replied with alacrity. First he assured the king that all friends of the abolition movement in England were 'earnestly desirous of raising [the African race] from their unmerited depression . . . and that as on the one hand nothing would recommend these interests more powerfully to all these various religionists than the Protestant observance of the Sunday in Haiti, so, on the other, nothing would tend more to damp their ardour than hearing that Sunday was not distinguishable in Haiti by men abstaining from the ordinary labours of their calling'.

He rejoiced that the Almighty had animated the king with the great purpose of improving the morals of his people as the surest means of promoting their happiness, and in this respect he could offer some practical assistance. 'A great variety of excellent little works have been published in this country of late years for the purpose of inculcating useful knowledge and good morals. Many of these, though professing to be intended for the use of young people may be read with advantage by persons of any age.' He promised to send off 'a considerable number of these' in the next ship bound for the island.

In his long letter to Henry of October 1818, under the heading 'Female Improvement', he told the king that Christianity was the only true method by which the females in his domain could be elevated, morally speaking. 'We boast in this country, not without reason, that, speaking of the higher circles, our women are much more generally faithful to their husbands than the ladies of any other country in Europe; Switzerland and Holland perhaps excepted.' He admitted that this had not always been the case; under Charles II's reign, and even under the first two Georges, 'our court was not pure', but George III's reign was characterised by the court's 'unpolluted purity'. Of Henry Christophe's court, Wilberforce was pleased to hear that the king had set an example of domestic virtue 'like that of our own king and queen'. To ensure that his court remained virtuous, Wilberforce told the king that only women of unblemished reputation should be received. 'If this could be introduced, I am persuaded that by degrees the standard of public morality would be raised.' He admitted that there would still be intrugues, but 'they would be kept secret and thereby would be prevented from producing public scandal'.

In his last letters Wilberforce expressed his concern not so much for Haiti's public but more for its political 'morality'. Understandably, Haiti never had a good press in Britain, not so long as Britain's sugar islands were populated predominantly by slaves who might at any time follow its example. Every sign, therefore, that the Haitians were behaving 'barbarously' towards each other was received with undisguised pleasure. 'Often has it been confidently affirmed by those who would support the old prejudices which so long obstructed the recognition of their just claim to the common rights and privileges of our nature', Wilberforce wrote in 1820, 'that one of the proofs of their inferiority was the violence and cruelty with which they were disposed to act towards each other in those contentions which too commonly take place in political society.' When one of the king's enemies was sentenced to death, Wilberforce begged the Haitian Government to remember that 'the course which they pursued may tend powerfully to gladden or depress the hearts of those, who, like myself, have long been their partisans and advocates'.[8]

Henry himself committed suicide when his army revolted soon after this correspondence came to an end. Zachary Macaulay and Wilberforce arranged to help his family to come to England. In autumn 1821 Macaulay wrote to his wife; '. . . you need be under no apprehensions respecting Madame Christophe. She is not likely to come near us. But if she had you might have rested perfectly easy on the score of morals. I have no doubt that the young women are perfectly modest and virtuous.'[9]

While Wilberforce and his friends were involved in teaching the blacks how to live a moral life, the slave trade conducted by their fellow-Englishmen continued despite the Abolition Act. Statistics of the numbers of slaves exported from Africa were hard to come by because of the trade's illegality, but the abolitionists soon became aware that the numbers had not appreciably diminished. There was one simple reason: the law of supply and demand. Now that the supply had officially ceased, the demand grew and with it the price of slaves. For high prices the traders were prepared to take the additional risks of capture and seizure to supply their customers in the West Indies. If only one in three voyages was successful they stood every chance of recouping their losses and making a profit.[10]

There was a song sung around many a living-room piano which captured the popular image of the heroic British navy rounding up the traders who exported blacks to the Americas. It was called 'The Slave Chase', and it recounted how an English cruiser chased a slave ship bound for Cuba.

> Alongside dash'd the cruiser's boat, to board and seize the prize.
> Hark to the rattling British cheer, that's ringing to the skies,
> And run aloft St George's Cross, all wanton let it wave,
> The token proud that under it there never treads a slave.[11]

The facts as the abolitionists were soon to learn were not nearly as heroic as that painted by songwriters and poets. The system of prevention created by the Abolition Act actually increased the evils it was supposed to eradicate. British cruisers did chase after slave ships, but their motives were not always noble. With rewards totalling £26 per slave family of man, woman and child, a full ship could bring in over £2,500 in bounty money. The naval squadron on the African coast became headhunters. Rather than stop the slave ships from leaving the coast of Africa which they were patrolling, the cruisers preferred to catch them at sea. They would remain hidden, waiting for the slave vessels to load on their cargoes and set sail. As soon as they were sighted on the open sea, the cruisers would fire a few warning shots and give chase. Then would follow scenes of horror surpassing almost anything that used to take place in the bad old days when the trade was legal. The slave captains would shove some of their cargo into specially prepared hiding-places, so small that the slaves would frequently die of suffocation, or else they would unceremoniously fling the slaves overboard to drown or be eaten by sharks. In this way they would avoid the penalties of capture and forfeiture.[12]

British slave ships and their captains sailed under assumed names such as Don Jorge Madre Silva of the *Gallicia*, who turned out to be George Woodbine of the *Queen Charlotte* sailing out of the Thames and bound for Africa and more slaves.[13] He and other British subjects were at least liable to punishment under British law, but how to deal with Spanish, Portuguese and American slavers was a problem that vexed the abolitionists for many years to come—and gave considerable cause for complaint from the foreign nations—especially the Americans—who objected strongly to having their ships seized by British cruisers and searched when they were doing what by the laws of their countries (excepting America) was perfectly legal.

For three years after the Abolition Act the abolitionists remained silent, but the information coming through to them was so disturbing that in June 1810 Henry Brougham who had only recently entered parliament, called the House of Commons' attention to the situation. He complained that Britain was doing nothing to end 'this abominable commerce'. She was always ready to use her power 'when the object is to obtain new colonies and extend the slave trade; then we can both conquer and treat; we have force enough to seize whole provinces where the slave trade might be planted and skill enough to retain them and the additional commerce in slaves their cultivation requires'.[14] When he sat down, James Stephen, who at that time was also a member of the House of Commons, declared that even if the exportation from Africa had not diminished by one slave, 'we have at least delivered ourselves as a nation from the guilt and shame of authorising that cruel and oppro-brious traffic'. This, in his estimation, was an advantage above all price. 'If we have effected nothing more I shall rejoice and bless God to the last hour for this happy deliverance.'[15]

An abiding concern for their own and the nation's soul almost to the exclusion of everything else, including the sufferings of their 'clients', was one of the least likable traits of the Clapham Sect and its associates. This selfishness and selfrighteousness had already earned them the nickname 'the saints' from their enemies; their friends, however, used it as a term of affection and approbation, and also to distinguish them from the counterfeit philanthropists. Since the end of the legal slave trade everyone, it seemed, was an abolitionist, even some of its former defenders. Mr Marryat, agent for Trinidad and a West Indian merchant, preceded Stephen in the same debate and called for stringent measures against the slave traders. Treat them as pirates, he said.[16] In 1810 this remedy was regarded as too drastic, though eventually parliament did declare them pirates;[17] but for the time being it satisfied itself with making trading a felony punishable by transportation of up to fourteen years.[18]

The abolitionists, though, had other plans. The meeting in Lincoln's Inn Fields which the Duke of Gloucester attended in July 1807 was for a very definite purpose. It was to estab-lish a new society—the African Institution. The names of the committee were familiar: Wilberforce, Brougham, Stephen, Clarkson, Sharp, Macaulay, and so on. The objects of the Institution were to keep a watch on the execution of the Abolition Act, to promote abolition in other nations, and to compensate the Africans for their losses. By the latter was meant 'the introduction of the blessings of civilised life'.

The motives behind the formation of the Institution accorded with abolitionist logic. The only satisfactory way in which to end the slave trade was to cut it off at its source. Teach the Africans to be Christians, to conduct themselves as Europeans (and British Europeans in particu-lar), and to sell commodities other than slaves, and the slave

trade must come to an end. The Institution declared that it
was no part of their plan to purchase territory in Africa
or to found colonies or even to carry on commerce itself, but
its first report added an ominously prophetic rider. 'Let
our benevolence interpose to . . . teach [Africa] the use of
her liberated faculties and we may soon discover . . . we
have only been laying a more solid foundation for the en-
largement of our own national prosperity.'[19]

In time the Institution took over the activities of the
Abolition Society which after 1807 became virtually mori-
bund. Though slavery was significantly absent from its
objects and no mention of the West Indies was made in its
first report, this did not protect it from virulent attacks by
its enemies, the merchants and planters who convinced
themselves that its sole object was to spy on their behaviour
to the slaves on the plantations. 'We are always reminded
in those unfortunate discussions of the power, rank, and
character of the African Institution. It is indeed great and
justly so in the private characters of its members', James
M'Queen, the editor of the *Glasgow Courier*, wrote in 1816.
'It is however here where the greatest danger lies because
evil-minded men shelter their destructive views under
highly respectable names. Their character induces thousands
to support measures . . . which they would not otherwise do.
. . . There are men among them who ought not to be trusted.'[20]

All this was still to come. With the abolition of the slave
trade and the sense of triumph and relief which followed,
the abolitionists almost persuaded themselves that they had,
indeed, liberated the African continent. As far as the slaves
in the West Indies were concerned most of them preferred
to go no further than Wilberforce. In 1811 he wrote: 'In
truth there is a peculiar call on our sensibility in the present
instance, for in proportion as the lot of the slaves is hard in
this world, we ought to rejoice in every opportunity of
bringing them under the influence of principles which may
cheer them under their present sufferings, and secure for
them a rich compensation of reversionary happiness.'[21]
He had in mind, of course, the consolations of Christianity.

One morning I had a hearty laugh at the expense of a woman who had purchased a female slave at one of these auctions. The girl in question had lately been imported. She appeared about sixteen, seemed very unwell, and had no other covering than a dirty blanket. She was placed on the table by the side of the auctioneer who frequently turned her round to the bidders to show her make and figure. He would also, at times, open her mouth and show her teeth, much in the same style as a jockey would exhibit the mouth of a horse for the inspection of his customers. One woman who appeared very eager to purchase outbid the rest under the full persuasion that the girl was *with child*, and of course a great bargain at the price. The girl got down from the table with much difficulty, and the woman went with her into the auction-room, for the sales are made in the street below the door. She was eager to examine the quality of the commodity she had bought, when, to her mortification, upon taking off the blanket, she discovered the girl, instead of being *with child* had got the *dropsy*. It was not his fault, the auctioneer said, if the lady had been deceived by appearances.

(*The Anti-Jacobin Review*, 1814)

A gentleman, Byam, who was the chief commissary of police in Mauritius, left with his wife in 1824. As Mrs Byam was on the point of getting into the boat which was to take them on board their ship, a slave woman called after her by name. . . . She recognised a poor creature to whom she had rendered some service and asked what she wanted of her. 'Madam,' said the woman in French, 'have you God in your country?' 'How can you ask such a question? God is everywhere.' 'No, Madam, God is not here. We have no God; if God is in your country, tell him what we poor slaves suffer. We have no God here!'

(*Antislavery Recollections*—Sir George Stephen, 1854)

Preachee and Floggee, Too

In an age of religious dissent few topics exercised the minds of theologians as did the subject of slavery. Did Christianity permit it or not? How could the apparent contradictions in the Old Testament be explained? Was the African part of a common humanity over which Christ's injunctions extended; if so, how was it possible that Christians could enslave him and treat him with barbarous cruelty; if not, how could the universality of Christ's Gospel be understood? The French philosopher, Montesquieu, stated the problem succinctly: 'If slaves are human, then we are not Christians.' Right up to the final emancipation in the 1830s in the British West Indies and in the 1860s in America Montesquieu's conundrum caused men who might in every other respect be united in common worship to react to each other with fierce and angry condemnation. In print, that is: when it came to a practical demonstration of beliefs in the slave countries themselves the gap between the dissidents was not nearly so wide.

There were two basic attitudes to the problem of Christianity and slavery: Christianity condoned slavery; Christianity condemned it. Four centuries before Europe was faced with the practical difficulty of having to solve the problem to save its own soul, St Augustine in the *City of God* had spoken of it as both a remedy and a penalty for sin. By God's judgment man was made a slave to other men because he had presumed by the exercise of his will to rise above his position in the natural order. By preserving the institution of slavery mankind could be disciplined and his self-aggrandisement corrected; and because no man was innocent, it was God's will alone who should be master and who slave.[1]

The close connection between slavery and sin, between perpetual bondage and punishment was one of the traditions handed down to the theologians of the eighteenth century who were questioning the institution. Another was that it was part of the natural order: as God had dominance over man, and man over beasts, so some men had dominance over others. The additional question raised by the enslavement of blacks, which did not arise in the ancient world where slaves might be of any colour or creed, was why only them?

The Reverend Raymund Harris was by no means the first, but he was one of the most prominent of the late eighteenth-century writers to consider the problems. In a book which appeared in that crucial year of anti-slave trade agitation—1788—he produced a wealth of scriptural evidence to support his contention that slavery, and particularly slavery of blacks, was in accordance with the word of God.[2] The datum upon which his argument rested was: 'That, as there can be no prescription against the authority of God, whatever is declared in any part of the scriptural records to be intrinsically good or bad, licit or illicit, must be essentially so in its own nature.'

He then went on to expound the Scriptures so as to show that they condoned the institution. In Exodus, God gave his ruling on the mode of employment for the Hebrew master and servant:

If thou buy an Hebrew servant, six years he shall serve; and in the seventh he shall go out free for nothing.
And if the servant shall plainly say, I love my master, my wife, and my children: I will not go out free

then the master was enjoined to bring the servant before a court which would adjudicate on the servant's status. This could be service in perpetuity to the one master, i.e. slavery. Leviticus, too, recognised slavery; and, more usefully, a certain category of slaves:

Both thy bondsmen, and thy bondsmaids which thou shalt have shall be of the heathen that are round about you; of them shall ye buy bondsmen and bondsmaids.

Then, of course, to link for ever the institution of slavery with one particular race of people there was Joshua's declaration to the people of Gibeon which has echoed down through the hundreds of centuries and can still be heard faintly in outposts of white imperialism:

Now therefore ye are cursed, and there shall none of you be freed from being bondsmen, and hewers of wood and drawers of water for the house of my God.

Turning to the New Testament, Harris quoted from Christ's Sermon on the Mount as the basis for his argument that Christianity recognised the existing systems and institutions of society:

Think not that I am come to destroy the Law of the Prophets; I am not come to destroy but to fulfil.

The silence of the first teachers of Christianity on slavery indicated that they never considered it, or had never been taught by Christ to consider it, as an infraction of any of the principles or moral precepts of his Gospel. 'Our blessed Saviour, though he attacked the Jews for irreligious abuses most severely, never reproved or even hinted the least disapprobation of the practice of slavery.' He went on to point out that even this silence was not total since Paul in his Epistle to Timothy says: 'Let as many servants as are under the yoke count their own masters worthy of all honour that the name of God and his doctrine be not blasphemed.'

Harris was finally faced with what was for religious apologists of slavery the most difficult for all Christ's teachings to explain away—to do unto others as you would have them do unto you. Ingenious as ever, he said that no Christian master can be said to carry out the Golden Rule unless he behaves to his slave 'with the same tenderness, justice and humanity as he would have his slave behave to him were the slave the master and he himself the slave'. Equally, no slave could be said to carry it out unless he served his master 'with the same fidelity, submission and respect which he would expect from his master were the latter his slave and himself the master'. Christ's maxim, therefore, served to enforce the reciprocal duties of master and slave 'in their different spheres'—an appropriate conclusion to a book dedicated to the mayor and aldermen of Liverpool, at that time the word's richest slave-trading port.

A dozen years before, Granville Sharp had applied his mind to the same problems.[3] In *The Just Limitation of Slavery in the Laws of God* he answered those who quoted Deuteronomy and Leviticus to support the argument that slavery was acceptable. He said that as far as the enslavement of the heathen was concerned this applied only to the 'seven nations' who were devoted to the destruction of the Israelites. In this respect, therefore, it was virtually self-defence, and was, moreover, only a temporary measure; not one extending to the British in the eighteenth century. For everyone else, God's command in Deuteronomy applied:

> Love ye therefore the stranger: for ye were strangers in the land of Egypt.

Regarding the enslavement of their own people indicated in the passage of Exodus quoted by Harris, Sharp said that a Hebrew could be made a slave only by his consent openly declared in court, which was a very different thing from the enforced slavery of the Africans who were made perpetual bondsmen against their will.

In his essay on *Self-love* Sharp dealt with Christ's Golden Rule in his usual detailed, pedantic manner and came to the conclusion 'that slavery is absolutely inconsistent with Christianity because we cannot say of any slaveholder that he doth to another what he would have done to himself. For he is continually exacting involuntary labour from the other without wages which he would think monstrously unjust were he himself the sufferer.'[4]

For Sharp, slavery was not God's punishment for the commission of sin; it was itself the sin which would bring down on the heads of all those involved in it the wrath of God. 'Let that man who endeavours to deprive others of their just privileges as brethren take heed lest he should thereby unhappily occasion his own rejection in the end when that dreadful doom which the uncharitable must expect will certainly be pronounced.'[5, 6]

Against this background of theoretical debate, more pressing practical problems had to be faced since slavery was an existing fact which until the eighteenth century had scarcely been questioned let alone been subjected to intense enquiry. The Church of England had, through its leading clergy, stated its position on a number of occasions. The Bishop of London in dealing with the question of the effect of baptism on ownership in a slave declared that conversion to Christianity did not make the slightest alteration in the duties arising out of the civil relationships of master and slave except that the converted slave would be under an even stronger obligation to perform his duties. The only freedom which Christianity gave him was the freedom from the bondage of sin and Satan.[7]

The Bishop of London, who had a particular interest in slavery since the care of the English plantations fell within his jurisdiction, addressed letters to the 'masters and mistresses of families' and to missionaries in these plantations in 1727, the gist of which was that not enough was being done to christianise the heathen by the propagation of the Gospel and by example. The Bishop was also concerned about Sunday observance. The planters objected to this on the grounds that it lost them a day's work from their slaves. The Bishop answered them firmly. 'I may well reason as St Paul does . . . that if they make you partakers of their temporal things (of their strength and spirit and even of their offspring) you ought to make them partakers of your spiritual things; tho' it should abate somewhat of the profit you might otherwise receive from their labours.'[8]

The Church of England had its missionary arm—the Society for the Propagation of the Gospel—which received its charter at the beginning of the eighteenth century. It was composed of the chief prelates and dignitaries of the Church and of 'several other lords and eminent persons in the state'. It had missions in Rhode Island, New England, New York, New Jersey, North and South Carolina, Georgia, and all the British sugar islands—everywhere, in fact, where there were slave populations. In addition it also owned plantations in Barbados with 300 slaves bequeathed to it by a wealthy slave owner, Christopher Codrington. By 1761 another 450 slaves were added to the original number.

'We . . . are become the innocent partakers of the fruits of this iniquitous traffic', said the Bishop of Gloucester, William Warburton, in a sermon preached before the Society in February 1766, making perhaps the first denunciation of the slave trade by any member of the Established Church. Slavery, however, did not worry him as much. He did not approve of it: 'Nature created Man free; and Grace invites him to assert his freedom'; but he did not suggest the Society should therefore emancipate the people they owned. Rather he delighted in the fact that the Codrington bequest enable the Church to redeem the heathen from the miseries of a brutal life and set them at ease in the accommodations provided for them by the Society. There the kindly treatment meted out to them would be an example to tyrannous masters on other plantations.[9]

In fact, the record of the Society's plantations never lived up to Warburton's expectations. The death-rate was about five-sixths the birth-rate, and its managers never showed any particular kindness to its slaves; even sixty years after Warburton's sermon the Society's plantations were behind the general standard of other plantations in the conditions provided for the slaves.[10]

With its power, wealth and influence the Church of England could have been an invaluable force on the side of abolition and emancipation had it chosen that course. However, partly because of its wealth and its total commitment to the sanctity of property it compromised itself all along the way with the West Indian merchants and planters, and acted instead as a brake on progress. The Dissenting Churches, however, though they inherited similar theological attitudes to slavery, did not have their freedom of action limited to such a degree by the need to conform to traditional social attitudes. They could, therefore, and did, adopt differing approaches to the problem of slavery and Christianity.

John Wesley's statement in his *Thoughts upon Slavery* was uncompromising. 'I absolutely deny all slave holding to be consistent with any degree of even natural justice. . . . Give liberty to whom liberty is due, that is to every child of man, to every partaker of human nature. Let none serve you but by his own act and deed, by his own voluntary choice.'[11] We have seen that the Quakers were also deeply disturbed by the existence of a system which seemed to them to be on every ground against the tenets of Christianity, though their concern at first was more the slave trade than slavery. They regarded the former as a sin, pure and simple, for which the nations involved would be punished by God. Anthony Benezet, one of the most prominent of the Quaker abolitionists, dismissing the idea that teaching slaves Christianity would improve them by quitting their minds of idolatry said, 'The end cannot justify the means. It was never intended that the gospel of peace should be propagated by the violation of every tender connection, by compulsion, and by fraud.'[12]

Though still members of the Church of England despite their calling themselves a 'Sect', the Claphamites shared with the Dissenting Church the hatred of the slave trade and the moral anxiety for the existence of the slave system in the colonies. This anxiety expressed itself more convincingly in the anti-slavery tracts and essays which Hatchards and other London publishers turned out monthly than in any purposeful action in the colonies. There were, of course, missions, but these tended to concentrate on the same aspects of slavery as did the Society for the Propagation of the Gospel and the nonconformist missions, namely, sabbath-breaking and the supposed sexual laxness of the slaves.

It was this last point which united all Christian denominations: the blacks, either because of their inherent nature or because of the inherent nature of slavery (depending on one's viewpoint) were immoral. In the evidence produced to the Privy Council in 1789 parliament was told that the missionaries had frequent occasion to see with sorrow 'how deeply rooted the habit of sin and the tendency to excuse it is in the minds of the negroes, who, when unconverted, are particularly given to an unbounded gratification of every sensual lust'. They lamented the slaves' 'hankering after the vain traditions of their forefathers' and recommended that the converted be separated from the unconverted lest the latter should seduce the others'.[13]

Nothing, of course, was done by the planters who were not nearly so bothered by their slaves' 'immorality' so long as they got a day's work out of them. The Reverend Joseph Hutchins complained to Lord Combermere in 1817: 'Nothing can be done successfully for promoting religion among the slaves without the general concurrence, approbation, authority and co-operation of their owners.' The Reverend George Foster, however, blamed the missionaries' failure to alter the slaves' attitudes on 'the extreme ignorance, debasement, and depravity of those on whom they are inculcated', and another missionary thought the slaves were 'a people of a very slow apprehension'.[14]

The one thing the slaves were very slow to apprehend was why they should have to give up any leisure time they were lucky enough to get to sit in a church and listen to sermons about a god that was not their own. They preferred to spend that time tending their little gardens if they had them, dancing and playing music, or simply blocking out of their minds the hell they lived in by getting drunk on cheap rum. Most of all there were the Sunday markets to meet friends and relatives, and perhaps to make a little money by selling vegetables grown in their gardens. A planter wrote in 1816: 'Sunday was only known to them as market day. . . . Their holiday time was only considered by them as a short respite from the service of the master and generally dissipated in idleness or intemperance.' However, where the missionaries had been permitted to work redemption and reform upon the slave, 'instead of the brutal appearance, the morbid sensibility, the stupid sensuality which stamped him as a disgrace to the form of humanity . . . consciousness has been awakened from the clod . . . and above all, his duty to his master is confirmed upon a much better assurance than ever, upon a principle of obedience inculcated by Scripture'.[15]

The enthusiasm expressed by this planter for the work done by the missionaries was not shared by all. Many thought more as Edward Long did. 'Some labourers in the Lord's vineyards have at times been men who were much better qualified to be retailers of salt-fish or boatswains to privateers than ministers of the Gospel', he wrote in 1774.[16] A distinction, however, was made between the clergy of the Established Church and the nonconformists. The latter were looked upon as potential revolutionaries since they were associated with the abolitionist fervour in Britain. 'Some of the Dissenting missionaries sent out were low, ignorant men who perhaps did more harm than good by their instructions, if they might be called. Instead of inculcating the plain practical duties which Christianity enjoins, they expiated on topics altogether incomprehensible to their ignorant auditors', was how the ex-sugar-estate manager, James M'Queen, saw the difficulties created by nonconformists. 'They [the slaves] became,' M'Queen said, 'in consequence of the fanatical cant of these pretended preachers more hypocritical, more assuming, more regardful of outward appearances, less cheerful and lively, full of fanatic gloom bordering on melancholy, and less attentive to the affairs of their families or the interest of their owners.'[17]

The planters much preferred the trustworthy clergymen from the Established Church. A West Indian reported in 1816 that the assemblies of the various colonies were of the opinion that the Bishop of London and not the missionary preacher was the 'regular and safe and effectual channel for promoting Christian knowledge' and he hoped that only 'true Church of England doctrines and discipline' would be disseminated among the slaves.[18]

The Dissenting missions were acutely aware of the prejudice against them. Later this grew to such violent proportions that it was impossible for them to ignore it. They tried everything they could to play down the attitudes of some of their more radical brethren who were not confronted by the daily burden of trying to preach Christianity to slaves whose masters considered missionaries to be dangerous. 'If Christianity meddles not with the civil relations of master and slave,' said the Wesleyan missionary the Reverend Robert Young in a sermon preached in Jamaica in 1824,

'let me admonish you, as bondservants, against being
dissatisfied with your condition. . . . It ought to be remembered that the situation of life in which Providence has placed
you is not without its comforts; for when you have performed your appointed work you are happily delivered from
all anxiety and tormenting care, and in the evening of
each day can return to your humble cabins with confidence,
being assured that no creditors will be found there. . . . Such,
however, are the trials of many of the labouring poor in
England.'[19]

It was not enough for the Dissenting missionaries to
point out to the planters that they meant them no harm;
they went further by showing that Christianity saved the
slaves from the corrupting fear and power of their own gods
—*obeah*; moreover, it inspired the slaves with principles of
honesty; and it made them sober and obedient. 'That the
Christian religion when fully imparted to the slaves greatly
enhances their value has, I flatter myself, been fully proved',
Robert Young, and his missionary colleagues, liked to believe.[20]

Towards the slaves and slavery the churches in general
and the Methodists in particular were expressing attitudes
similar to those they held about work discipline and the
poorer classes in Britain. Throughout the eighteenth century
there were continual complaints about the idleness,
corruption, and immorality of the working class from
clergymen of all denominations, but it was the Methodists
who set about actively doing something to correct the
manners and behaviour of the poor. Their answer was—
as it was with the slaves in the West Indies—Christianity.
The only way to make people work, Arthur Young said in
1771, was to keep them poor. Poverty, however, made no
one happy and unhappy people tend to be indisciplined.
The Methodists' solution was to teach submission through
preaching the blessedness of poverty. Robert Young's
message to the slaves was: be happy with your lot because
God has placed you there and anyway it has its comforts.
Similarly the Methodists in Britain were telling their flock
not to complain about being poor, but to regard themselves
as fortunate. 'The box-like, blackening chapels stood in the

industrial districts like great traps for the human psyche', was how the historian, E. P. Thomson, so aptly put it.[21]

Just as the Methodists in the West Indies congratulated themselves when their slave converts were not involved in the frequent rebellions which took place, so their brethren in England patted themselves on the back when their working class converts did not take part in the riots and disturbances which occurred in Britain in the first few decades of the nineteenth century. 'I hope no considerable portion of our brethren is found among the Radicals', wrote a correspondent to the Methodist minister, Jabez Bunting, in 1816.[22]

In the West Indies also, the Methodists and, in fact, all the churches of whatever denomination kept themselves out of trouble as far as possible by concentrating not on the theoretical problems raised by the system—that was reluctantly left to the theologians in the home country—but on the morals of the slaves. 'The Sunday market has been abolished by law in this island', triumphed Edward Eliot, archdeacon of Barbados, in 1830. 'The duty of putting an end to the unchristian usage of marketing on the Lord's Day is now generally acknowledged throughout the British West Indies. . . . It has been urged . . . that the master is unwilling to abridge the comforts of his slaves by depriving them of the little gains which the privilege of a Sunday market affords them, or by forbidding the recreation of the Sunday revel or dance. There is something selfish in this boasted kindness. The master is favouring himself at the expense of God. He refuses to grant any portion of the time which is his own, while he gives away, with an ostentatious liberality, the time which is not his, but his Lord's.'[23]

It would be difficult to find a more glaring example of religious hypocrisy, of tortuous charity and distorted benevolence than in the churches' attitudes towards the slaves in the West Indies or wherever the slave system existed. The cartoonist Cruickshank caught the cruelly twisted values of the Christian missionaries in a sketch called 'Pigmy Revels'. It showed a parson sermonising to a black slave who answered him with a remark which had become a current catch-phrase:

'One thing at a time, Massa; if you please. If you floggee, floggee; if you preachee, preachee, But no preachee and floggee, too.'

The law respecting negroes there [in America] my Lord, is the law of property, consentaneously the law of England. By this law they are made real estate, for the purpose of descent, and goods and chattel quoad the payment of debts. This is the original and fundamental law concerning negroes. I do not remember ever to have seen the word slavery made use of, in any law, of any colony in America. I admit that the negroes are there termed slaves, but I will tell your Lordship why. In the criminal law, where they become necessarily the objects of punishment, it is essential that they should have some descriptive name or title given to them. It is for this reason, therefore, that they are there, and there only, so called. As they had been already defined as property, as negroes, it could not be said that if property should strike his master, property shall be punished; but it is said that if a slave should strike his master, this slave shall be punished accordingly.

(Considerations on the Negro Cause—Anon, 1772)

Names	Age	Colour	Country	Manner of Death or how Disposed	Conspicuous Marks	Remarks
William	40	mestiffe	Creole	suicide	none	hung himself (or otherwise as the case may be)
Edward	13	mulatto	Creole of Grenada	dysentery	none	—
Jenny	50	black	Africa	dropsy	country marks on face	had been a long time sick

(Specimen Annual Return of the Increase and Decrease of Slaves for the Registry of Slaves, Grenada, 1821)

The creoles, particularly if cooks or mechanics, such as tailors, carpenters, or the like, are valued at twenty or thirty or even sixty pounds more than untried Africans; who, besides requiring to be taught, may prove to be subject to some malady, or may fall sacrifice to the seasoning. Women, and boys sixteen or seventeen years old, are considered to be of nearly equal value; but are somewhat cheaper than the men.

(Pinckard)

Registration, Amelioration, and Mr Canning

The life of the West Indian slave scarcely altered for the better after the abolition of the slave trade, contrary to the expectations of the abolitionists. They had strongly maintained that if the supply of slaves from Africa was cut off the slave owners would be forced to treat those they owned well to keep them alive and useful for longer. In the event they were proved wrong, as they were proved wrong about the cessation of the slave trade itself. Their great achievement, the Abolition Act, for which they had striven so hard and which, at their moment of triumph they had equated with the liberation of Africa, turned out to be a dead letter.[1]

Discipline on the plantations remained as rigid as ever. At four o'clock in the morning the bell would ring to call the slaves to the field. For five hours they would work without a break, then at nine o'clock they would take a break for breakfast. From 9.30 to lunch they continued with field work, then after lunch until sunset, again without a break. During crop time the work was less arduous, but some industrious planters would have their people labouring at the sugar mills and boiling houses all night. The whip was the planter's badge of authority and he resorted to it for the slightest infringement or the briefest falling off of work. If life became too hard to bear and the slaves ran away, they faced death from starvation, or recapture and terrible punishment.[2]

Most plantation owners treated their slaves with casual but unpremeditated cruelty. To whip a child, to send a man off to the treadmill to tread until the skin came off his legs, or to keep an old woman in stocks for days without food, these and other acts were perpetrated in the ordinary course of the day. Occasionally, however, a planter would exceed the acceptable limits and act in an exceptionally ferocious way. Edward Huggins, a Nevis planter, was one such man. He had been plagued by a series of runaways and at last he caught and drove twenty slaves to the centre of town. There, with his two sons and two practised whippers, Huggins flogged the runaways—up to 365 lashes for the men and 291 for the women. He was charged with cruelty, and despite the fact that the floggings had been witnessed by five magistrates and had gone far above the maximum permitted by Nevis law, Huggins was acquitted. Arthur Hodge of Tortola was not so fortunate. He was found guilty of killing either personally or under his orders nearly one hundred blacks by cruelty, torture and whippings. Three of his slaves, Tom, Prosper and Cuffy, had been stretched out on the ground and whipped continuously for over an hour until they died. Boiling water had been poured down the throat of the plantation cook, and a hot iron had been placed in another's mouth. Young slaves had been beaten, dipped in boiling liquid, nearly drowned, then hung up and horsewhipped. All this was too much even for the white magistrates, and despite the fact that seven members of the all-white jury recommended mercy, Hodge was hanged.[3]

The leading abolitionists were not so busy with the immorality and heathenism of the East Indians and Africans to ignore what was happening in the West Indies. Stephen especially came to acknowledge that the Abolition Act had failed to improve the lot of the slaves. At the beginning of 1812 he met with others at the home of the law reformer, Sir Samuel Romilly, to discuss his plan for registering the slaves. If each colony was required to keep a register of the number of slaves in that colony, together with details of births, deaths, punishments, and so on, and these registers were sent from time to time to London, it would be possible to know if there was any illegal importation of slaves, and also to have some idea of the general state of the slave populations, whether they were increasing through humane treatment or decreasing through cruelty. As Stephen's son said in his *Antislavery Recollections*, the market-place of a West Indian colony was a sealed book to the British public.

The register would, it was hoped, open that book for all to see.[4]

The abolitionists thought about the idea of the register for a long time before anything was done about it. They concentrated their parliamentary activities on the foreign slave trade, particularly since, with the defeat of Napoleon and the gathering of the European Powers for peace talks, the moment presented itself for 'urging the consideration of the wrongs of Africa'. Wilberforce moved a resolution 'that His Majesty's Government would employ every proper means to . . . implore other members of the commonwealth of Europe to signalise the restoration of its order . . . by the prohibition of this detestable commerce'.[5]

Zachary Macaulay was sent by the African Institution to Paris to assist Lord Castlereagh, and a declaration was finally signed by Britain, France, Russia, Austria, Prussia, Sweden, Spain and Portugal condemning the trade as 'repugnant to the principles of humanity and universal morality' and expressing 'the sincere desire of concurring in the most prompt and effectual execution of this measure by all the means at their disposal'. Empty words. Despite the agreement by Britain to pay Portugal an indemnity of £300,000 against any losses, the slave trade went on.[6]

James Stephen's Registry Bill, which had been pushed aside by these considerations, was finally introduced into parliament. Lord Grenville said in the House of Lords in March 1816 that the Abolition Act might be made completely effective by such a Bill,[7] and immediately Lord Holland, who had been an ardent abolitionist, advised caution about entering into 'a system of polemical legislation for our colonies'[8]—the argument which the West Indians were to use to great effect during the next few years. Registration, they maintained, was an internal matter and could therefore be left to the colonial assemblies to establish if they should so wish; if not, parliament ought not to interfere.

As in the past, events played into their hands. In the same year there was an uprising in Barbados and unrest in other islands. The planters immediately blamed the abolitionists and the African Institution in particular for causing trouble by their demand for registration. 'If anything could stop

these philanthropic Quixotes in their career of mischief,
the recent event at Barbados would have imposed silence
on their tongues and restraint on their pens', thundered
The Anti-Jacobin Review in July. 'For that insurrection and
projected massacre in that devoted island was as much
produced by the discussion on the Registry Bill, and by
the pamphlets of Messrs Stephen and Macaulay as the horror
in St Domingo proceeded from the encouragement of their
fellow-labourers in France.' The *Review* accused them of
obstinacy, of claiming Papal infallibility, and rather than
the 'miserable cant and whine of puritanism' called for
'plain manly sense' to prevail.

Where better to find that than in parliament? 'Persons
have been found assuming the sacred office of religious
instructors, making their way into the interior of the islands,
instilling into the mind of the negroes doctrines subversive
of the public tranquillity, mixing with the truths of Christianity the dreadful principles of insubordination and insurrection', raged one West Indian in the House of Commons.[9]
'The minds of the slaves have been filled with discontent',
said another, 'and those of the masters with alarm. Wilberforce has produced calamities of which no man can foresee
the conclusion. That such a change can have happened to
such a man is indeed painful to know! The Registry Bill
comes out, the ferment begins, the appearance of every
packet is eagerly expected [in the colonies] with the order
for emancipation, and when the last packet arrives without
such order disappointment explodes in a nearly general
revolt. The members of the African Institution live in a
world of delusion and error.'[10]

Speaking on behalf of the Government in that tone of
grovelling humility which cabinet members usually adopted
when in the presence of irate West Indians, Lord Castlereagh
apologised that the Registry Bill might have been responsible for the recent calamities. His Majesty's ministers could
never have had in mind emancipation. The idea was preposterous, a delusion. 'We owe it to the deluded negroes to
dispossess them of the wild opinion that anything so preposterous was sanctioned by the government of this country.'
He suggested that Wilberforce should withdraw the Bill

immediately to settle the minds of the blacks.[11] The debate ended with the reading of a dramatic letter from a planter: 'Pray tell Mr Wilberforce that until the negroes heard of the Registry Bill . . . I slept with doors and windows open, but now, although under the guns of a fort, I have loaded pistols at the side of my bed every night.'[12]

Leave it to us, the West Indians said. The slaves are our problem and we will register them and also introduce measures in our assemblies to improve their conditions if this is what was wanted. But it must be left to us, otherwise everything will get out of hand and a general slave war will probably take place. The British public, tired of wars and suffering from post-war distress and discontent, gravely exacerbated by the introduction of the Corn Laws in 1815, was only too happy to leave the problem of slavery to the colonies, and for the next couple of years, apart from the Government promising to show parliament the acts of colonial assemblies purporting to ameliorate slavery or register slaves but never doing so because there were no such acts, the West Indies were left undisturbed.

Then during 1818 and 1819 parliament once again considered the problem of the treatment of slaves. Despite one planter's loud complaint that 'our purity and innocence should be placed on record',[13] the Huggins case and other instances of cruelty were cited to show that the slave owners were not only doing nothing to improve the conditions of their slaves, they were making life even harder for them. The West Indians were furious. 'Whatever punishment is mentioned', said Mr Grant, 'the House hears of the cart-whip and so conveying an idea of severity and cruelty in the treatment of slaves.' 'Was the instrument of punishment not a whip?' asked Sir Samuel Romilly. 'Most undoubtedly it was', replied Mr Grant. 'But why use the odious and invidious term "cart-whip", implying a brutal infliction of severity instead of a necessary correction.' The workhouse and a sentence of labour in chains, he went on to point out, was 'rather intended to promote their health than to gain anything by their industry in this situation'.[14]

Not many people, however, were taken in by excuses such as these, and the Registry Bill was passed in 1819. It provided for the establishment of a Registry of Slaves in Great Britain and for the appointment of a Registrar of Slaves whose task it was to ensure that every slave in the colonies was registered; no slave could be bought or sold, or sent from one island to another, and no money could be lent on the security of a slave unless he or she was registered.[15]

Again the abolition leaders thought they had gone as far as they could; again their opponents within the movement—and their numbers were steadily growing—maintained that they had not gone far enough. 'I know I have been considered too moderate by many', admitted Wilberforce during one of the debates on the Bill.[16] More radical abolitionists pointed out that the Registry Act only confirmed the recognition by the British parliament of ownership in man; and later on the West Indians themselves argued that by recording the identification of every slave and by making the registration of him the responsibility of public officials, and, moreover, the indispensable evidence of title, the legislature had *de facto* as well as *de jure* ratified the title to property in man. They further maintained that having thus induced people to purchase or to lend money on the faith of a title recognised by parliament, it would be unconstitutional to declare such property invalid.[17]

At that stage no one was talking publicly about emancipation. A new epilogue had been added to an old play—*The Padlock*, by Isaac Bickerstaff:

> O sons of freedom! equalise your laws,
> Be all consistent, plead the negro's cause;
> That all the nations in your code may see
> The British negro, like the Briton, free.[18]

But the 'sons of freedom' were otherwise engaged. Wilberforce, speaking on slavery at the Cape of Good Hope confessed that 'perhaps of late we all have been chargeable with not having paid due attention to the subject', and admitted that registration, too, was not proving an adequate protection for slaves.[19]

The years passed. The slaves continued to be exported from Africa in their thousands, continued to be ill-treated on the plantations in the West Indies. Then came 1823, and like 1788 it was marked by an extraordinary upsurge of emotion for the slave. In January the London Society for the Mitigation and Gradual Abolition of Slavery was founded, and during the next year and a half no fewer than 750 petitions against slavery were presented to parliament. One of the London Society's greatest enemies, James M'Queen, pointed out that its members were the same as those of the African Institute which 'Proteus-like assumes every shape as suits its purpose'.[20]

In March Wilberforce introduced in the House of Commons a petition of the Quakers, praying for the abolition of slavery throughout the British dominions. 'I now regret that I and those honourable friends who thought with me on this subject have not before now attempted to put an end, not merely to the evils of the slave trade, but to the evils of slavery itself.' He excused himself by putting some of the blame on 'the immediate friends of abolition' who were satisfied with the Abolition Act, 'which might perhaps extenuate my own guilt in not having sooner proposed the termination of that evil against which the prayer of the petition . . . is directed'. Incorrigible as ever, he then gave the West Indians their next weapon by tentatively suggesting they might be entitled to compensation of some kind, 'never forgetting that we have no right to pay British debts with African freedom'.[21]

By now Wilberforce was only the figure-head; the real burden of the parliamentary battle fell on Thomas Fowell Buxton who was thirty-seven. Wilberforce was a small, bird-like man, reputedly a wonderful orator with a lilting voice; in contrast Buxton was 'in stature a giant . . . a thorough sportsman',[22] but not an exciting or attractive speaker. He was connected to the Quaker families of the Gurneys and the Frys and after coming down from Trinity College, Dublin, he joined Truman and Hanbury, the brewers. In 1818 he entered parliament. Wealthy, intelligent, ambitious, but above all, a profoundly serious man who was haunted by a sense of responsibility for others, he was an ideal successor to Wilberforce.[23] He was one of those referred to by his illustrious contemporary, Lord Macaulay, as 'the most enlightened generation of the most enlightened people that ever existed'.[24] He knew right from wrong. He knew what was good for himself, and more important, what was good for others. He carried into the middle of the nineteenth century the same irritation with 'the heathen' for being 'immoral' and the same obsessive desire to convert them to his way of life and to his religion that had characterised Wilberforce and his generation. He also made the same mistakes when it came to dealing with West Indian interests in parliament.

Buxton opened his first parliamentary attack on slavery[25] by insisting that he harboured 'no species of prejudice either against the whole body or against any individual of the body of persons connected with the West Indies'. Because they did not create slavery, but inherited it, 'I consider them as eminently unfortunate . . . rather than culpable.' Then he proceeded to tell the West Indians what he and his colleagues had in mind. Like Wilberforce he started on a strong, forceful note: 'I hope I shall not be deemed imprudent if I throw off all disguise and state frankly and without reserve the object at which we aim. The object . . . is the extinction of slavery—nothing less than the extinction of slavery—in nothing less than the whole of the British dominions . . .' Straight away, then, in case he might excite too much acrimony, he added, '. . . not, however, the rapid termination of that state—not the sudden emancipation of the negro—but such preparatory steps, such measures of precaution as by slow degrees and in a course of years first fitting and qualifying the slave for the enjoyment of freedom shall gently conduct us to the annihilation of slavery'. His words were well chosen: preparatory, precaution, slow, gently. 'Nothing can more clearly show that we mean nothing rash, nothing rapid, nothing abrupt, nothing bearing any feature of violence than this—that if I succeed to the fullest extent of my desires, confessedly sanguine, no man will be able to say, I even shall be unable to predict that at such a time, or in such a year, slavery will be abolished. . . . We are far from meaning to attempt to cut down slavery in the full maturity of its vigour. We rather shall leave it gently to decay; slowly, silently, almost imperceptibly to die away and to be forgotten. . . . To a nation thus steeped in this species of iniquity', he went on, 'we do not ask that you should suffer punishment . . . we do not even say, cease to enjoy those acts of criminality which you have begun, but take the full benefit and fruition of past and present injustice; complete what you have commenced, screw from your slave all that his bones and muscle will yield you: only stop there; and when every slave now living shall have found repose in the grave, then let it be said that the country's satisfied with slavery and has done with it for ever.'

Anyone closely reading a report of Buxton's speech would have been justified in wondering whether he ever honestly intended there to be emancipation. Buxton knew as well as, if not better than, most people that the illegal slave trade ensured that no time would exist when 'every slave now living' would be dead. So long as slavery existed in the West Indies there would always be slaves; and so long as there were slaves, the institution would continue to exist unless parliament at some stage declared: emancipation now! Buxton made it abundantly clear that he was not asking parliament to do that. 'Now for the existing slaves. Slaves, I fear, they must too generally continue. . . . The slave is not ripe for liberty. If I deemed them ripe for deliverance my moderation would be small.' So apart from sounding courageous and impressive, Buxton's words were virtually empty of meaning.

This, and the fact that his 'moderation' was excessive, did not prevent his opponents from attacking him. 'If any measures are taken for abolishing slavery', said one of the West Indians, 'the inevitable consequence will be that the whole of the islands will be lost to this country.'[26] Another well-known representative of their interests, Charles Ellis, took up the argument which the abolitionists had been the first to state—the slaves were not fit for freedom. 'If the result of emancipation was to be that the negroes were . . . to revert to their former habits of savage life . . . shall we have performed our duty towards them?'[27]

The atmosphere of *déjà vu* which permeated the whole debate was strengthened by the Colonial Secretary, George

Canning, who performed the task on behalf of the present
Government which Henry Dundas had performed for
Pitt's Government in 1792. He brought the movement
towards possible reform to a gentle but firm halt. This was a
fearful question, he said; one rash word, perhaps even one too
ardent expression might raise a flame not easily to be extinguished. The British parliament had for ages tolerated,
sanctioned, protected, and even encouraged slavery; it could
not now legislate as if it was legislating for a new world.
He did not think that, though emancipation was 'a great
national object', it was fair to accomplish it at the exclusive
expense of any one class of the community. What he proposed, therefore, were resolutions which would go a long
way towards ameliorating the conditions of slavery in
the West Indies. They included suggestions for laws to
encourage marriage among the slaves, to permit slaves to
give evidence in court against their masters, to encourage
religious instruction, to reduce punishments for all and end
whipping of female slaves, to prohibit the removal of slaves
from their homes to satisfy their master's debts, and finally
to remove some of the restrictions on manumissions. The
British parliament would not bring in enactments in respect
of these ameliorative steps—that would be legislating for
the colonies—but it would strongly recommend to the
colonial assemblies that they do so immediately.[28]

On the strength of what appeared to be far-reaching
measures to improve the slaves' condition, Buxton agreed to
withdraw his motion for the gradual emancipation of the
slaves. Mr Canning had his resolutions carried without
opposition. 'It has generally been received as truth that
these resolutions of Canning were preconcerted by him with
the West Indian Committee', George Stephen said.[29] They
gave 'the substance to the West Indians and the shadow to
the slave'. It took the abolitionists fifteen years to overcome
the nullifying effects of Henry Dundas's machinations on
behalf of his West Indian friends at the end of the eighteenth
century. It took their successors only slightly less—ten years
—to overcome Canning's. 'I regarded him as our very worst
adversary on all that related to West Indian affairs,'
Macaulay was told by Henry Brougham. '[He] affected

to have the same object in view, and pretended to be waddling towards it by another and more roundabout road, while he is in reality running in the very opposite course.'[30]

The British parliament could now turn to other matters, satisfied that it had done all it could for the slaves which would not cause irritation to the West Indian slave owners and merchants, nor unrest among the slaves themselves. 'Rulers, who neither see, nor feel, nor know', wrote Shelley of England in 1819. His words applied even more so in 1823.

> Religion Christless, Godless—a book sealed;
> A Senate—Time's worst statute unrepealed,
> Are graves, from which a glorious Phantom may
> Burst, to illuminate our tempestuous day.

A phantom was about to burst, but not in Britain. In a small island thousands of miles away. And not glorious either, but ugly and violent. It did, however, illuminate their 'tempestuous day' for years to come.

A gentleman of my acquaintance who had purchased at the same time ten Koromantyn boys and the like number of Eboes (the eldest of the whole apparently not more than thirteen years of age) caused them all to be collected and brought before him in my presence to be marked on the breast. This operation is performed by heating a small flame of spirits of wine, and applying it to the skin which is previously annointed with sweet oil. . . . When the first boy, who happened to be one of the Eboes, and the stoutest of the whole, was led forward to receive his mark, he screamed dreadfully . . . but the Koromantyn boys, laughing aloud, and immediately coming forward of their own accord, offered their bosoms undaunted to the brand, and receiving its impression without flinching in the least, snapt their fingers in exultation over the poor Eboes.

(*The History of the British Colonies in the West Indies*—
Bryan Edwards, 1793)

Being one morning at her house, while sitting in conversation we suddenly heard the loud cries of a negro smarting under the whip. Mrs — expressed surprise on observing me shudder at his shrieks; she exclaimed with a broad smile, 'Aha, it will do him good! A little wholesome flagellation will refresh him. It will sober him; it will open his skin, and make him alert.'

(Pinckard)

I am an advocate for humanity, and in consequence of this principle not an advocate for the liberation of the slave. I am an advocate for all that can make him comfortable and happy, for his removal from his natal soil, that he may taste the comforts of protection, the fruits of humanity, and the blessings of religion.

(William Beckford Jnr—*The Gentleman's Magazine*, 1788)

Demerara, 1823

The Times, Monday, October 13th, 1823: 'Accounts of a very alarming nature were received on Saturday by the Leeward Islands' mail from Demerara of an insurrection having broken out among the slaves in that colony on the 17th or 18th August. According to one of the letters, the whole colony was in a state of insurrection. Three thousand negroes of the different estates had revolted, and formed a junction . . . The utmost apprehension exists among the merchants trading with Demerara, and the next intelligence from thence, as well as from the West India islands, is expected with much anxiety.' The report added as an aside that 'there is reason to hope that the statements, as is very usual in cases of this nature, have been much exaggerated'.

Tuesday's edition confirmed this. 'The reported insurrection at Demerara appears, as we expected it would, to have been much exaggerated. Advices received by way of Barbados state that the number of insurgent negroes did not exceed 1500 and after they had been dispersed by the soldiery, the insurrection was suppressed.' A later report stated that the governor of the colony, accompanied by his staff and eight or ten of the militia, had parleyed with the blacks from some estates to persuade them to return to work. The slaves told him that they had been promised their freedom by the English king; the message had come from England to that effect, but as the Governor was withholding it from them, they were determined to take it for themselves. The parley accordingly failed, and the military operations were set in motion which resulted in the deaths of hundreds of slaves.

On Wednesday, October 15th, *The Times* published a copy of the Governor's proclamation in which he said that because of the misconduct of the slaves, 'they are at this moment suffering all the horrors attendant on the existence of martial law, which I have been compelled to put in force in that part of the colony with all its accompanying severity'. A court martial had been hastily organised and had commenced to hear details of the insurrection. The conspiracy, *The Times* was told, had deep ramifications and was contrived by men of superior quality. A letter from Demerara dated the 31st August said that the lines of communications which had been set up to direct the revolt were so complicated that they could never have been thought of by negroes. Three white men had been arrested.

On the next day the news was out that two of the arrested men were Methodist preachers. Immediately the Methodist Society inserted an advertisement in the press in the form of an open letter from its secretaries. They denied that missionaries belonging to their Society had ever been implicated in any attempt to produce disturbances. They assured the public that none of the names of the men who were being held in custody were Wesleyans, and to prove this they quoted from their instructions to their men going out to the West Indies: 'your only business is to promote the moral and religious improvement of the slaves to whom you may have access without in the least degree, in public or private, interfering with their civil condition'.

Fifteen days after the first news arrived from Demerara came the report that one of the white men who had been arrested was a Mr John Smith, a missionary belonging not to the Wesleyans but to the London Missionary Society. The latter also immediately published its own advertisement in which it also quoted from its instructions to missionaries, 'from which it will appear . . . how improbable it is that our agents would act so directly contrary' to them. These instructions were even more stringent that the Wesleyans'. 'Not a word must escape you, in public or private, which might render the slaves displeased with their masters or dissatisfied with their station. You are not sent to relieve them from their servile condition, but to afford them the consolations of religion and to enforce upon them the necessity of being subject.'

During the next week the London newspapers revealed to their readers that the principal ringleader of the revolt, a slave named Quamina, had been shot after attempts had been made to take him alive. His son had been taken into custody, and the two white men were awaiting their trial. On Quamina's body a Bible had been found which had been clearly marked at the 8th chapter of the Book of Joshua.

And the Lord said unto Joshua, 'Fear not, neither be thou dismayed: take all the people of war with thee, and arise, go up to Ai: see, I have given into thy hand the king of Ai, and his people, and his city, and his land; And thou shalt do to Ai and her king as thou didst unto Jericho and her king; only the spoil thereof, and the cattle thereof, shall ye take for a prey unto yourselves: lay thee an ambush for the city behind it.

'There is but one opinion amongst all classes in the colony,' said a despatch from Demerara, 'that the missionaries from the London Society should leave the colony and their places be immediately supplied by clergymen of the Established Church of England or Scotland.' The despatch also quoted from a report of the Registrar of Slaves, which *The Times* reminded its readers should be taken very seriously since the Registrar was appointed by the King and Council. 'Efforts to create disaffection have originated . . . where the missionaries have been most encouraged. It would be satisfactory could persons in Europe who encourage these men by their very general hostile disposition against West India proprietors have the opportunity of personally ascertaining the progressive but silent amelioration and augmentation which have been going on in the condition and happiness of slaves within the last twenty years.'[1] The finger was being pointed directly at the chief abolitionists who were themselves directly or indirectly connected with the missionary societies.

The *Guiana Chronicle*, quoted in *The Times*, put the blame squarely on the abolitionists. A resident of Demerara writing an open letter to Canning said, 'This party, formerly denominated "Saints" and now "Philanthropists" have so wonderfully increased in numbers and political influence as at length to have become powerful in the House of Commons, whilst in the country their labours are discoverable in every village! Busily employed in plans which subdue the spirit, cripple the energies, and destroy the industry of the people. . . . In the present truly portentous situation of these affairs, the West Indians, Sir, look towards you with intense interest; you are the rock on which they rest the anchor of their hope.'[2]

The Wesleyans could now breathe a sigh of relief since they were no longer implicated in the plot. On December the 11th they published in *The Times* an advertisement which glowed with smug satisfaction. 'We have now to state that . . . the estates on which our missionaries preach and catechise remained in perfect submission; that the people of one of them assisted in placing their master in safety, out of reach of the insurrectionists . . . and that on another the slaves brought in the cutlasses and laid them before the manager to show that they had no disposition to join the rebels.'

The events the London newspapers were describing had, of course, all taken place months before, and by the end of 1823 the missionary, John Smith, had been tried. Of the other white man nothing more was heard. Smith had been charged with promoting discontent and dissatisfaction in the minds of the slaves towards their lawful masters, managers and overseers with the intention of exciting the slaves to break out in open revolt. He had also been alternatively charged with advising the leader, Quamina, about the revolt, or, that he had known of the revolt and had failed to inform the authorities.

He pleaded not guilty. Numerous slaves were brought forward to give evidence against him, an extraordinary exception to the time-honoured rule that no black could give evidence against any white in a West Indian court. They all said the same thing: that they had attended Smith's prayer meetings and that he had referred to passages in the Bible which were intended to be interpreted as both an incitement and a justification for rebellion. Manuel, for instance, deposed that Smith had at one particular meeting quoted the words: 'Jesus came out and He stooped down and looked and He wept: He looked down upon the city and said this city shall be destroyed because it did not believe in God.'

Smith was tried by a military court, and not before ordinary magistrates, the authorities realising that a civil court might have been more lenient towards him, and, more important, that there would be no automatic right of appeal to a high court in England. Their pretext was that since Smith had refused to take up arms against the slaves on religious grounds, the case fell within the jurisdiction of a court martial. The rules of evidence, including the one about the evidence of slaves, could therefore be, and were, bypassed to suit the court. Smith's journal was produced and parts of it selected to show that he had all the while been contemplating a slave revolt. In any other court the evidence would probably have been thrown out, but not by these judges. They listened to the prosecutor reading out statements like: 'It appears to me very probable that ere long they will resent the injuries done to them', and drew the conclusions they were determined to draw.

Inevitably, Smith was found guilty on all charges and sentenced to death. This being a rather drastic departure from tradition—executing a white man for stirring up a black revolt—the court recommended mercy so that the Governor would be free to take whatever steps he considered suitable in the circumstances. Smith was taken to gaol, there to await his fate. He was already a sick man at the time of his arrest, and as a result of his suffering, his health had rapidly deteriorated. Within a few months the news came through that the King had remitted the death sentence and had ordered that Smith be expelled from Demerara and the rest of the West Indies. It was too late.

On February 6th, 1824, Smith died in the colonial gaol where he had been confined since the 26th of December.³ A sanctimonious report from the *Barbados Mercury* read: 'We are happy to state by personal inquiry and inspection that this unfortunate man had the utmost attention and kindness shown to him by the humane keeper of the prison. . . . His apartment was airy and commodious, and he had always at his command every comfort which his taste fancied, or his necessities required. He has left a widow to deplore his fate and lament his loss.'[4] Unfortunately for him he did not know that a full pardon from the King had been received by the Governor on the day of his death.

John Smith's tragically unnecessary death was peaceful by comparison to what happened to the slaves he was accused of having incited. Against them the white inhabitants of Demarara unleashed their murderous anger, aggravated by their fear of a repetition of the slaves' action. Though the rebellion was restricted to only a few plantations and resulted in the death of two white men—managers who had attempted to resist the insurgents—the colonists treated their slave population, the rest of the West Indies and, of course, the British public to a display of bestiality that was exceptional even for those 'Eden islands of the West'.[5] Within a month of the revolt, apart from more than a hundred killed in battle, forty-seven slaves had been executed by hanging and by the various other methods the colonists used to dispose of their recalcitrant blacks. Others were literally torn to shreds under the whip. The *Demerara Gazette* of January the 16th, 1824, five months after the revolt, was still giving its readers details of the punishments currently being meted out: Louis of Porter's Hope, 1,000 lashes; Mercury of Enmore, 700; Austin of Cove, 600; Jessamin of Success, 1,000; John Otto, 200; and August of Success, 300. Some of those who recovered from these beatings were then condemned to work the fields for the rest of their lives shackled by heavy chains. Still, the colonists were anxious because the Governor had decided to reprieve one of the rebel chiefs, Jack Gladstone, who had given evidence against Smith. The *Demerara Gazette* came to the conclusion that: 'His Excellency, no doubt, very justly considered that if no distinction were to be made between the blood-thirsty and humane, the negroes, in the event of another revolutionary effort, would have little cause for displaying towards us what had not been shown towards themselves.'[6] An odd, but typically colonial interpretation of Christ's Golden Rule.

Those blacks who had not been involved in the rebellion were rewarded with the Governor's congratulations and were allowed their usual Christmas holiday, but the masters of all slaves were positively forbidden 'to admit of any dancing or indulgence whatever among them'. By way of explanation, the Governor wrote about the terrible punishments to Earl Bathurst of the Colonial Office in sorrow. 'With respect to the executions consequent upon the revolt, which it has been my most distressing duty to fiat, I have been guided by those principles which your Lordship has done me the honour to expect I should be actuated by.'[7]

The Wesleyan missionaries met in the Kingston, Jamaica, in September 1824 to bring to an end, once and for all, the insinuations made against them in the colonies since the Smith affair. The meeting examined each of the allegations against them: that they believed slavery to be incompatible with Christian religion; that their doctrines were calculated to produce insubordination among the slaves; that they were secretly attempting to put into operation means to effect the emancipation of the slaves; and that they were connected and in secret correspondence with the African Institution. They denied all these emphatically, and declared their belief that Christianity did not interfere with the civil condition of slaves; that if the ideas of the emancipationists were carried into effect it would be a general calamity—injurious to the slaves, unjust to the proprietors, ruinous to the colonies, deleterious to Christianity, and tending to the effusion of blood. The meeting took the view that the methods of the emancipationists of 'blending most absurdly religion with politics, or interfering with other men's properties under the profession of Christian Philanthropy' was not only immoral, 'but altogether repugnant to the whole Christian code'. A copy of the meeting's resolutions was sent to the Governor of the colony with its express thanks for the goodwill shown towards the spread of morality and religion among the slaves.[8]

Soon after the Demerara revolt, another riot took place in Barbados. A crowd of whites broke into Reverend Shrewsbury's Methodist chapel and threw bottles of acid at his congregation, mainly the blacks. Shrewsbury complained to the authorities, but they did nothing about it. After publicly declaring their intention, the same crowd later attacked the chapel again, smashing the windows and doors, breaking the benches, pews and pulpit, and tearing up and jumping on a large collection of Bibles and tracts intended for use by the slaves. They then stoned the minister's home.

Shrewsbury managed to escape from the island to St Vincent. A year later, on the anniversary of the destruction of his chapel—'an anniversary more dear to true Barbadians than Trafalgar to Britons'—as their public declaration stated, the white mob turned on the house of a black woman 'where Methodism again begins to rear its hideous head'. They warned that if anyone resisted he would 'be sent to sleep with his forefathers'.[9]

What made the whites suddenly turn with such fury on the missionaries who, clearly, did all in their power to stay out of politics and whose teachings would, if anything, prevent and not encourage the slaves to revolt? John Smith of Demerara, though he was later made into a martyr, was not, by any stretch of the imagination a champion of the slaves as the statement he made at his trial clearly shows: 'Soon after my arrival in Demerara I requested permission to remove the chapel to the side of the public road that I might be farther from the negroes. . . . I was very cautious not to apply to the negroes those parts of scripture which related to temporal possession. . . . If they themselves read the Bible, and so applied it, the fault must be charged upon their ignorance, and shows the necessity of their having more instruction. . . . I have not interfered in any manner with the temporal concerns of the negroes, save in such cases as were intimately blended with their spiritual concerns; as for instance, in settling their disputes, rebuking their members for offensive language, taking two wives, and immoral conduct in general. . . . In admitting [negro evidence] the court ought to be well aware of the negro character, and to be very cautious as to the degree of credibility to be attached to their evidence. . . . They are general incapable of narrating a transaction, neither can they relate with any tolerable accuracy even the shortest conversation.'[10]

The Reverend Mr Shrewsbury's father-in-law was a planter in the West Indies and he himself was anything but a member of the emancipationist movement. After fleeing from Barbados he wrote to his former black parishioners: 'Never speak disrespectfully of any in authority. . . . Let no slave who is a Methodist be dishonest, or lazy, or impertinent either in speech or behaviour. . . . And as to political matters, whether ye be bond or free, never meddle with them, but mind higher and better things relating to God and eternity.'[11]

Fear and hate were driving the colonies to this kind of desperate action which they must have known would eventually redound against them. They blamed the emancipationists for the Demerara uprising and for all their other problems which were rapidly gathering around their heads. For years, since before the Registry Act, they had been working themselves up into a frenzy against Wilberforce, Macaulay, and others. 'The virulence of our West Indian friends knows no respite. The newspapers are filled with their abuse and invectives', Macaulay wrote to his wife in 1816.[12] In partnership with Babington he had set up a merchant company which traded with East India and Africa, particularly Sierra Leone, the colony of former slaves of which he had once been the Governor. '. . . his traffic in philanthropy has filled his coffers and introduced him to respectable society', *The Anti-Jacobin Review* said of him.[13] James Stephen was charged by the West Indians with nepotism in the appointment of his son, James, as law-clerk to the Colonial Office. 'The access which this appointment gives his father and through him the whole party to all papers in the Colonial Department and the opportunities thus afforded them of exposing and aggravating every occurrence that can tend to disparage the legislatures and inhabitants of the West India colonies in the public estimation, omitting everything that would redound to their honour, renders it as a source of great mischief and irritation which will never cease so long as this interference of a party who see all West India objects with a jaundiced eye continues to be exercised', was how Joseph Marryat, representing the West Indians, breathlessly stated their complaint.

Curiously enough the only man who was spared the worst

of the West Indian invective was Wilberforce, though he was still the acknowledged leader of the opposition party. Macaulay and Stephen were both forced to resort to the courts to protect themselves from libel. Not Wilberforce; his reputation as a saint whose motives and actions were above reproof must have been strong enough to shield him against even their hatred.

The abolitionists blamed George Canning and his resolutions for the unrest in the colonies, particularly the resolution abolishing the whip as a means of driving the slaves to work each day. This abolition had been incorporated into an order-in-council[15] which had been sent to the colonial governors and had been received, like the rest of the resolutions, with 'every symptom of dissatisfaction and disgust'.[16] Wilberforce's reaction to the order-in-council was one of horror. 'What! have they given such an order without preparation and without explaining its purpose to the slaves—why it is positive madness!'[17] Similarly Macaulay: 'You will recollect how I held up my hands in utter astonishment at hearing that ministers had begun their operations by abolishing the whip,' he wrote to Thomas Buxton, 'by an act, in short, of the most direct interference between master and slave, and that an act of the utmost delicacy and difficulty. The whip . . . is the grand badge of slavery in the West Indies. Its use is identified with the servile state. Can we wonder that the poor slaves confound this ever-present symbol of slavery with slavery itself, and that they should regard its abolition as but another name for emancipation?'[18]

In Britain, Demerara became a rallying cry for all those who opposed the slave system. 'The effects of this great debate cannot be overestimated', wrote Thomas Clarkson; 'this single case of a persecuted individual, falling victim to these gross perversions of law and justice which are familiar to the colonial people produced an impression far more general and more deep than all that had ever been written or declaimed against the system of West India slavery.'[19] Henry Brougham, speaking in the House of Commons about Smith's trial, claimed that there had taken place more illegality, more violation of justice 'in substance and in form than in the whole history of modern times'.[20] And

Buxton asked, 'Was there ever such a train and cluster of enormities?'[21] These statements are remarkable coming from men who supposedly had devoted their lives to the cause of black slavery. What if not persecution, perversions of law, illegality and violations of justice had the slaves been suffering for two centuries? What was all the excitement about now when one man was condemned to death (but not executed), and another driven from his home when countless numbers had been driven from their homes and condemned to slow painful deaths? The answer is, of course, that Smith and Shrewsbury were white, and were missionaries.[22]

So long as the colonists had confined their cruelty to black men the British public, though it complained and remonstrated, did little about it. But by attacking white missionaries they had brought the whole of the Dissenting Church in Britain against them, and had forced the Established Church to take notice lest it be next in line for attack. The colonists were acting blindly, under pressure from circumstances, mainly economic, which they found almost impossible to control. For those with eyes to read, the writing was on the wall for the West Indies.

Extract from the evidence of Major-General Sir John Keane, K.C.B.

Question: Have you an interest in property in the West Indies?

Keane: None whatever. The remarks I have made [arise] out of my own personal observation.

Question: Did it come to your knowledge that any complaints have arisen on the part of the negroes as to their supply of food in any way?

Keane: Never.

Question: Do you think they would be likely to complain if there was any occasion?

Keane: I am sure they would.

Question: Do you think that any cruel proprietor of slaves, or any cruel manager would, in the present state of society in Jamaica, be tolerated?

Keane: Decidedly not.

Question: You are aware, of course, that slaves receive no wages from their masters?

Keane: They know very well that they are the property of their masters; they work for their own protection and for their existence and are well taken care of, are well fed, and are little worked, I will be bold to maintain; and they are in sickness and in health taken care of, and are well clad; and what more can they expect?

Question: Do negroes in Jamaica in general look healthy and well?

Keane: They are a magnificent race of people, very much so.

Question: Are they cheerful?

Keane: Always singing. It is a most extraordinary thing they are always singing and seem excessively delighted.

Question: When they work in gangs do you mean to say that they display this hilarity and cheerfulness?

Keane: They do invariably, cracking their jokes and singing from one end to the other.

(Minutes of evidence before a committee of the
House of Lords, (?) 1790)

Wampum, Swampum, and Other Comic Characters

The dialectics of slavery threw into sharp relief the figures of the noble savage and the depraved black. They also reinforced in the public's mind a third stereotype: the black man as a figure of fun. During the early 1800s he appeared frequently in this guise in cartoons and satirical sketches. He was shown as the grinning black servant serving food and drink to upper-class whites; he was seen aping the white man by affecting his clothes and manners. His wife was usually portrayed as fat and ugly, but his children, like himself, were roly-poly, laughing creatures: childlike, silly and harmless. In the sketch satirising the current catchphrase, 'the march of the intellect', he was seen in the dress of a footman strutting about with cockaded hat and long cane. He even had names by which he could easily be identified and placed like Sambo and Mungo.

Mungo was the slave of Don Diego in Isaac Bickerstaff's *The Padlock* which David Garrick's company first produced in 1768. It was said to have been as popular as Gay's *The Beggar's Opera*, and it remained so well into the nineteenth century.[1] The plot was loosely based on Cervantes's novel, *The Jealous Husband*, and concerned an old man, Diego, who wanted to marry a beautiful young girl who preferred a handsome young student. Tricked by his maid-servant, Ursula, and by Mungo, the old man was finally forced into agreeing to the marriage. Early in the play he suspected the girl was seeing the student. He asked Mungo, 'Do you know of any ill going on in my house?'

Mungo: Ah, Massa, a damn *deal*.

Diego: How, that I'm a stranger to?

Mungo: No, Massa, you lick me every day with your rattan; I'm sure, Massa, that's mischief enough for poor negar man.

Mungo, dressed in white and pink striped trousers and jacket, black stockings, white round straw hat, and a blue sash, hopped about the stage, alternatively cringing and grinning. The student gained access to his beloved by tempting Mungo with two supposedly typically 'black vices', drink and music; but in the end it was the slave who suffered though he was only one of the conspirators. Ursula, Don Diego's servant, received money from the reformed old man at the end of the play; but not Mungo.

Mungo: And what you give me, Massa?

Diego: Bastinadoes for your drunkenness and infidelity.

The man who made Mungo such a popular character was a young actor and composer, Charles Dibdin, who scored his first West End success in both categories. One of eighteen children, he had started to study for the church, but gave this up and at seventeen began writing music for the stage. *The Padlock*'s music established him as one of the leading song-writers of the day. After 1787 he started speculating in theatre ownership without success, so he turned then to writing 'entertainments' which consisted of anecdotes, jokes, songs and patter. A memoirist wrote: 'His principal songs became universally popular; they were sold in every music shop, seen on every lady's pianoforte, and sung in every company.'[2]

Dibdin always included in his entertainments songs and stories about blacks, for which, since Mungo, he was especially well known. One of his favourite jokes was about two black slaves who met one day as one was returning to his master with the jug of rum he had purchased for him. He also had with him a letter he had been asked to deliver to his master. His friend stopped him and suggested they have 'a lilly sup' of the rum. Cudjo refused. He was frightened, he said, in case the paper he was carrying would speak and tell his master what they had done. His friend suggested they hide the letter under a stone so that it would not see. Cudjo agreed. The letter was hidden and they started to sip the rum. Unfortunately, they took more than they intended and the friend suggested they top up the jug with water. When Cudjo returned with a full jug, his master drank some and spat it out. 'You've had some of this,' he shouted at his slave, 'and filled it up with water.' 'Ah, Massa,' Cudjo replied, 'don't you vex. Indeed, I do nothing.' 'What!' shouted the master. 'Don't you think I can't read?' And he pointed to the words on the jug's label which stated the percentage proof of the rum. 'Ah, Massa,' said Cudjo, 'if I no tell Buddy so, dat dam paper suree talk very wicked for poor negro man.'

One of Dibdin's most popular 'nigger' songs was 'Kickeraboo'. The word meant 'to die', and Dibdin made use of it in his entertainment, *Christmas Gambols*.

> One negro say one ting, you take no offence,
> Black and white he one colour a hundred years hence.
> And when massa death kick him into a grave
> He no spare negro Buckra nor massa nor slave.
>
> Then dance and sing and banjer thrum thrum,
> He foolish to tink what tomorrow might come.
> Lilly laugh and be fat de best ting you can do,
> Time enough to be sad when you kickeraboo.[3]

The use of dialect has always been a sure way of getting a laugh on the English stage, 'Nigger' dialect was particularly favoured: it sounded so good in songs, as countless white minstrels since the early nineteenth century have realised and profited from.

> Nelly Bly! Nellie Bly! bring de broom along,
> We'll sweep de kitchen clean, my dear,
> An' hab a little song.
> Poke de wood, my lady lub;
> An' make de fire burn,
> And while I take de banjo down;
> Just gib de mush a turn.

Dialect for authenticity's sake, as opposed to its use for comic effect, sometimes produced unconsciously absurd results,

as in the following serious poem which appeared in the
Gentleman's Magazine in 1793.

> Here in chain poor black man lying
> Put so tick dey on us stand,
> Ah! with heat and smells we're dying!
> 'Twas not dus in negro land.[4]

Dibdin died in 1814, but his form of entertainment had
been passed on to others, complete with 'nigger' costumes,
stories and dialects. In the 1820s Charles Mathews was
considered the funniest comedian on the London stage;
his routines were so popular that when they appeared in
print they were eagerly bought up. One of the best acts
was his entertainment, *A Trip to America*,[5] in which he told
of his journey through the United States, convulsing the
audience with his jokes about Americans, white and black.
The Londoners particularly enjoyed his use of English
words in a typically American way—though this did not
endear him to his American audiences—and his impersona-
tions of 'niggers' which he assumed when he recounted his
tales of his arrival in the States.

'Some tourists travel to explore foreign parts to find
black men or brown women,' Mathews would begin, 'but
the motive that induced me to cross the Atlantic was to
find out and secure the *yellow-boys* [gold].'

On his arrival in New York he found himself surrounded
by crowds:

> 'There are Yankees and Niggers all gazing and pressing so,
> While we so merrily through the crowd dash,
> And the Nigger a portmanteau there is caressing so,
> To find out the virtue of English cash.'

Mathews was approached by a black man. ' "Massa, you
come wi' me. I take you to de best hot-hel in New York," the
black man offered. "How many Blacks have you got in
your house?" "Twenty, Massa." "Twenty! Then yours is a
house of mourning!" ' ['Blacks' being understood by the
audience to mean 'funeral clothes'.]

'I went to a theatre called the Niggers' Theatre,' his patter would go on, 'where I beheld a black tragedian in the character of Hamlet.' Mathews, dressed in his 'nigger's clothes of bright candy stripes, would then assume the pose of Hamlet at the grave. 'To be or not to be, that is the question. Whether it is nobler in de mind to suffer, or tak' up arms against a sea of trouble, and by *opposum* end 'em.' No sooner was the word *opposum* out of the tragedian's mouth than his audience burst forth in one general cry, 'Opposum! Opposum! Opposum!' and the black tragedian came forward and informed them that he'd sing their favourite song:

> 'Opposum up a gum tree,
> Have no fear at all.
> Opposum up a gum tree,
> Him never tink to fall.
> Opposum up a gum tree,
> Him hop and skip and rail;
> But nigger him too cunning,
> So he pull him down by de tail.'

Like Dibdin before him, and generations of comedians after him, Mathews had his story about the stupid 'nigger'. He called his Maximilian. When Mathews was sitting having dinner with a friend he put on the table his snuff-box. Now, unknown to the 'nigger', Mathews was a ventriloquist, and whenever Maximilian entered the room with food for the table Mathews would throw his voice from the snuff-box, making it talk or cry like a child. This would cause Maximilian to giggle, laugh and upset his tray over the other diners.

Another favourite character was the fat, lazy runaway slave, Agamemnon, who was sold to Jonathan Doubikin by his Uncle Ben, their conversation going like this:

' "Well, Uncle Ben, I calculate you have a nigger to sell?" "Yes, I have a nigger, I guess. Will you buy the nigger?" "Oh, yes, if he's a good nigger, I will, I reckon; but as this is a land of liberty and freedom, and as every man has a right to buy a nigger, what do you want for your nigger?"

"Why, as you say, Jonathan, this is a land of freedom, and independence, and as every man as a right to sell his nigger, I want sixty dollars and twenty-five cents. Will you give it?" "Oh, yes, but now the nigger has proved a bad one; I've lost him and Uncle Ben's got the money." '

To the white man the colour white was always the ideal; black the opposite. Black was associated with the devil, with evil and sin; white with angels, goodness and purity. William Blake's 'Little Black Boy' was born in the southern wild:

> And I am black, but O! my soul is white;
> White as an angel is the English child,
> But I am black, as if bereav'd of light.[6]

Shakespeare was always sure of capturing his audiences' attention when he had his characters speaking lines loaded with allusions they would understand and appreciate, such as Iago in *Othello*:

> Even now, now, very now, an old black ram
> Is tupping your white ewe. Arise, arise;
> Awake the snorting citizens with the bell,
> Or else the devil will make a grandsire of you . . .[7]

By the end of the eighteenth century colour had become a self-conscious comic device. George Colman Jnr, used it in his musical comedy *Inkle and Yarico* to sustain long passages of otherwise banal dialogue. He was a skilled theatrical craftsman who knew what would appeal to his audience, and in *Inkle and Yarico* he combined in nearly equal proportions the sentimental and the comic view of the slave. The story of Mr Inkle who sold his lover, Yarico, who had rescued him from her people, had been known since the early years of the century. The essayist Richard Steele told it to his readers in *The Spectator* in 1711, and confessed that he was so touched by it that he left the room in tears on first hearing it. Enlarged and expanded into a musical comedy by Colman, it was first acted in 1787 at the Haymarket, London, and had the rare distinction of being performed in that and another London theatre, Covent Garden, simultaneously for many years.

In a later edition of the play (1816) Mrs Inchbald, a distinguished serious actress and novelist, introduced it by mentioning that 'it might remove from Mr Wilberforce his aversion to theatrical exhibitions, and convince him that the teaching of a moral duty is not confined to particular spots of ground; for in those places, of all others, the doctrine is most effectually inculcated where exhortation is the most required—the resorts of the gay, the idle, the dissipated'. She went on to say that the play had the honour of preceding the great debate on the slave trade, and that 'it was the bright forerunner of alleviation to the hardships of slavery'. Her only criticism of it was that Yarico, the slave girl, meets Inkle in America and not Africa. 'As slaves are imported from Africa, the audience in the last two acts of the play feel as if they had been in the wrong quarter of the globe during the first act. Inkle could certainly steal a native from America and sell her in Barbados, but this is not so consonant with that nice imitation of the order of things as to rank above criticism.'

Colman structured the play so that the story of Inkle and Yarico appealed to the romantic, sentimental mood of his audience, while the parallel story of Trudge, Inkle's manservant, and Wowski, his Indian maid, provided the comedy. Jokes about colour abounded; some of them looked forward nearly two hundred years to reflect current prejudices.

Inkle: I have been comparing the land here with that of our own country.

Medium: And you find it like a good deal of the land of your own country—cursedly encumber'd with black legs, I take it.

Shipwrecked on the coast of America, Inkle and Trudge go off to find help, watched by two sailors.

Sailor: Foolish dogs! Suppose they are met by the natives.

Mate: Why then the natives would look plaguy black upon 'em, I do suppose.

Trudge does not want to go. He is frightened they will be

captured, and 'all my red ink will be spilt by an old black
pen of a negro'. They approach Yarico's cave.

Inkle: Talk again of going out and I'll flay you alive.

Trudge: That's just what I expect for coming in. We
shall stand here, stuff'd for a couple of white wonders.

The scene of Inkle and Yarico's meeting was one of the
most popular in the play.

Yarico: Ah! What form is this! Are you a man?

Inkle: True flesh and blood, my charming heathen, I
promise you.

Yarico: What harmony in his voice! What a shape! How
fair his skin, too.

While they are getting to know each other, Trudge meets
Wowski. She tells him that she learnt to speak English and
smoke a pipe from a sailor who was eaten by her chief.
But she says she will save Trudge who promises to take her
back to England.

Trudge: Damme, what a flashy fellow I shall seem in the
city! I'll get her a *white* boy to bring up the tea-kettle.
Asked if she is married, she answers:

Wowski: No, you be my chum-chum!

Trudge: So I will. It's best, however, to be sure of her
being single; for Indian husbands are not quite so complacent
as English ones. . . . But you have had a lover or two in your
time, eh, Wowski?

Wowski: Oh iss—great many—I tell you.

They then go into a duet:

Wowski: Wampum, Swampum, Yanko, Lanko, Nanko,
              Pownatowski,
          Black men—plenty—twenty—fight for me,
          White man, woo you true?

Trudge: Who?

Wowski: You.

Trudge: Yes, little Wowski.

Wowski: Then I leave all and follow thee.

The scene shifts to Barbados where Inkle and Yarico,
Trudge and Wowski disembark. Inkle is betrothed to the
Governor's daughter, so that when he is offered a price for
Yarico, greed and ambition tempt him to sell her despite
his declarations of love and fidelity. Trudge, on the other

hand, spurns offers for Wowski. However, he, too, has a previous attachment—to Patty, the Governor's daughter's maid.

Patty, in contrast to Trudge, is a bigot, and when she is told about Inkle and Yarico, she reacts with horror.

Patty: How! A tawney?

Trudge: Yes, quite dark; but very elegant, like a Wedgwood teapot.

Patty tells him she would never let a black kiss her because 'he'd make my face all smutty'.

Trudge: I'd have you know that blackamoor ladies, as you call em, are some of the very few whose complexions never rub off. (Aside) 'S'bud, if they did, Wows and I shou'd have changes faces by now.

Patty's and Trudge's contrasting attitudes are expressed in their two solo songs. Patty sings:

> Tho' lovers, like marksmen, all aim at the heart,
> Some hit wide of the mark, as we wenches all know:
> But of all the bad shots, he's the worst in the art
> Who shoots at a pigeon, and kills a crow—O ho!

Trudge sings:

> Your London girls, with roguish trip,
> May boast their pouting under-lip,
> My Wows would beat a hundred such,
> Whose upper-lip pouts twice as much.

In the end Inkle's betrayal of Yarico is found out and he is shamed into reforming. Trudge is rewarded by the Governor for his loyalty to Wowski by being made his personal manservant.

Trudge: Orare! Bless your honour! Wows! you'll be a Lady, you jade, to a Governor's Factotum.

Wowski: Iss—I Lady Jacktotum.

In the finale he sings:

> 'Sbobs! now I'm fixed for life,
> My fortune's fair, tho' black's my wife.

But it is Patty who had the last word.

Let Patty say a word—
A chambermaid may sure be heard—
Sure men are grown absurd,
Thus taking black for white!
To hug and kiss a dingy miss,
Will hardly suit an age like this.

George Colman had another success with *The Africans*, which was first performed at the Haymarket—the theatre which by now he owned—in 1808. Here, too, he managed to combine the tragic with the comic and achieve the rather remarkable result of making slavery appear to his audience horrible and amusing at the same time. He portrayed the noble savages acting out dramatic captures, departures and deaths against a background in Africa showing 'a large tract of romantic country'; but what ensured the play's success were Mr Mug, the white man kidnapped and sold as a slave, and his beloved, Sutta, a black slave. 'Mug' became, as the notes to a later edition point out, 'the cognomen for any cocking Adonis whose constitution and countenance were uncommonly concupiscent and charming'.

In the first act there was the inevitable dialect song:

Kouskous and sinkatoo, for king Ali Beg, oh!
But Serawooli king he eat antelope's leg, oh!
Sing shannawang, sing sharrawang,
Sing shongo!
Good wife had Kickawick, she drowny one night, oh!
But Kickawick no fish again, for fear him wife bite, oh!

There were also plenty of jokes about colour.

Mug: Oh, nature! since you form'd me amorous, why did fortune cast me on a soil where to be fair is to be ugly?

Sutta: Turn your face t'other way, massa Mug, cause when you look me full, it make me jump.

Mug: Jump! What for?

Sutta: Skin like tooth—white all over.

Mug: Why I tell you, as I told you over and over again, white is the handsomest.

Sutta: Ah, black for me.

There followed a good song about colour distinctions: the duet between Mug and Sutta:

> *Sutta:* Oh, the jet feather'd raven, how lovely it look, ah!
> When he spread him black wing to fly over brook, ah!
>
> *Mug:* Oh, the white swan he swims in the Thames mighty smugly,
> But he hides his black legs 'cause they look so damned ugly.
>
> *Sutta:* But I be Afric—I be Afric;
> Blacky man he be my delight, ah!
>
> *Mug:* And I'm a Cockney—I'm a Cockney:
> I love black when I can't get white, ah!

Mr Mug's most famous song, and one of the most popular of the day, 'Won't you come, Mr Mug?', was a series of puns on colour.

> *Mug:* My skin is lily white, and the colour here is new,
> So the first man that they sold me to, he thump'd me black and blue.
> The priest who bought me from him, in a tender-hearted tone,
> Said, come from that great blackguard's house, and walk into my own.

The jokes and remarks about colour in these plays are noteworthy for their innocent quality, and for their lack of real malice. The black girls and the white boys may mock each other's different characteristics, but they end up happily together despite them. So long as the slave was a slave—and, therefore, not a real threat to white superiority—the white man could accept with equanimity the situation of racial intermarriage presented to him in romantic or comic guise on the stage. He could also accept jokes made against the absurdities of his own prejudices and presumptions.

By the middle of the nineteenth century a self-consciousness had crept in and with it a loss of innocence. The black man had become someone to contend with, at least as far as Britain and the northern states of America were concerned. The jokes against him became crueller, the caricatures more distorted, and black and white relationships a subject for tragedy, not comedy.

An early example of a play in which colour prejudice was the motivating factor and not simply a comic ploy was *The Black Doctor*. It was a French drama, translated by I. V. Bridgeman and first performed in England at the Royal Victoria on November 13th, 1846. Fabian, the black doctor, was a creole ex-slave who suffered insult, imprisonment and finally death for his love of Pauline, a wealthy white plantation owner from the French colony of Bourbon. She returned his love and they were married in secret since it was impossible to do so openly. 'This division of colour,' one planter commented, 'is a prejudice, if you choose to call it, but an inflexible and implacable prejudice which our susceptibility will neither discuss nor reason on: the pride of our race is in us—in our very veins, and will never leave them but with the last drop of our blood.' He cannot understand how any white person will allow the black doctor to treat them. 'There was my poor old cousin who was at the last extremity. He [Fabian] could have saved her, but she preferred to die. Her conduct was grand—it was sublime—it was heroic!'

When Fabian and Pauline return to France they find that racial prejudice there is almost as strong as it is in the colony. Pauline says of her mother that it was for her 'a second religion'. Fabian, who pretends to be Pauline's servant, is described contemptuously by a footman as 'a mulatto, a liberated slave whom Mademoiselle de la Raynerie brought with her from the Island of Bourbon as a kind of memento, a sort of curiosity of the country'.

Pauline's mother intends that her daughter marry an aristocrat, and when she learns of Pauline's marriage to Fabian she arranges that he be sent to the Bastille. There he languishes until the revolutionary mob set him free, by which time he has gone mad. But Fabian is the good 'nigger' *par excellence*—the continental version of the character which Mrs Harriet Beecher Stowe was to introduce to the public six years later, Uncle Tom. At the end of the play in which the audience has seen him endure incredible humiliation with resignation—like the true Christian the whites would like to be but never are—Fabian saves Pauline from the anger of the mob and receives the fatal stray bullet meant for her.

Because Fabian is free and not a slave, because he is a thinking man trained in the arts of medicine, and not merely a brave, beautiful but mindless prince like Oroonoko, because he is a man and not a woman like Sutta or Wowski, and has married a white woman—the creature which the white man, sensing his inadequacy and fearing for his virility, always puts on a pedestal when he feels threatened by the black man, because of all these factors, colour prejudice in *The Black Doctor* is no longer a joke. The white man, faced by a free black man, responds by making the latter the victim of humiliation. On the stage where he can play out his fantasies he punishes the black man for presuming to be his equal. More than a hundred years have to pass before racial differences become again the subject of comedy, but by now it is the black man who is the comedian and the white man the butt of *his* jokes.

OROONOKO.

MR. SAVIGNY in the Character of OROONOKO.

Oro. I'll turn my Face away, and do it so.

Published Nov.ʳ 23, 1776 by J. Lowndes & Partners.

Oroonoko. The death of Imoinda. Frontispiece to the 1776 edition of **Thomas** Southerne's play. (See page 113 on) *(Trustees of the British Museum)*

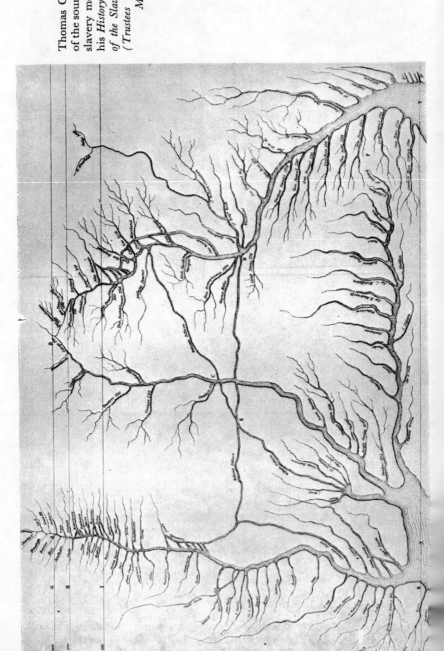

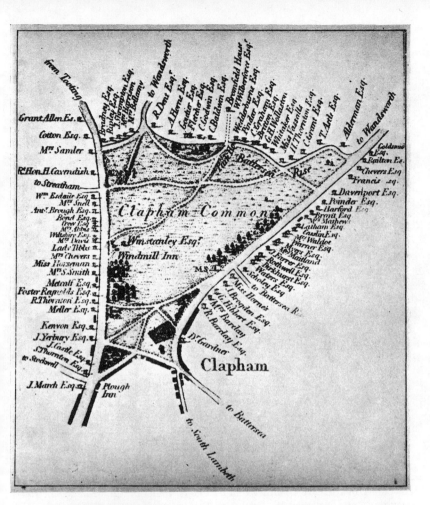

Clapham
(*Above*) A street map of Clapham Common, circa 1801. Note the homes of Wilberforce, Thornton, Grant, etc. (*Clapham Antiquarian Society*)

(*Opposite*) The medallion of the anti-slavery movement, donated by Josiah Wedgwood. (*Reproduced by permission of Josiah Wedgwood and Sons Ltd.*)

The entertainer, Charles Mathews, in his two costumes of Agamemnon, the runaway slave, and Jonathan W. Doubikin, Agamemnon's young master. From *The London Mathews*, 1823. (See page 181) *(Trustees of the British Museum)*

PART THREE

Berbice

Criminal Demand vs. negro Willem

Demand and Conclusion made and presented to His Excellency Henry Bears, Esquire, Governor, and the Honourable Court of Criminal Justice of the Colony of Berbice and its Dependencies.

The Fiscal R.O. states that the negro Willem, alias Sara, alias Cuffey, a Creole or native of this colony, belonging to the plantation Buses Lust, situated on the east bank of the River Berbice, the property of Major General Murray, stands accused of treasonable practices, by deluding the minds of the negroes belonging to the plantation . . . and causing to be danced the Minje Mama dance. . . . That he has taken upon himself to rectify abuses, presuming to judge and prescribe punishments; and in execution of such punishments on the aforementioned negress Madalon, to cause and occasion her death. That the power of taking away life is confined solely to regular constituted authorities. . . . And whereas the horrid crime of murder is strictly prohibited by the law of God . . . So it is, that the Fiscal of the Colony, R.O. making his demand in the name of our Sovereign Lord George the Fourth, by the Grace of God of the United Kingdom of Great Britain and Ireland King, defender of the Faith, concludes that the negro Willem, alias Sara, alias Cuffey, be convicted by the Honourable Court of the charges preferred against him, and condemned to be taken to the plantation, there delivered into the hands of the public executioner in the presence of this Honourable Court, to be hung by the neck on the Mangoe tree under which the negro woman Madalon was suspended, until he be dead; his head then severed from his body, and stuck on a pole, there to remain till destroyed by the elements, or the birds of prey; or such other greater or more mitigated sentence as this Honourable Court in their wisdom shall deem consistent with law and the circumstances of this case.

Berbice, 14th January, 1822

M.S. Bennett (Fiscal R.O.)

(Papers on the Slave Trade—State Papers, Vol. XVIII, 1823)

The Old Guard and the New Radicals

Hero-worship makes bad history. This is particularly true of the history of the abolition movement and William Wilberforce. His friends exaggerated his virtues and achievements during his lifetime; his sons sanctified him in their biography, and subsequent generations of writers continued the tradition. The historian Sir Reginald Coupland, whose biography of Wilberforce first appeared in 1923, said of him that more than any other man he 'founded in the conscience of the British people a tradition of humanity and responsibility towards the weak and backward peoples whose fate lay in their hands'.[1] Today this might be regarded by some as more an insult than a compliment, but schoolchildren are still taught that Wilberforce led the British anti-slavery movement almost unaided and that without him the slave traffic would never have been stopped and the slaves never emancipated.

In 1825 the Society for the Mitigation and Gradual Abolition of Slavery met at the Freemasons' Hall to record, among other things, 'their deep sense of the misfortune they have sustained in the recruitment from public life of their late revered leader, Mr Wilberforce', and to pay tribute to 'the invaluable services he has rendered to the oppressed natives of an entire quarter of the globe; that with a self-devotion of the most rare and unrivalled description he deliberately sacrificed the most brilliant prospects of political distinction at the shrine of justice and humanity; and that to the opportunity of mixing on equal terms among the statesmen of Europe, he preferred the steady pursuit of extended usefulness in a path which led, not to the acquisition of wealth or power, but to the alleviation of human misery, and the unwearied promotion of the highest interests of man'.[2]

Wilberforce helped to alleviate some human suffering; but he also helped to cause much human misery through the later political application of the intolerant ideas about blacks which he made acceptable and respectable. It was for saving Britain's soul, for 'freeing his native land from her foulest stain' that his saintly friends most revered him.[3] That by doing so he neither ended the slave trade nor freed the slaves was something they either did not appreciate or, if they did, preferred to forget. To minimise his successes would be to minimise their own.

In 1823 Wilberforce published his *Appeal in Behalf of the Negro Slaves in the West Indies*, his first and last on the subject of slavery itself. It is a tract typical, not only of Wilberforce, but of the Clapham Sect and others who had taken upon themselves the plight of the slaves among a number of their benevolent projects. He began and ended in his usual manner by excusing the non-resident West Indian proprietors. 'I have ever wished myself to keep in remembrance and observe in practice . . . that while we expose and condemn the evils of the system itself, we should treat with candour and tenderness the characters of the West India proprietors.'

He then went on to enumerate the physical cruelties which slaves were subject to. He admitted that they were of no small amount, but added that 'to a Christian eye they shrink almost into insignificance when compared with the moral evils that remain behind'. As he saw the situation—and he hoped the bulk of his countrymen would agree with him—'though many of the physical evils of our colonial slavery are cruel, and odious, and pernicious, the almost universal destitution of religious and moral instruction among the slaves is the most serious of all the vices of the West Indian system'.

He realised that it was hard for Europeans in general—and vulgar minds in particular—to feel anything but contempt for, 'even disgust and aversion' to the personal peculiarities of the negro race, 'but raise these poor creatures from their depressed condition, and if they are not yet fit for the enjoyment of British freedom, elevate them at least from the level of the brute creation into that of rational nature. . . . Taught by Christianity they will sustain with patience the sufferings of their actual lot, while the same instructors will rapidly prepare them for a better; and instead of being objects at one time of contempt, and another of terror . . . they will be soon regarded as a grateful peasantry.'

For an anti-slavery tract, Wilberforce's *Appeal* was not very helpful. Far more radical statements were being made on the subject by people associated with the movement. A year after his tract was published Elizabeth Coltman produced another tract which stated with force and determination quite a different point of view.[4] Wilberforce did not like women in the movement despite the fact that they were the most ardent abolitionists and attended meetings in greater numbers than the men. In a letter to Macaulay he said that he would prefer that the latter did not speak of ladies' anti-slavery societies in his monthly *Anti-Slavery Reporter*.[5] When the chairman of one of these societies heard of this, she wrote to a friend, referring scathingly to the title of the main Society for the Mitigation and Gradual Abolition of Slavery. 'Men may propose only *gradually* to abolish the worst of crimes, and only *mitigate* the most cruel bondage. . . . I trust no Ladies Association will ever be found with such words attached to it.'[6]

Elizabeth Coltman had no time for the timidity and caution of the Wilberforce/Buxton parliamentary leadership. She attacked their tactics and arguments, admitting that her opposition to them was probably presumptious and hopeless. She contended that the idea of gradual emancipation was 'a very masterpiece of satanic policy'. one which the enemies of slavery had fostered to the ruination of their cause. 'It is marvellous that the *wise* and the *good* should have suffered themselves to have been imposed upon by this wily artifice of the slave holder—for with him must the project of gradual emancipation have first originated.' So long as it was maintained that the slave was not 'fit for freedom', he would remain a slave since it was the system itself which prevented him from every being 'fit' for anything but slavery. To say, therefore, as did Wilberforce and Buxton, that the slaves had to remain slaves until they were fit to be free was condemning them to perpetual bondage. The planters realised this; why not the abolitionists?

She considered the annual petitioning of parliament for gradual emancipation was a waste of time, and worse, the delays the petitions caused lost them ground and supporters. She accused the leaders of the movement of being fooled by the threats made by the West Indians of the consequences which would follow emancipation. 'It is no marvel that slave holders should cry out against immediate emancipation as they have done against all propositions for softening the rigours of colonial slavery. "Insurrection of all the blacks—massacre of all the whites"—are the bugbears which have been constantly conjured up. . . . The panic was the same, the outcry just as violent when an attempt was made about forty years ago to abate the horrors of the Middle Passage by admitting a little more air into the suffocating and pestilent holds of the slave ships.' What did amaze her, however, was that the abolitionists should have 'caught the infection—should be panic-struck . . . should be diverted from their purpose . . . that they should be so credulous, so easily imposed upon'.

Their cause, the authoress said, was betrayed rather than supported 'by all softening, qualifying concessions. Every iota which is yielded of their rightful claims impairs the conviction of their rectitude and consequently weakens their success.' Her final attack went to the very root of abolition policy up to that date. The leaders had, she said, not gone about their work in the right way. Their 'apprehension of *losing all, by asking too much*, has driven them into the danger of losing all by asking too little'. While they were arguing about trifles and irrelevancies, the miseries they deplored continued. Slavery had to be crushed at once. 'While the abolitionists are endeavouring *gradually* to enfeeble and kill it by inches it will *gradually* discover means of reinforcing its strength.' Liberal people in England thought it an act of Christian virtue to supply the Greeks with arms and ammunition to enable them to achieve their independence. 'Let us first liberate our own slaves', Coltman concluded, 'which we may do without furnishing them with arms or ammunition.'

In 1826, two years after Miss Coltman's, another tract appeared which was written anonymously by someone close to the abolition leadership. Called *Letters to the More Influential Classes*,[7] it caused some dissension in the ranks because in its advertisement the reader was told that the title and contents had undergone considerable alteration as a result of the author's correspondence with one of the leaders of the movement. 'From this privilege', the advertiser pointed out sourly, 'it is feared that the following pages will evince that the writer has profited but very partially.'

Like Coltman the writer attacked the policy of gradual emancipation as one which was 'secretly sapping the foundation of public virtue, paralysing its resolution, familiarising us to crime, rendering us a nation of hypocrites . . . who expose and reprobate crime, not to extirpate but to tolerate and foster it'. Consistency required that the disclosure of the cruelties of slavery should be followed up by unremitting exertions for its speedy and utter extinction. He added the further point that by holding out for gradual emancipation the abolitionists were making it worse for the slaves who would suffer the anxieties of uncertainty in addition to their other miseries. He also attacked the timidity of the leadership for allowing the planters to frighten them with tales of ruin and destruction. 'If by the ruin of the planter is meant only temporary embarrassment and humiliation we candidly say—"'tis a consummation devoutly to be wished".'

What worried this author, as it had worried Miss Coltman, was the relationship which existed between some of the leading abolitionists and the West Indian proprietors. Many of them, he said, were personal friends. With heavy irony he characterised the proprietors as 'men of education and liberal attainments—of humanity and religion. . . . These accomplished, humane, and pious slave holders assert that their slaves are incapable of making the right use of their freedom; that immediate emancipation would be destructive of their own happiness, as well as the property and lives of the masters; and men of such high character *must* be believed—those who are in habits of intimacy with them *cannot* withhold their assent'. But, he added, '*we can*—and *we do* withhold ours'.

In both tracts Coltman and the anonymous author had touched on the one difficulty which the conventional abolition leadership found impossible to overcome and which inhibited them in their efforts on behalf of the slaves: their background and environment. They were, like the West Indian proprietors, men of considerable property who were subject to all the fears and fantasies associated with property. They respected it as something sacred, and slaves were, whether one liked it or not, property. Accordingly slaves represented ownership; they were connected intimately with intangible but very real concepts like mortgages, annuities, inheritance. Attacking the slave trade had been easier for them. Trade of any kind was something a little less than respectable; in addition the slave trade was a horribly brutal business conducted by men they would not have invited to their homes, the profits of which did not directly benefit them or any of their circle of friends. To attack slavery, however, meant attacking the sanctity of ownership and property, to attack, in other words, the very essence of the way of life in which they all believed. From this they shrank back.

They shrank back, too, from facing the problem of a West Indies without slaves. Plantation cruelty was easier to understand than the complexities of plantation economics. They knew slavery was evil; but to know is one thing, to change it is another, and here another of their defects became apparent—a singular failure of imagination for which, perhaps, they could not altogether be blamed. Slavery and sugar were inextricably connected and had been since the seventeenth century and earlier. The end of slavery would mean, as far as the old-guard abolitionists were concerned, the end of the plantation system and probably the end of the colonial empire in the West Indies. They considered themselves as patriots and to a patriot the economic and social health of the colonies was a matter of vital importance. They were too close to the situation to realise that these colonies were sick and declining rapidly. They were reformers, not revolutionaries. They were prepared to see things alter gradually, but not to alter altogether, at least not in their lifetime. For their time they had as much courage as anyone and a good deal more than many; but they were not heroes and they were not what some of them liked to believe themselves to be—and what publicists later made them out to be—saints.

George Stephen tells an anecdote about Thomas Buxton which very well describes the kind of man he was, but more so the kind of society in which he moved so easily. On one occasion, while he was riding through St James's Park on his horse, John Bull, he was passed by the Prince Regent in his carriage. The Prince saw Buxton's horse and took a fancy to it immediately. He sent his equerry to make an offer for it. 'Give my dutiful respects to his Royal Highness,' Buxton replied, 'and tell him that I like a good horse as well as he does. John Bull is not to be bought at any price!'[8] Stephen added that 'the only matters of the kind in which he appeared to me to take a personal interest were the points of a horse or the make of a gun'.[9]

Admittedly the sketch was drawn by a man who challenged the leadership of the old guard and was probably, therefore, tinged with a certain amount of prejudice, but it is clear from it that Buxton resembled far more the typical West Indian merchant or non-resident proprietor living in London on the proceeds of his slave-run plantations than the idealised version of the abolitionists that came to be accepted in the later years of the nineteenth century and is still—to some extent—the popular image of them. By trying to elevate men like Buxton and Wilberforce, by casting them in the roles of untarnished saints, a disservice has been done to other members of the movement, especially to the young radicals who took over the active leadership at the end of the 1820s. They, as we shall see, finally forced the issues which their predecessors tried to avoid, but even at the end it was the old guard with their restricted vision who helped the West Indian interests. Their lack of courage and determination, their reluctant sympathy for the plight of men of property being deprived by legislation of property which they had either bought or inherited allowed the West Indians to pull victory out of apparent defeat.

Political radicals who were agitating for economic reforms and for greater social justice hated the old-style philanthropists like Wilberforce for their complacency and indifference to poverty in their own country while fighting against the same thing abroad. In a ballad which became famous in Yorkshire, Michael Sadler told the true story of a factory child who had died from overwork. In the last verse he says:

> That night a chariot passed her while on the ground she
>   lay,
> The daughters of her master an evening visit pay,
> Their tender hearts were sighing as negro wrongs were
>   told,
> But the white slave lay there dying who earned their
>   father's gold.[10]

The radical, Francis Place, called Wilberforce 'an ugly epitome of the devil',[11] and William Hazlitt wrote a portrait of him, showing him to be a man who, despite his preaching Christian humility as the greatest virtue and public popularity as its greatest danger, did all in his power to court and keep public esteem.[12]

'We can readily believe that Mr Wilberforce's first object and principle is to do what he thinks right: his next (and that we fear is of almost equal weight with the first) is to do what will be thought so by other people. . . . He does not seem greatly to dread the denunciation in Scripture, but rather to court it—"Woe unto you, when all men speak well of you!" We suspect he is not quite easy in his mind because West India planters and Guinea traders do not join in his praise. His ears are not strongly enough tuned to drink in the execrations of the spoiler and oppressor as the sweetest music.' He wished to give no offence, said Hazlitt, nor to do any harm to himself or his reputation. His views and actions never went so far as to banish him from the best circles. 'He preaches vital Christianity to untutored savages, and tolerates its worst abuses in civilised states. He thus shows his respect for religion without offending the clergy.' Hazlitt accused him of cant and trickery.

His patriotism was servile; his humanity ostentatious; his loyalty conditional; his religion a mixture of fashion and fanaticism. He appeared to remain independent of factions without attracting their disfavour. 'Mr Wilberforce is far from being a hypocrite,' the essayist concluded, 'but he is, we think, as fine a specimen of *moral equivocation* as can well be conceived.'

Hazlitt felt that even in the question of the abolition of the slave trade Wilberforce fluctuated a great deal, leaving much of the battle in Pitt's dilatory hands, particularly when he thought that the 'gloss of novelty was gone from it'. He believed that Thomas Clarkson should have received far more of the credit. So did Clarkson. When Wilberforce's sons tried in their eulogising biography to raise their father above everyone else connected with the movement, Clarkson was so incensed that he published a rejoinder in which he said that the 'Committee would have been formed as it was, and would have done what it did had Mr Wilberforce never existed; they would have found out some other parliamentary leader, though I am sure they could not possibly have found in the then House of Commons any man so well qualified to take the lead'. A couple of years after Wilberforce's death Clarkson was even more biting. To the poet Coleridge he commented that Wilberforce 'cared nothing about the slaves, nor if they were all damned provided he saved his own soul'.[13]

Another member of the movement who was very critical of Wilberforce—and incidentally of most of the old guard—was James Stephen's son, George. He became one of the leaders of the radical emancipationists at the beginning of the 1830s. He said that Wilberforce was a man of 'busy indolence'. 'He worked out nothing for himself; he was destitute of system, and desultory in his habits; he depended on others for information and laid himself open to mis-guidance.' Stephen also accused him of indecisiveness and of lacking confidence in his own judgment. 'It was a common saying of him . . . that you might safely predicate his vote for it was certain to be opposed to his speech.' Like Hazlitt, Stephen thought that Wilberforce felt 'too much deferential regard for rank and power'.[14]

In another man these faults would have been neither very serious nor important, but in Wilberforce's case it was different. They mattered because of the position in which he placed himself as the public arbiter of other people's morals, and because of the position in which public opinion subsequently placed him as an example, *par excellence*, of British Humanitarianism. There is yet another reason to try to see the man as he really was: he was not only the leader, but also the most prominent representative of a whole group of similarly-minded men and women whose arrogance, smugness and self-righteousness became that of Britain's in the nineteenth and part of the twentieth centuries. It is really only since the Second World War that these haughty attitudes which brought so much unhappiness to so many people in other parts of the world have been discredited; but not entirely, for they still linger on.[15]

For the abolitionists the 1820s were years spent in fruitless activity in trying to overcome the anaesthetising effects of the Canning resolutions. 'Still nothing was said about emancipation,' George Stephen remembered, 'or if said, it was in a whisper. Colonial abuses, colonial obduracy, colonial hypocrisy were the only topics for agitation, but colonial castigation and colonial emancipation were tabooed.'[16] The rest of the country, however, was vibrant with activity: a financial boom during the first half of the 1820s had turned to a slump in the second half; there were continuing troubles in Ireland; industries were expanding, techniques improving; there was agitation for parliamentary reform—an end to privilege and rotten boroughs—and agitation for Catholic emancipation. But there was also a series of weak, short-lived Governments that did not accomplish very much.[17]

By the end of the decade things began to change. The patience of the abolitionists was growing thin. 'The progress of the colonies is so slow as to be imperceptible to all human eyes save their own', said Mr Brougham in the House of Commons in 1828. 'They are standing still instead of advancing towards the goal at which it was the wish of the House they should gradually but certainly arrive.' What, in fact, had the colonies done during all this time to improve the condition of the slaves as envisaged in Canning's resolutions? 'Out of twenty heads of regulation and improvement recommended to them there are no less than nine in which not a single colony has take a single step. In Jamaica and Barbados with populations together of nearly half a million slaves not one step has been taken with respect to sixteen out of twenty heads proposed to them by the Colonial Department', Brougham claimed.[18] The Government lamely replied that it was their desire 'to introduce a system which will be beneficial to the slaves without infringing on the rights of private property'.[19]

In June 1829 a new note of urgency was sounded in the Commons; not by the official leader of the abolition party, Thomas Buxton, but by another member who was associated with the new radical wing of the party which had grown tired of the time-serving of their leaders, of the excessive politeness and accommodation shown by them to the West Indians. Mr Otway Cave rose to speak to a resolution calling for the freedom of all children of slaves born after 1830. 'I am sorry, Sir, on this occasion to be under the necessity of appearing to act independently of those influential persons who . . . urged me to postpone my motion for another session. The best moment is the very moment. I have consented, much against my will, to the delay which has already taken place, and I cannot, consistently with my duty, allow wishes or convenience of individuals, however eminent or meritorious, to weigh against the lives and liberties of millions of our fellow-subjects.' He reminded the House that nearly forty years had elapsed since slavery was first brought before parliament, but because 'of our having lost sight of principles, and bewildered ourselves with endless details' the slave holders, whose only hope was in delay, had gained to their loss.[20] Mr Cave stood little chance of having his resolution accepted, particularly when William Smith, one of the founder members of the Clapham Sect and a close colleague of Wilberforce and Buxton, rose to answer him. 'I cannot give my support to these resolutions', he said emphatically. 'They are connected with a question of too much importance to be agitated in such a manner.'[21]

History would remember the philanthropists like Smith

and forget those like Cave who eventually achieved what the others have been given the credit for. Wilberforce, said George Stephen, was not qualified 'either by taste or habit or physical power for that very rough labour which was yet to be performed'. The African Institution, drooping under 'an accumulation of political bias, aristocratic ascendancy, and, worse than either, of tame monotony' had given way to the Mitigation and Abolition Society.[22] This, too, was about to be threatened—from within, by its own lack of forcefulness; and from without by the young emancipationists who had the energy and the determination their elders lacked; and the imagination to envisage the West Indies without slaves.

In walking through Kingston I observed . . . sixteen or eighteen negroes linked in a sort of harness, and forming a regular team, were drawing an immense trunk of mahogany conducted by a driver with a cart-whip, who went whistling at their side and flogging them on, precisely as an English carter does his horse.

We went a little off the road to approach four, almost naked females working in a cane field. We found that they were labouring with the hoe, to dig, or cut up the ground preparatory to the planting of sugar; and that a stout, robust-looking man, apparently white, was following them, holding a whip at their backs. Observing that he was the only one of the party who was idle, we inquired why he did not partake of the task, and were told in reply that it was not his business—that he had only to keep the women at work, and to make them feel the weight of the whip if they grew idle, or relaxed from the labour.

(Pinckard)

Extract from the evidence of the Agent of Jamaica

Question: Would it be possible to cultivate the lands in the West Indies by the labour of free negroes?

Answer: Impossible.

Question: Would it be possible to cultivate the West-India islands to advantage by the labour of Europeans; or could their constitutions subsist in such a climate under the labour necessary?

Answer: Utterly impossible. Under no government they would commit every excess; nine out of ten would die within three years.

(Evidence before the committee of the Privy Council, 1788)

Sugar Gardens Tilled by Slaves

In the 1820s people were beginning to think the unthinkable and say the unsayable things about the West Indies. 'The frame of West Indian society, that monstrous birth of the accursed slave trade, is so feeble in itself . . . its continued existence seems little less than a miracle,' Henry Brougham announced in a debate in 1824.[1] In the same year a former resident of the West Indies, T. S. Winn, wrote: 'England, by getting rid of her West Indian colonies would be relieved from an enormous expense and incumbrance.'[2]

In 1825 in the debate on colonial policy, William Huskisson, who was to reform the colonial system from one based on monopolies to one based on preference, raised the issue which was to prove as vital to the interests of the West Indies as the emancipation question. An open trade, he said, was infinitely more valuable than any monopoly. Could Britain with her monopolistic system based on her colonies compete with other countries and their freedom of trade? When one came to examine the position, he added with a note of contempt, the West Indies were merely a collection of plantations—sugar gardens tilled by slaves, for the benefit of masters resident in Great Britain.[3]

Adam Smith had anticipated Huskisson by fifty years. In *The Wealth of Nations* Smith had written: 'The exclusive trade of the mother countries tends to diminish or, at least, to keep down below what they would otherwise rise to, both the enjoyments and industry of all those nations in general, and of American colonies in particular. It is a dead weight upon the action of one of the great springs which puts into motion a great part of the business of mankind. By rendering the colony produce dearer in all other countries, it lessens its

consumption, and thereby cramps the industry of the colonies, and both the enjoyments and the industry of all other
countries, which both enjoy less when they pay more for
what they enjoy, and produce less when they get less for
what they produce.' The exclusive trade, Smith maintained,
was 'a clog' because it inhibited consumption.[4] Since
consumption was the purpose of all production the consumers'
interest ought to be paramount, 'but in the mercantile
system the interest of the consumer is almost constantly
sacrificed to that of the producer'.[5]

By raising tariffs against the produce of other countries
and permitting the produce of the West Indies—sugar, in
particular—to enter at a cheaper price, the people of Britain
may have benefited in the early days of the colonial system,
but long before the end of the eighteenth century slave-
grown sugar had proved to be more expensive than sugar
grown by free labour. Cheap sugar had therefore become
dear sugar, and the only people who continued to benefit
from the system were the West Indian merchants and the
plantation proprietors, as Smith had warned.

The call went out to end the West Indian monopoly,
and open the trade to competition from other sugar producing countries.[6] The heated debate which took place between
the free traders and the West Indian monopolists was
further aggravated by the East Indian merchants whose
sugar was not tainted with slavery and was, more important
still, cheaper to produce though more expensive to buy in
England. They launched their first major campaign against
the West Indian planters a few weeks before Thomas
Buxton's initial speech against slavery in 1823. The Society
of West Indian Planters and Merchants, correctly antici-
pating the close co-operation which would exist between
the abolitionists and the East Indian interests, recommended
a series of reforms for the improvement of the slaves' conditions which, had they been implemented at the time,
would have satisfied the most demanding abolitionist.[7]

This identity of interests between the abolitionists and
the East Indians expressed itself wherever possible. In 1824
the abolitionists organised a boycott of West Indian sugar
in favour of the sugar from the East Indies; and as the

East Indian economic pressure grew stronger, so the abolitionists' case against the slave system was strengthened.[8] Both were aided, indirectly by a general tendency to transfer attention from the empire in the West to the empire in the East,[9] and directly by the economic situation in the West Indies. This was seldom stable; it fluctuated between periods of great prosperity and near bankruptcy. It is unlikely that a British parliament would have felt it necessary to introduce legislation as far back as 1732 enabling creditors to recover their debts more easily in the West Indian and American colonies unless there were sufficient creditors already demanding that their claims be satisfied.

Forty years later parliament had once more to come to the aid of the resident West Indians by permitting foreigners to lend money to them, and to recover their debts even if the foreigners were at war with Britain. The West Indian debt became in time as notorious a factor in eighteenth-century economic life as the celebrated wealth of the sugar island. The debts, however, belonged in the main to the colonists; the wealth to those non-resident proprietors whom Wilberforce so admired. It was they who held the mortgages over the plantations and who earned the interest on the capital lent to the residents to run their plantations.

Because sugar was the major source of income for the colonies, resident and non-resident proprietors alike depended on it being sold at a good price with a high margin of profit. But an increased duty had been imposed on the product in the 1790s, ostensibly to help pay for the war effort and to maintain the West Indian naval patrol. The duty, to the disgust of the West Indians, remained long after the war with France was over. In 1812 planters from Barbados and Tobago petitioned parliament for help in their distress, resulting from 'the depreciation in the price of sugar'. 'The distress of West Indian planters have increased to an extent hitherto unexampled', read one petition. The result, they threatened, 'must deprive the Petitioners of the means of affording their negroes many essential necessaries'.[10] By the end of the 1820s petitions to parliament from the West Indian planters to reduce the sugar duties became as regular as petitions from the abolitionists to end slavery.[11]

So anxious were the West Indians becoming that in 1830 some of them were even hinting at reintroducing the slave trade so that they could compete with the Brazilians, for example, who still legally imported slaves. 'Notwithstanding all our exertions, 700,000 slaves have been brought to foreign colonies since the peace of 1815 to extend cultivation there', complained one West Indian in a debate on the reduction of sugar duties.[12] Another said that two million was spent on putting down the slave trade and British vessels were kept cruising on the unhealthy coast of Africa at a heavy annual expenditure, and yet British colonists were the only people prevented from importing slaves while such immense advantages accrued to the foreigners who continued the trade.[13] A year later Mr Keith Douglas pointed out that the price of slaves in British colonies was £100 while it was only £40 in Brazil and Cuba; freshly imported slaves were more effective than colony-bred ones; thus, he computed, the English planter had only thirty-four effective labourers out of 100 slaves, while the Brazilians had fifty-five.[14]

At the same time as the West Indians were petitioning to reduce their sugar duties, they were also petitioning for relief. Long before slavery was ended, the West Indians were asking parliament to remember that slaves meant property and property, money, and that if ever it was parliament's intention to deprive them of their property, they ought to be compensated. 'It is not freedom that revolts the minds of West Indians', wrote a resident proprietor in 1824, 'but the loss of property and the total ruin of their temporal interests.' The same author repeated the threat that the West Indians would look to America for assistance. 'America is near: she is independent, aspiring, and powerful; the advantages of her protection have already been contemplated; and although the balance inclines at present in favour of the mother country, it may not possibly be always so.'[15]

'Our West Indian white subjects now broadly hint that unless allowed and without control to continue their slave system they may transfer their allegiance to some other power, and it seems the American States are to be preferred by the proffer. Well, (waving the penalty of rebellion, and the right and power of Great Britain over her Colonies) let them make the experiment whenever they please, and try whether any nation will indulge them as much (too much) and protect them as England has done,' was T. S. Winn's answer to the threat. 'The American States,' he said, 'like most other nations, are already supplied with an abundance of sugars and other tropical produce for the home and foreign markets much cheaper than the people of England, and are not likely to burden themselves, or shackle their commerce with high prices, bounties, protecting duties, and etc., merely to bolster up West Indian interests to the exclusion of cheaper products.'[16]

If the colonists were also concerned about giving the blacks social equality, the non-resident proprietors were even more concerned about the price of that equality because the mortgages they held over the plantations and the loans at high interest would become valueless since they depended largely for security on slaves. Richard Pares in his study of a wealthy West Indian family, the Pinneys,[17] came to the conclusion from the records of the family that its wealth in the first half of the nineteenth century was derived not mainly from the plantations it owned in the West Indies, but from the interest on money lent to the other planters. Some of the debts owing to the family went back as far as 1750, and by 1819, when the prosperity of the West Indies was over, the total amount owed in the West Indies to the family was £200,000. As the economic situation in the sugar islands worsened so the Pinneys and other creditors began to foreclose on their mortgages. Pares says that between 1820 and 1831 the Pinneys took possession of eleven plantations in satisfaction of debts due to them.

When Lord Dudley and Ward said in the House of Lords as far back as 1826, 'if any measure for the abolition of slavery, likely to be injurious to the interests of the planters, is carried into effect, they should be allowed full and fair indemnification',[18] he probably had already realised that slaves as a means of production had become uneconomic, but slaves as a security for loans were still extremely valuable. Where slavery ended, he added, compensation began.

Certainly, judging from the number of petitions for compensation presented to parliament even before the leading
abolitionists were committed to immediate abolition,
West Indians, it seems, were preparing the way for a profitable encashment of their securities. That by doing so they
were selling the colonists down the river was another matter.
They had their fortunes to think about.

This, of course, did not stop them trundling out the usual
arguments against emancipation even when compensation
was the topic of the debate. They had to appear to their
friends in the islands to be doing all in their power to protect
their interests and their way of life. But from 1830 onwards
the petitions were not against emancipation, but for compensation. Month after month they came in: petitions for
the reduction of sugar duties; petitions to aid West Indian
distress; petitions for 'compensation—if property was
interfered with in the West Indies'.[19] In 1831 a select
committee of the House of Commons was appointed to
enquire into the state of the colonies and the 'cause of its
present distress'.[20] In the same month the Barbados and St
Vincent Importation Bill was passed which ended the
monopoly of supplying these islands with food and provisions.
A year later the Crown Colonies Act was passed, the purpose of which was to provide funds for the relief of the
colonies: £500,000 to Jamaica, £500,000 to the others.[21]

This kind of money was not nearly sufficient to make the
West Indies profitable once more. In 1832 a crowded
meeting of people connected with the colonies heard Lord
Harewood plead the cause of those who had only their
West Indian property to depend on. 'I wish,' he said, 'to
come *in forma pauperis* before the Government to give us
relief.'[22] Poor Lord Harewood who, in a few years' time, was
to receive many thousands of pounds as compensation for
the slaves he owned, said that slave property was the
only type of property that could not be got rid of if it was
bad, or did not produce any returns. No longer were slaves
thought of as the sinews of the colonial system; they had now
become the main cause of colonial distress. The banker
John Smith pleaded even more eloquently for those West
Indians who were now suffering. Their children, he told

the House of Commons, had now no means of acquiring education except in parish schools, and he himself had known a most amiable and virtuous lady of high rank who was now reduced to utter distress. 'I cannot condemn my fellow-subjects to this misery,' he said. 'It will be unjust and base to liberate the slave with one hand, and with the other condemn my friends and acquaintances to poverty, destitution and misery.'[23] The Colonial Secretary himself recognised the plight of the West Indian proprietors. He said that they were among the most helpless and unprotected class of the community. 'A strong necessity is imposed on this House to look at this question of money compensation, not in a grudging and niggardly, but in a liberal and comprehensive point of view.'[24]

The abolitionists were well aware of the fact that the planters, when they saw that their slaves were unlikely to remain for very much longer their property, would seek to convert them into cash. But in this as on the question of immediate and gradual emancipation they were divided. The anonymous author of *Letters to the More Influential Classes* said that 'we would resist all pretensions to compensation in this question from a conviction that every iota which is conceded to the loud and importunate demands of the slave holder is deducted from the silent yet powerful claims of the slave. To the slave holder nothing is due; to the slave everything.'

That, however, was in 1824. In the end his viewpoint was overlooked in that last great slave sale of all—the emancipation of the British West Indian slaves.

But I must first say that it is not true that slave owners are respected for kindness to their slaves. The more tyrannical a master is, the more will he be favourably regarded by his neighbouring planters; and from the day that he acquires the reputation of a kind and indulgent master, he is looked upon with suspicion, and sometimes hatred, and his slaves are watched more closely than ever. . . .

The Captain sold my aunt, Betsy Bristol, to a distinguished lawyer in the village, retaining her husband, Aaron Bristol, in his own employ; and two of her children he sold to another legal gentleman named Cruger. One day Captain Helm came out where the slaves were at work, and finding Aaron was not there, he fell into a great rage and swore terribly. He finally started off to a beech tree, from which he cut a stout limb, and trimmed it so as to leave a knot on the butt end of the stick, or bludgeon rather, which was about two and a half feet in length. With this formidable weapon he started to Aaron's lonely cabin. When the solitary husband saw him coming he suspected that he was angry, and went forth to meet him in the street. They had no sooner met than my master seized Aaron by the collar, and taking the limb he had prepared by the smaller end, commenced beating him with it, over the head and face, and struck him some thirty or more terrible blows in quick succession; after which Aaron begged to know for what he was so unmercifully flogged.

'Because you deserve it,' was the angry reply.

(*Twenty-two Years a Slave, and Forty Years a Freeman*—
Austin Steward, 1857)

St. Vincent

Extract from the Return of All Persons Committed to the Common Jail

Year	*Names*	*How disposed of*
1814		
9 Sept	Charles—A negro man taken up at sea and committed by the honourable John Grant; says he is a free man of Martinique	2 Dec. Died in prison
1815		
25 Aug	A black man named Pierre, a Frenchman, picked up in an open boat between St. Lucia and this island	11 Dec. Sold; the net proceeds of the sale carried to the credit of the public
1820		
11 Aug	A negro named Guy, belonging to the estate of George Ottley; committed as a runaway	18 July 1821. Released to the executors of George Ottley deceased, the prisoner proving to be an insane slave belonging to the estate of Ottley

(Papers on the Slave Trade—State Papers, Vol. XVIII, 1823)

The People Must Emancipate the Slaves

The Anti-Slavery Society meetings were getting out of hand. In May 1830, 2,000 people packed the Freemasons' Hall to hear their leaders denouncing the slave system.[1] By that stage even William Wilberforce was saying that they had to exert themselves to put an end to it. He was a tired old man and his voice was so feeble it could hardly be heard, especially by the rowdy and impatient young radicals who were there in force to embarrass their elders with demands for emancipation after the 1st of January 1831.

'We should strike at the root of the evil at once, and instead of mincing and huckstering about minor points of good and bad treatment, assert and insist upon for the negro the inalienable right of every British subject.' said Mr Pownall to loud cheers. Mr Drummond added: 'The friends of humanity have slept too long at their posts while the enemy never slackens his endeavours to perpetuate the present abuse by which his avarice is fostered. Indeed I fear that until some black O'Connell or an African Bolivar devotes his unceasing energy to effecting emancipation of his negro brethren, the condition of the slaves . . . will never change.'

The audience again cheered loudly, especially at the mention of the Irish Member of Parliament, Daniel O'Connell, who was in the hall. When Henry Brougham, now Lord Chancellor, attempted to calm down the meeting by reminding it that there was no open day in parliament for the introduction of the resolution which had been suggested —and deprecating the haste—O'Connell challenged him. 'Let us make a beginning,' he said. 'Whatever day we propose we will be met with the answer, "you are too hasty; you do not give enough time to educate the young descendants of slaves before they come to man's estate, and make them fit for freedom." The resolution is a distinct and tangible proposition upon which we should take our stand.'

But the old guard with its fear of too rapid a movement towards emancipation won the day. The meeting ended in uproar. The young radicals were dissatisfied and it was clear to them than unless they acted independently of the leaders, very little would be achieved. George Stephen summed up the conflict, thus: 'The Antislavery committee consisted of some half-a-dozen members of Parliament; sometimes more, and a few gentlemen out of Parliament. The M.P.s always thoroughly understood the inside of the House, and the outsiders did not; hence the latter were by no means slow in urging motions to be made and resolutions to be passed, and notices to be given which the former honestly believed would do mischief. The M.P.s said "Trust to Parliament", the outsiders replied, "Trust to the people". The M.P.s rejoined, "The people know nothing about it". The outsiders retorted, "The House cares nothing about it".'[2]

As in the 1780s so now in the 1830s it was left to a few individual Quakers to take the first steps towards directing the new spirit. The official committee had rejected a suggestion to start up subcommittees in the suburbs of London and in the provinces. James Cropper, a Quaker, liked the idea and introduced its proposer to a group of Quakers at dinner. 'The projector was desired to explain almost before the first glass was passed round', Stephen recalled; 'a Quakerish fashion against which I enter my protest.'[3]

The plan was to divide the country into districts, and to send a lecturer to each, armed with facts and information about slavery and fired by an enthusiasm to convert new audiences around the country to emancipation. The Quakers accepted the idea immediately and Cropper advanced £500 out of his own pocket. The prosperous Birmingham Quaker, Joseph Sturge, who was to play such an important role in the later history of emancipation, advanced £250. Wilberforce gave £20 and James Stephen ten guineas. Within two weeks a new committee was formed by a number of young radicals to put the plan into action. Calling itself the Agency Committee because it depended upon its separate agents to spread the word, it took offices in the building in Aldermanbury, London, occupied by the main Society so as to avoid the suggestion of dissension within the movement.

The Committee met every day; three was a quorum and the first to arrive was the chairman. After a while the pace was too great for most of the original eighteen members, and the bulk of the work fell on the shoulders of George Stephen and the two Quaker brothers, Emanuel and Joseph Cooper.

Simplicity was the keynote of the Agency Committee's tactics. In their letter of instruction to their agents they stated their credo: 'To uphold slavery is a crime before God, and the condition must therefore be immediately abolished.' There was no talk of improving the system of slavery, or preparing the slaves for freedom, or granting the children freedom while their parents laboured on as bondsmen— in other words, none of the time-wasting tactics adopted by the official leadership. 'If in your opinion the first part of this proposition remains doubtful,' stated the letter of instruction, 'it is scarcely necessary to add that your services will not be accepted by the committee.' To them emancipation meant simply 'the simultaneous establishment of a system of equality with the freeborn subject in the enjoyment of civil rights'.

The agent's duty was to revive the waning enthusiasm of existing antislavery societies, and to establish and guide new ones. He had to endeavour to win over the provincial press in favour of emancipation, and above all to lecture and give as much accurate information about slavery to as many people as possible. His lectures had to deal with the biblical and historical arguments in favour of emancipation, then proceed to the economic and political arguments in its favour. The instructions stated, 'in urging the practical duties which this view of the whole subject entails upon those who admit its truth, you cannot be too rhetorical or declamatory. National honour, political consistency, domestic feeling, and Christian principle, all come into play here, and all must tell.'

The agent was also reminded that, though specific instances of violence practised by planters on slaves were useful to illustrate the cruelty of the system, he was not to rely on atrocities to stir up interest in the cause. In this respect the new emancipationists differed from the slave trade abolitionists who had relied on painting the trade as vile as possible to win public support. But as one of the radicals correctly pointed out, 'occasional atrocities are mere aggravations of the crime and ought not to make us lose sight of the main question—the utter illegality of slavery itself. The great and fundamental truth at issue is not less than whether the law of the land acknowledges or not that man can be the property of man.'[4]

Good agents were not easy to find. The Committee had only six paid agents, but the number of unpaid agents soon began to grow. A proof of its efficiency is that the number of affiliated societies multiplied in the course of one year from twenty to nearly 1,300.[5]

The Agency Committee's different approach to 'the occult science of agitation',[6] as Stephen called it, was partly the result of its own deliberate policy and partly the result of changes in the political and social environment. In 1831 a Reform Bill, which extended the franchise by giving the vote to occupiers of houses rated over £10, had been introduced in parliament, but had been defeated. Within the next year it would be passed, and the young emancipationists knew that not only could they seek the support of an enlarged electorate, but could also now rely on a different kind of labourer in the cause. The working bees, said Sir George Stephen, were homely but earnest. 'They gathered more honey, however, than more illustrious men.'[7] Like their predecessors in the abolition movement, their work entailed influencing public opinion, except that now the public was much larger and, after the passing of the Reform Bill in 1832, politically much more powerful.

In preparation for a reformed parliament, the emancipationist movement, through more than 1,200 affiliated societies sought to win over as many new candidates and new voters to their cause as possible. They found their support in the most unexpected places. 'Be you a candidate for Lords or

Commons?' asked an old Lincolnshire farmer of one of the candidates in the 1833 parliamentary elections. 'For the Commons, my friend,' he replied. 'There are no elections for the Lords.' 'Well, sir, I know nothing about that, but which votes against slavery? Lords or Commons, he shall have my vote, and not the king himself if he don't.'[8]

Their work was greatly assisted by the newspapers, some of which had adopted a forward-looking approach to questions of the day and were explaining to their readers the new rights and duties which would devolve upon them once they were represented in parliament. The anti-slavery societies were quick to point out that emancipation was one of the first political duties. The press also gave a lot of space to reporting their meetings which were being held regularly all over the country. They resembled more what would today be called 'teach-ins', rather than the stately proceedings which the old Society conducted with the Duke of Gloucester presiding and the parliamentary leaders outdoing each other in proposing lofty but useless resolutions. The agents, equipped with their facts and figures about the slave system, were in attendance to explain to the audience everything they wished to know. As Stephen said, 'they challenged enquiry, they courted controversy . . . in an open arena, before the world'.[9]

The West Indians did not sit back and do nothing. They may have become obsessed with sugar duties and possible compensation, but they made sure of putting their views to the public at their own meetings. Sometimes it became a race as to which party would be first in a town because the winners would book the best hall, and, more important, try to predispose the press in their direction. In London the West Indians sent tough labourers from the sugar-baking houses and clerks in the counting-houses to break up the anti-slavery meetings. George Stephen, who was one of the most active members of the Agency Committee, arranged to have the police at one meeting. The next day a newspaper reported: 'Brutal attempts having been made by certain individuals . . . to prevent public lectures on the important subject of slavery . . . which attempts last night were attended by menaces and gestures of personal violence

... the friends of the cause will not fail to notice this conduct as it deserves, and it is hoped will rally around those who are thus arduously fighting the battle.'[10]

Economic uncertainty and anxiety of not knowing the final outcome of the emancipation question continued to cause unrest in the colonies. At the end of 1831 there occurred a major slave rebellion in Jamaica led by a Baptist convert, Samuel Sharpe. 400 rebels were killed, 160 properties were damaged or destroyed, the loss amounting to over half a million pounds. In retaliation for the death of three or four whites, 100 slaves were shot, hanged or whipped to death at the rate of about twenty a week, and once again, as in Demerara eight years before, the white colonists blamed the missionaries. 'Shooting is . . . too honourable a death for men whose conduct has occasioned so much bloodshed, and the loss of so much property', the *Jamaica Courant* raged. 'There are fine hanging woods in St James and Trelawny, and we do sincerely hope that the bodies of all the Methodist preachers who may be convicted of sedition may diversify the scene.'[11]

Whether or not John Smith and Demerara had taught the colonists caution, they did not hang any missionaries, but limited their revenge to expelling some of them from the islands in as humiliating manner as possible. 'We were then paraded through the town,' wrote some Baptist missionaries to their Society in London, 'and went on board an *open canoe* about twenty minutes before twelve o'clock. . . . We were seven hours in this open canoe, treated civilly enough by our guard, but compelled to hear language very painful to a Christian's feelings. Let British subjects, British Christians, judge if they can what our feelings must have been. . . . Let them picture to their imaginations three *British* subjects, Christians, and missionaries in a British colony and professedly under British laws, about to be forced from their wives and children without being permitted to see them, and then let them repress their indignation if they can.'[12]

Once again, as after the Demerara affair, the British public which had for the most part successfully repressed its feelings about black people being forced from their wives and children without being permitted to see them for

the rest of their lives, reacted with rage at the mistreatment
of white missionaries. 'This sort of excitement in this cause
it is absolutely in vain to attempt to control', Zachary
Macaulay wrote to Henry Brougham, now Lord Brougham
and Vaux. 'The religious persecution in Jamaica had roused
the immense body of Methodists and Dissenters throughout
the land to a feeling of the most intense and ardent description. . . . I stand astonished myself at the result.'[13]

Once again the emancipationists channelled the excitement and aggression against the colonists into anti-slavery
agitation. The pace was now increasing as the last unreformed parliament drew to a close. The Jamaica persecutions could not have come at a better time. William Knibb,
one of the missionaries who had been thrown into gaol
for inciting rebellion, committed to trial and eventually
freed, toured England, his lectures attracting large crowds.

Another Methodist, though not a missionary, Henry
Whiteley, was also forced to leave Jamaica, and on his
return to England wrote a tract called *Three Months in
Jamaica*[14] which sold an incredible 200,000 copies in two
weeks.[15] Whiteley admitted that when he arrived on the
island—with a view to be employed on a plantation—he
believed that there was more real slavery in England than
in any of the colonies—a belief held by many especially
in the manufacturing districts. 'I blamed such gentlemen
as Mr Buxton for making so much ado in parliament
about colonial slavery and neglecting the slavery of the
poor factory children at home with whose condition I was
well acquainted.' However, after seeing the ruins of a
Methodist chapel which had been destroyed by whites
during the recent riots, he began to change his opinions.
He got a job as a bookkeeper on a plantation and was able
to witness the casual manner in which barbaric punishments were meted out to slaves on the smallest pretext.
The legal maximum number of lashes permitted was thirty-
nine; this had also become virtually the minimum. And,
as he pointed out in his tract, who on a plantation was to
say that the master had inflicted more than the maximum.
He asked one slave about punishments. The old man
had been in charge of the sheep and had been flogged

many times. ' "And what were you flogged for?" I enquired. "When sheep go astray—when sheep sick—when sheep die —then," he said, "Busha put me down and flog me till me bleed." "And how many lashes?" I asked, "did Busha ever give you?" "Ah, Massa," said the poor old man, "when me down na ground, and dey flog me till me bleed, me something else to do den for count de lashes." '

Whiteley's interest in the slaves on the plantation aroused suspicions; his belongings were searched and a letter was found addressed by him to a Wesleyan missionary. That was enough for the highly sensitive whites. It was rumoured that unless he left immediately, he would be tarred and feathered. He did not wait to find out. When he was formally confronted by a group calling themselves the Colonial Church Union and told to leave, he left.

'Whiteley, Whiteley, nothing but Whiteley,' Thomas Buxton complained at the extravagant success of his book.[16] He and his colleagues in the Mitigation and Abolition Society had other complaints. They did not like the Agency committee's policy of immediate emancipation; they did not like the way in which the committee was canvassing new parliamentary candidates by demanding that they pledge themselves to an anti-slavery vote in the reformed parliament, and going even further by publishing shedules in daily newspapers of all eligible, ineligible and doubtful candidates. The result of these lists was that letters poured into the committee's offices from prospective candidates, pledging themselves to vote on immediate and unconditional abolition, and mentioning any fact which might help them; one, for instance, said he had dined with Wilberforce; another knew Macaulay, and a third had purchased a slave's manumission.[17]

The older Society also complained about the Agency Committee's posters which Buxton described as 'incendiary'; about the doggerel rhymes and schoolboyish electioneering slogans which George Stephen thought up and distributed;[18] and about the intransigent attitude the young radicals had adopted towards compensation. But most of all they complained about the dissension their attitudes had caused. 'I cannot bear to let you remain under the painful impressions which in a mind of any feelings must be produced by the supposition that they who ought to be our friends are misconceiving and calumniating us', wrote a sorrowful old Wilberforce to an equally sorrowful old Macaulay.[19]

'It cannot be doubted,' George Stephen said, 'that with a reformed parliament popular feeling would have been more respected . . . and it had long been advancing in favour of the slave, but the advance (under the old Committee) was slow, it was the creeping of a tortoise.' While he and his committee were working hard to persuade the public to their way of thinking, the old guard were still busy dissecting and criticising the slave codes in the colonies. 'The "Young England" abolitionists were a hundred miles ahead of them!' Stephen maintained. 'The Agency Committee did not of itself accomplish the work, but they accelerated its accomplishment by at least one generation.'[20]

The old parliament was dissolved in December 1832; the hopes of the emancipationists which rested on a liberal Whig majority in an anti-slavery House of Commons were shaken when in the Speech from the Throne at the start of the new parliament in 1833 no mention at all was made of the subject of slavery. There had, in fact, been a lot of behind-the-scenes activity in the Colonial Office to explain this, and also what happened later. Two permanent members of the Colonial Office, James Stephen, Jnr, and another, both committed emancipationists, had been working under Viscount Goderich, the Colonial Secretary, on schemes for emancipation. Their ideas, particularly Stephen's, were far more progressive than Earl Grey, the Prime Minister, was prepared to accept.

Grey began to put pressure on Goderich to resign, and eventually succeeded in April 1833. The man who replaced him as Colonial Secretary was Edward Stanley, the 14th Earl of Derby, destined to become three times Prime Minister. Immediately on taking office he rejected the Goderich proposals in favour of his own plan for the emancipation of the slaves.[21]

Thomas Buxton had been warned by Goderich not to expect too much from the new administration. He was told that an issue would be made of compensation, and he knew that to fight it, though the emancipationists might have the strength in parliament eventually to succeed, would take many sessions. He preferred, as usual not to press too radical a line in case by asking too much he got nothing. The official Anti-Slavery Society had a meeting at Exeter Hall and obtained from the members a partial assent to a concession on compensation. The young emancipationists wanted nothing of it. One of their outstanding leaders, Joseph Sturge, wrote to a friend in March 1833: 'It is now time to stir ourselves . . . agitate, agitate, agitate. We must all become Radicals and Unionists, for if we sit down quietly with our hands before us Government will laugh at us. The people must emancipate the slaves, for the Government never will . . .'[22]

Having collected themselves into a body about one o'clock in the morning, they proceeded to the fort of Port Maria; killed the sentinel, and provided themselves with as great a quantity of arms and ammunition as they could conveniently dispose of. Being this time joined by a number of their countrymen from the neighbouring plantations, they marched up the high road that led to the interior parts of the country, carrying death and desolation as they went. . . . In one morning they murdered between thirty and forty whites, not sparing even infants at the breast, before their progress was stopped. Tacky, the Chief, was killed in the woods. Of three who were clearly proved to have been concerned in the murders committed at Ballard's Valley, one was condemned to be burnt, and the other two to be hung up alive in irons, and left to perish in that dreadful situation. The wretch that was burnt was made to sit on the ground, and his body being chained to an iron stake, the fire was applied to his feet. He uttered not a groan, and saw his legs reduced to ashes with the utmost firmness and composure; after which one of his arms by some means getting loose, he snatched a brand from the fire that was consuming him, and flung it in the face of the executioner.

The two that were hung up alive on the gibbet which was erected in the parade of the town of Kingston never uttered the least complaint except only of cold in the night, but diverted themselves all day long in discourse with their countrymen who were permitted very improperly to surround the gibbet. . . . I remember that both he and his fellow sufferer laughed immoderately at something that occurred—I know not what. The next morning one of them silently expired, as did the other on the morning of the ninth day.

(Edwards)

The Colonial Secretary Presents His Plan

One spring day in London in 1833 an unusual sight caught the attention of pedestrians and carriage passengers passing along the Strand and Whitehall. The thoroughfare had been taken over by a large, sombre, orderly procession of clergymen and Dissenting ministers all dressed in black. They were marching to Downing Street to present to the Prime Minister on the eve of the great emancipation debate their call for immediate and unconditional emancipation without the payment of compensation.

A few weeks before the march, the Agency Committee had circularised its associate societies with a protest against compensation. Emancipation, the committee maintained, was founded on the illegality of the slave system; compensation to the former owners of slave simplied the exact opposite: the acceptance of the legal basis of slavery. The Agency Committee also sent Joseph Sturge all over Britain to drum up enthusiasm for their policy, and on his return to London a meeting of nearly 350 delegates from the country took place. They expressed in no uncertain terms their dissatisfaction with the parliamentary representation of their cause by Thomas Buxton, William Smith and the others.[1] They knew that Buxton would compromise with the Government, and they wanted to make sure that the Government was aware of the large section of the public who wanted to have no truck whatsoever with the West Indians who, as one writer put it, were 'like an angry child that threatens to beat its Mammy unless she humours it in all its whims and vagaries'.[2]

Buxton was against the idea of a protest march, but notwithstanding his disapproval it took place. It was followed up by petitions for immediate emancipation from all over the country. One from Leeds was signed by 18,000 people, but the largest of all was presented by the Ladies' Anti-Slavery Societies which contained 187,000 signatures. In his *Antislavery Recollections* George Stephen pays frequent tribute to the work done by women in the campaign. He says that only after they were admitted to meetings were the halls crowded. 'It is simple nonsense to attribute this to gallantry, for I never yet knew staid men of business seduced from their offices and counting-houses by mere gallantry. . . . I impute it more to the affectionate influence which women rightfully exert in persuading their male relatives to join in matters that interest their best feelings; . . . yet their admission was long resisted on the ground that their presence lowered the dignity of the subject.'[3]

In parliament Buxton moved for the abolition of slavery, but the Government persuaded him to withdraw his motion since the Colonial Office was preparing a plan of its own.[4] On May the 14th the Colonial Secretary, Edward Stanley, rose to present the ministerial proposals to end slavery.[5] Parliament was crowded with members and spectators, and they listened in rapt silence to Stanley's three-hour-long speech. His peroration was a stirring one. He spoke of the history of the system, of the speeches in the past. He told of the failure of the Orders in Council to change substantially the situation of the slaves; he spoke of depopulation and distress for black and white in the colonies. Then he came to the core of his speech—the Government's plan for emancipation; and the faces of those who were hoping for the complete and final end to slavery grew longer and longer.

The plan was in the form of resolutions. The first provided for the abolition of slavery throughout the colonies. 'I propose that every slave, on the passing of the Act, shall have the power of claiming to be put in a situation . . . in which they would be entitled to every right and every privilege of freemen subject to this condition, and to this condition alone—that for a certain period they shall contract to labour under their present owners but now their employers.' In justification of this proposal Stanley came back to the old 'fit for freedom' argument. 'To throw the slave suddenly into freedom will be to destroy all his inclinations to industry; it will be exposing him to the temptation of recurring to his primitive habits of savage life, from which he has but lately been reclaimed.'

Stanley went on to explain that of the total time the ex-slave worked as an apprentice he would work three-quarters of the time for his master and one-quarter of the time for himself. During the latter period the slave would be at liberty to employ himself elsewhere.

After dealing with the resolution which provided for immediate freedom of children under the age of six and those born after the Act, Stanley came to the question of compensation. 'We propose a loan,' he said, 'for the West Indian planters of £15 million.' The method of repayment of the loan was ingenious. 'It is quite clear that the repayment must be borne either by the produce of the negro labour, or by the revenue of this country,' he continued without explanation for that extraordinary assumption; 'it cannot in justice be borne by the planter.' The planter was 'sacrificing' one-quarter of the labour of his slaves, so it was only just that the slaves should be asked to contribute their share to the repayment. There was another reason why the slaves should pay the money back out of their earnings. 'I think it likely that the negro will be encouraged to continue his industry and exertions if out of his wages for the fourth of his labour some deduction should be made for the purpose I have adverted to . . . . [It would be] more conducive to create in him habits of industry and of self-denial than if, having all his wants provided for by the planter in consideration of three-fourths of his labour, he should feel that the only object of employing the remaining fourth would be, at his own option, to provide himself with superfluities.'

Cutting out the racist nonsense, what the Colonial Secretary was proposing was that the slaves buy their own freedom from their masters. The British Government still accepted, therefore, that slavery was legal, that slaves were property recognised by law, and that in order to end the system they would have to be bought out of slavery and not simply emancipated, the British Government lending the money for this purpose.

Stanley, an ardent churchman though not one of the 'saints', was just as keen as the latter that the blacks should be properly educated in Christian principles, the practical application of which he had just so ably demonstrated. 'With the young our responsibility will immediately commence. . . . We must endeavour to give them habits, and to imbue them with feelings calculated to qualify them for the adequate discharge of their duties here; and we must endeavour to instil into them the conviction that when those duties shall be discharged they are not "as the brutes that perish".'

Stanley then took the opportunity to pay tribute to William Wilberforce as 'one of the most religious, one of the most conscientious, one of the most eloquent, one of the most zealous friends of this great cause'. Wilberforce had only two months to live and Stanley, knowing that he was a very sick man, hoped that he would live to see 'the final consummation of the great and glorious work which he was one of the first to commence, and to exclaim like the last of the prophets: "Lord, now let thy servant depart in peace." ' Stanley could not conclude without the obligatory self-commendation on the wonderful humanity displayed by a British parliament. He offered up an ardent prayer that they 'will for a second time set the world a glorious example of a commercial nation weighing commercial advantages light in the balance against justice and religion'.

To put it very simply, therefore, Stanley's humane plan was to buy the slaves from the planters, and to force the slaves to pay back the money out of the wages they earned in their free time. That way, no one would be out of pocket, and the ex-slaves would be forced to remain on the plantations. Despite what it has always believed of itself, the British parliament has seldom been known for its generosity, but the original scheme for the emancipation of slaves must surely go down in history as one of its least generous acts, as far as the slaves were concerned.

When Stanley sat down, Viscount Howick rose and said that the whole speech had left him with feelings so painful 'as hardly to leave me the power of utterance'; yet he managed to speak for the next two hours, picking holes in the proposals, but not seriously damaging them.[6] A few speakers liked the plan, though none wholeheartedly. One said that it would be received with 'unbounded joy' by the slaves, and it would 'bind them to this country by their interest and rivet them to it by gratitude and affection'; and also, of course, though he did not add this, by a debt of fifteen millions.[7] Mr Hill thanked His Majesty's Ministers from the bottom of his heart for the great service they had rendered to the cause of emancipation. However, he thought the plan was neither one thing nor the other; the blacks would be too much freemen to be coerced as slaves, and they would be too much slaves to be actuated by the motives that actuated freemen.[8] Mr Marryat, the agent for Trinidad, got to the root of the matter by recognising that compensation was the keynote of the plan and that without it the whole measure 'must be a complete failure'.[9] But Colonel Conolly thought the proposals were attended with all the evils of massacre and conflagration—of loss of property and life.[10]

Conolly's style of threatening ruin in answer to every suggestion concerning slaves had become old-fashioned. In general the response of the West Indian body to the Colonial Secretary's plan was, for them, relatively quiet and unhysterical. Slavery, as it had existed, might be at an end; but what had replaced it was not as bad as it could have been. More important—especially to the non-resident proprietors and creditors—a loan of £15 million had been granted. This was in May. By June the 3rd the loan had been changed to an outright grant and the amount of compensation raised from £15 to £20 million. 'A pretty strong step' was how one of the abolitionist described with incredible understatement the Colonial Secretary's financial conjuring act.[11]

Twenty million pounds could go a long way to paying off a lot of debts, the West Indians realised. 'Debts which were considered bad debts in April last,' said Buxton, 'are considered good debts now. Individuals who were bankrupts in April are now solvent.'[12] He called it the luckiest windfall that could have befallen the West Indian interest. In return, he suggested to parliament, complete emancipation should be given. If it was not, he warned, there might be a general insurrection.

The Colonial Secretary was on his feet, objecting to Buxton's words; if they were reported to the slaves they might lead to the result he feared. Buxton replied: 'The right honourable gentleman has done me the honour to say that the language I hold towards the negroes might have some influence upon them. If that is the case, I will say to them: "The time of your deliverance is at hand; let that period be sacred—let it be defiled by no outrage . . . let not a hair of the head of a single planter be touched. Make any sacrifice—bear any indignity—submit to any privation, rather than raise your hand against any white men; continue to wait and to work patiently." Help,' he added, 'was coming. "Trust implicitly to that great nation and paternal Government who are labouring for your release." '13

By this absurd display of insensitivity Buxton might have hoped to have endeared himself to his opponents, but as far as the radical emancipationists were concerned the speech—and Buxton—were entirely irrelevant. Mr Buckingham said that the Bill was defective in principle and therefore ought to be opposed. 'I only regret that those who consider themselves leaders on this great question should not have so opposed it.'14

Two closely related issues received considerable attention from speakers in the debate: the 'fit for freedom' issue and the issue of race and colour. The two had always been closely identified in the minds of most whites—slaves were not fit for freedom; slaves were black; blacks were not fit for freedom. Now they became firmly welded together, though members were at pains to keep them separate lest they should appear to follow their fellow members and to the world outside motivated by prejudice, pure and simple.

'There are physical as well as moral causes which obstruct the settlement of the question, and make it one of great embarrassment,' was how Robert Peel, the future Prime Minister delicately put it. 'There is the distinction of colour. I do not allude to this as implying any inferiority between black and white,' he added hastily. 'I merely allude to it as a circumstance which throws a difficulty in amalgamating the slave population with the free. In the United States,' he continued, 'in those states where the equality of all classes is recognised, it has to be admitted that amalgamation does not take place satisfactorily.' The other problem which worried Peel was the slaves' 'aversion to labour'. The slave was not to be trusted with the power of labouring for his own subsistence since his 'elysium was repose'. The West Indies were so fertile that only a few days' labour were needed to procure not only the necessaries of life, but also the luxuries.[15]

Another member had the same anxiety. From the possession of necessaries to the desire for luxuries was a regular progress which the negroes still had to go through, he pointed out, revealing how inextricably linked in his mind were the supposed inherent racial characteristics of the blacks and the institution of slavery. The nouns 'black man' or 'negro' and 'slave' were interchangeable. 'They must be educated to habits of industry by increasing their wants. . . . If they are to be suddenly let loose without that sort of education I am afraid they will only indulge their love for pernicious beverages. . . . I compare them to children; and no rational being, after subjecting children to a strict rule, will at once indulge them with unlimited freedom.'[16] Wilberforce had said something very similar over forty years ago, only then he had compared the slaves to men coming out of fainting fits whose first convulsions would be 'dangerous at once to the party himself and to all around him'.[17]

A number of speakers agreed with Sir Robert Peel that liberty to the negro or slave meant the least amount of work. 'I fear that the whole negro population will sink into weak and dawdling inefficiency,' said a Mr Macaulay, 'and will be much less fit for liberty at the end of the period of apprenticeship than at its commencement.'[18]

Viscount Howick attempted to separate race from the institution of slavery. 'I am aware that we have often been taunted with our ignorance of the negro character; my belief is that . . . we commit a grievous error when we suppose that the moral circumstances attendant upon slavery have so changed the physical character of the negro as to unfit him for freedom. It is a most dangerous error to attribute that to the physical qualities of the negro which results solely from the moral conditions which slavery has superinduced. It yet remains to be seen whether the negro is less industrious or less anxious to better his condition than other men.'[19]

Howick was speaking for the old-guard abolitionists. The younger men had fewer reservations. 'We have been proceeding with so much caution and have taken our steps so very gradually that after thirty years of continued efforts for the abolition of slavery up to the present time the slaves are no more free now than they were then, and any improvement in their condition is so slight as to be imperceptible,' complained Mr Buckingham. Then, going straight to the crux of the matter with a logical simplicity which appears to have completely escaped the older abolitionists, he added: 'We can never prepare them for freedom but by making them partake of its enjoyment. Emancipation must therefore precede improvement.' Replying to Peel, Buckingham said that the only reason why the African race was looked upon with 'such feelings of contempt for its inferiority by the European race is that the constant association of the condition has led to the constant assumption of their inferiority of blood and nature. The testimony of all history, whether ancient or modern, and the evidence of all experience goes to show that in countries where no such idea of slavery is associated with darkness of colour, these physical causes are not at all in question.'[20]

Daniel O'Connell, the Dublin member, neatly summed up the nonsense of the 'fit for freedom' argument with the words, 'Men who can bear slavery most assuredly offer a very strong presumption that they can bear freedom.'[21]

In the Colonial Secretary's original plan the slaves were divided into two types—praedial labourers who were attached to the soil such as field workers whose apprenticeship was to last for twelve years; and non-praedial labourers such as domestic servants and artisans who were to be apprenticed for a shorter period. When it looked to the radicals that their cause was lost and that they would not get immediate emancipation, they tried to bargain with Stanley. George Stephen records their conversation.

Stephen: Are we to understand that you will not reduce the term?

Stanley: It is impossible.

Stephen: Not to five years?

Stanley: I cannot reduce it by a single year; I am pledged to the West Indians; they regard it as the best part of the bill, and I cannot abate an hour of the apprenticeship.

Stephen: Then, sir, the country will be dissatisfied, and we must appeal to it.

Stanley: I am well aware of your power; you have caused us much annoyance, and you may cause us more. But there is no help for it; the apprenticeship must stand or the bill must go with it.[22]

Stanley was right about the radicals causing him more annoyance. Stephen had already sent out advertisements for a meeting at Exeter Hall for the day of the second reading of the Bill. The Hall was packed by angry and frustrated crowds of abolitionists. The newspapers reported the meeting in full and soon after the apprenticeship scheme was altered. The term for praedial labourers was reduced to seven years; the term for non-praedials to five. The abolitionists could not claim a victory; nor could the West Indians, though their pockets were fuller and they were assured of labour for their plantations for a few more years to come. The slaves, of course, had neither freedom nor money.

Wilberforce died in July 1833, the month before the Bill became law. James Stephen had died the previous year and Macaulay had only five more years to live. Wilberforce's old age had been disrupted by financial worries, but in his public life he was still venerated. An Italian official once remarked at the opening of parliament: 'When Mr Wilberforce passes through the crowd everyone contemplates this little old man as a sacred relic—as the Washington of humanity.'[23] He was buried at Westminster Abbey with full honours, close to the tombs of Pitt, Fox and the man who had done so much harm to his cause, Canning. 'A great part of our coloured population who form here an important body', wrote a West Indian clergyman, 'went into mourning at the news of his death.' And his sons reported that 'the same honour was paid to him by this class of persons at New York . . . and their brethren throughout the United States were called upon to pay marks of external respect to the memory of their benefactor.'[24]

The so-called Abolition Act was passed in August 1833.[25] What thoughts went through William IV's mind when he gave his assent to it are unfortunately not known, but it must have hurt him, the former Duke of Clarence and fiery defender of West Indian interests, to have to sign the Act whose preamble began: 'Whereas divers persons are holden in slavery within divers of His Majesty's colonies, and it is just and expedient that all such person be manumitted . . .' What is interesting to note is that, right to the end, despite over fifty years of abolitionist activity and propaganda, they never succeeded in persuading supposedly the most humanitarian legislature in the world that slavery was immoral; unjust perhaps, inexpedient certainly, but not wrong. In the preamble to the clause dealing with compensation, the keynote of the plan as the agent for Trinidad had pointed out, the Act stated specifically that 'the persons at present entitled to the services of the slaves' be compensated 'for the loss of such services'. One cannot help admit to a grudging admiration for the sheer effrontery of a legislature that can, with complete equanimity, reduce nearly 300 years of inhumanity, cruelty and oppression of one people by another to that single, bland word—'services'. Finally, by the very act of compensating the slave owners, the British Government of 1833 recognised, as had all its predecessors, the right of one man to own another.

The Act came into operation on the 1st August 1834. More than 800,000 blacks were now ostensibly free, but still apprentices and as such still subject to the strict regimen of the plantation. Did they riot, burn and rape as the planters had warned they would do ever since they bought the first slaves? The answer came in a despatch from the Marquis of Sligo, the Governor of Jamaica, to the Colonial Office.

'The first prophecy [of the managers] was blood and destruction on the 1st August; in this they were wrong. The second was that this scene would take place at Christmas; in this they were wrong. The third, that the apprentices would not work for wages; in this they were wrong, as I know of no instances in which the usual wages were offered and were refused. The fourth was that the crop would not be taken off; in this they were wrong, as it had in many cases been taken off much earlier than usual.'[26]

As the ex-slaves complained, it was adding insult to injury to call them apprentices since they had no need to undergo an apprenticeship to a way of life which they already knew all too thoroughly.

Slavery Abolition Act

Extract from an Account of the Averages of Sales in the several Colonies affected by the Act for the Abolition of Slavery, upon which the Sum of Twenty Millions, voted as Compensation to the Owners of Slaves, was apportioned among the several Colonies, of the periods for which those Averages were taken; and of the Rate of Compensation per Head which was allotted to each:

Colony	*Average of Sales of Slaves from 1822 to 1830*			*Rate of Compensation per Slave*		
	£	s	d	£	s	d
Bermuda	27	4	11¾	12	10	5
Bahamas	29	18	9¾	12	14	4¾
Jamaica	44	15	2¼	19	15	4¾
Honduras	120	4	7½	53	6	9½
Barbados	47	1	3½	20	13	8¼
Cape of Good Hope	59	6	0	12	1	4¾

Extract from Sums of Money Awarded for Slavery Compensation on Uncontested Claims:

British Guiana   *6 December 1837*

Date of Award	*No. of Claim*	*Name of Party to whom Payment is made*	*No. of Slaves*	*Sum*		
Jan				£	s	d
1836	2288	H. M. Bunbury	478	24,169	1	3
	2289	Hugh Duncan Baillie	456	23,024	6	5
	2290	Charles Bean	319	16,852	5	0
	2291	Thomas Bell	159	8,219	16	8
	2292	(litigated claim)	171	8,735	11	1
	2293	Edward Bunbury	65	3,393	4	3
	2294	(litigated claim)	26	1,419	12	10

				£	s	d
	2295	Frances G. Bayley	9	346	18	11
	2296	Mrs A. E. Burton	33	1,819	0	5
	2297	Samuel Bruton	1	63	0	1

Jamaica
1835

				£	s	d
28 Sept	22	Sir Henry Fitzherbert bart.	88	1,613	7	0
	23	The Earl of Harewood	112	2,599	0	4
	24	Alexander Bravo	114	2,372	18	11
28 Sept	74	Frances Jackson	5	106	13	3
	75	(litigated claim)	237	—	—	—
28 Oct	76	William Jackson	259	5,427	6	0

Extract from a Statement of the Average Value (in Sterling Money) of a Slave as appraised by the Sworn Valuators, and of the Compensation awarded for such Slave of each Class of the Several Divisions of Praedial Attached, of Praedial Unattached, and of Non-Praedial, in each of the Colonies where Compensation has been granted:

Cape of Good Hope

Divisions	Classes	Average Value of a Slave as appraised by the Sworn Valuators			Compensation per Slave		
		£	s	d	£	s	d
Non-Praedial	Head tradesman	151	2	5	61	8	6¼
	Inferior "	100	16	0¼	40	19	5¼
	Head people employed on wharfs	98	0	0	39	16	8
	Inferior people of the same description	100	5	5¼	40	15	1¾
	Head domestics	115	0	4¼	46	15	0¼
	Inferior "	71	13	1½	29	2	6¼
	Children under six years of age on 1st Dec. 1834	16	4	7	6	11	11¼
	Aged, diseased or otherwise non-effective	13	18	5½	5	13	2¼

(Accounts of Slave Compensation Claims—
House of Commons Session Papers, 1837–8, Vol. 48)

Slavery in Disguise

'The Christian proprietor will never desire to return to
an order of things which is undoubtedly opposed, if not
immediately, yet in its indirect and more remote consequences
to the religion of Christ. The Christian apprentice will, by a
quiet submission to the laws of the land, and by doing
voluntarily the work which before was exacted through
compulsion, satisfy his former master that the change in his
condition has not made him a worse man, or a less profitable
servant.' Thus did Edward Eliot, the Archdeacon of Barbados, see the continuing relationships between former
masters and slaves. The emancipated slave had cause, not
for boasting but for gratitude; gratitude to Almighty God
from improving his earthly condition; gratitude to the
government of Great Britain 'for zealously coming forward
in his behalf, and submitting to a great pecuniary sacrifice
in order that his condition may be improved and his comforts increased'; and, finally, gratitude to his master 'for
consenting to an arrangement which takes power out of
his own hands and places it at the disposal of another'.[1]

Notwithstanding Eliot's sermons and doubtless the many
other similar sermons preached in the churches in the West
Indies after the Abolition Act, the apprenticeship system
was difficult to administer since neither ex-master nor
ex-slave knew exactly what was expected of him. The only
section of the Act which would be executed with relative
ease was that dealing with compensation. A Compensation
Board was set up and claims in all the colonies were dealt
with as quickly and as efficiently as possible, the most
difficult ones being where mortgagees and other creditors
fought over the proceeds.

Little of the £20 million went into the pockets of the planters themselves, but to the creditors who had been working so effectively to bring the whole unsatisfactory slave economy to a conclusion profitable to themselves. The Pinney family, according to Richard Pares, received out of the £145,000 paid to the planters of Nevis £18,500 directly and £14,000 indirectly; in other words, between 20 and 25 per cent of the total compensation due to that island —and they were only one family.[2] Another family which received very large sums were the Gladstones whose most famous scion, William, had made his maiden speech in parliament in the emancipation debate, complaining of the unpleasant references to the treatment of slaves on one of his father's estates. The Earl of Harewood, who earlier had pleaded poverty on behalf of himself and all his friends at a planters' meeting, had many claims under his own name and possibly more under the names of nominees; and a number of church dignitaries received substantial sums; the Bishop of Exeter, for example, was paid over £12,700 for 665 slaves.[3]

The accounts of the claims published later showed the differing values of slaves in the various colonies. The average price of a slave in Jamaica was £30; in Antigua, £27; in Honduras, £60.[4] In the Cape Colony, where the bulk of the claimants were of Dutch origin and owed no allegiance, except by law, to the British crown, the price paid to them in compensation caused much dissatisfaction and, according to those who left the Cape to trek into the interior of the country, was one of the main reasons for their move. Another was their horror at being treated on equal footing with 'heathen' blacks.

During 1834 and 1835, except for the few who had seen the Abolition Act for the hypocritical fraud it was, the British public seemed satisfied that it had successfully responded to its humanitarian instincts by ending the slave system in the colonies, if in name only. However, by 1836 the news coming from the colonies was disturbing enough to prompt parliament into appointing a committee to enquire into the workings of the apprenticeship system.[5]

The committee included Buxton, Dr Lushington, O'Connell, Grey, and representing the planters, William Gladstone. In view of the vastness of the subject and the short time available to produce its report, the committee limited its enquiry to Jamaica. From March to May it heard about fifteen witnesses and sifted through masses of documentary evidence. From the Governor it received letters addressed to him by fifty-three magistrates on the island in response to his request for information about the industry and conduct of the ex-slaves and the treatment of them by their former masters. The letters tended to approve of the behaviour of the ex-slaves: 'obedient and orderly'; 'gradually improving'; 'working well'; 'complaints against them decreasing'; 'civilisation, and with it some sense of moral obligation making progress among them'.

Some, though, had nothing good to say about them: 'the children growing up in total ignorance and in habits of indolence and dishonesty'; 'for the most part sullen and obstinate'; 'open acts of violence prevented only by the fear of punishment'. But the general impression conveyed to the committee was that the apprentices were 'docile and obedient as ever' which meant 'just like slaves'.

The magistrates had good and bad things to say about the masters as well; but here again the general impression was that they were behaving in a fair, judicious and encouraging manner. There had been instances of 'petty tyranny', but these were becoming fewer. Only one man was accused of 'not setting a good example; too generally living in a state of concubinage and inebriety'.

As part of their duties magistrates had to make returns of the punishments meted out to the apprentices. These, too, were produced to the committee for its inspection. It is from them that one can get a small idea of just how brutal life must have been for the slaves in the past if, in fact, the statistics represented—as presumably they were meant to do—a very great change in their circumstances as apprentices since the passing of the Act.

These returns included the name of the planter or manager, the period, the number of apprentices punished, the reasons for and the details of the punishments. The following are only a few examples from the depressingly long schedule produced to the committee:

April to July

William H. Alley—94 days—240 males, 44 females: 30 to flogging, 6 to imprisonment, 3 to the treadmill, 6 to the penal gang, 17 to solitary confinement, &c.

Donald M'Gregor—1 year—355 males, 171 females; 100 for insolence: 231 to flogging, 10 to imprisonment, 94 to the penal gang, 60 to solitary confinement, &c.

Charles Hawkins—265 days—322 males, 293 females: 246 to flogging, &c.

Edward Fishbourne—295 males, 134 females: 193 to flogging, 39 to the penal gang, &c.

Edward Baynes—365 days—640 males, 407 females; 674 for neglect of duty, 215 for disobedience, 42 for insolence: 221 to flogging, 106 to imprisonment, 11 to the treadmill, 53 to the penal gang, 92 to solitary confinement, 62 to switchings, 511 fined.

'The system of apprenticeship in Jamaica is working in a manner not unfavourable to the momentous change from slavery to freedom which is going on there', the Committee concluded in its report delivered to parliament. 'The mutual suspicion and irritation . . . appear to be gradually subsiding, and on the part of the negro population, industrious habits and the desire of moral and physical improvement seem to be gaining ground. Under these circumstances your committee feel bound to express their conviction that nothing could be more unfortunate than any occurrence which had a tendency to unsettle the minds of either class.'

The radicals outside parliament were not satisfied. Joseph Sturge was receiving communiqués from contacts in the West Indies who had very different things to report. One lawyer described the apprentices as emancipated prisoners who were liable substantially to the same punishments and laboured under the same disabilities as before.[6] He decided at the end of 1836 to see for himself, and what he witnessed in the West Indies confirmed his suspicions that the apprenticeship system was a failure.

He collected a wide range of complaints from the apprentices which varied from not enough salt fish to brutality, unjust punishments, being defrauded of their extra time, and a complete lack of hospitals and doctors. In Barbados he paid a visit to the treadmill where he saw women being brutally flogged while working the infernal machine. On one morning a group of them had been up on the treadmill four times before Sturge arrived and were due to go back twice more. He saw one woman literally suspended by the bend of the elbow of one arm, her legs knocking against the revolving steps of the mill until the steps were spattered with her blood. 'There she hung, groaning, and anon received a cut from the driver to which she appeared almost indifferent.' During the time he was there, the Barbados legislature was holding its sessions not more than thirty yards away from the treadmill.[7]

After visiting Antigua, Martinique, Montserrat, and Dominica, as well as the larger islands, Sturge returned to England and immediately published his journal of the voyage. In addition he published the story of an ex-slave whom he had fully manumitted, James Williams, which resulted in an abusive reaction from the West Indies. 'I have been flogged seven times since the new law came in', Williams wrote. 'I said it was not an earthly man that made the world, but the Man that made the world would come again. For this I was charged with insolence, and sent to the house of correction to dance the treadmill for seven days, and received twenty lashes.'[8]

Sturge was regarded as an agitator and Williams an ungrateful black. Even the Antislavery Society turned Sturge down when he applied to use the organisation and influence at its command to bring the apprenticeship system to an end. He returned to Birmingham and there formed a new committee. As August 1838 approached when the non-praedial apprentices—those who were not 'attached to the land'—were due to receive unconditional freedom, agitation grew to end the system for all apprentices. The evidence which Sturge and others produced to the public convinced many that the twenty millions Britain had paid had been taken by the West Indians under false pretences since they were entirely ignoring the Abolition Act other than collecting their compensation.

Petitions began to arrive at parliament for the immediate abolition of the apprenticeship system. One had been signed by Thomas Clarkson, now an old man in his seventies but still very much in touch with what was happening. The same Bishop of Exeter, former plantation proprietor and slave owner, presented a petition from the Wesleyan Methodists of Bath, from the Society of Friends of Sutton, from 3,175 females resident in Bradford, and from several Dissenting congregations in that town. He observed: 'I was one of those who were not very sanguine in my expectations of the results which would probably attend the emancipation of the negroes. I did not think that the negroes were sufficiently prepared for the reception of that great boon. But from all that has since transpired and from all the evidence which has been collected on the subject, I feel thoroughly convinced that the negroes are now fitted for it.'[9]

Lord Brougham, presenting the petitions to the House of Lords, quoted an opinion of the Lord Chief Justice on the Abolition Act. 'This compromise, like a thousand other attempts to reconcile right and wrong, is admitted on all hands to have failed; compulsory apprenticeship, which was another name for slavery, and could only be justified by expediency, is proved to be inexpedient, and nothing remains but the duty of the mother country to afford all her subjects the protection of equal laws.'[10] With these strong words the highest legal authority in the land condemned fifty years of parliamentary inactivity under the guise of ameliorative legislation on behalf of the slaves, and condemned, moreover, the final act of hypocrisy for the fraud it was.

Viscount Howick, on behalf of the Government, pointed out that in every country a system of forced labour made labour of all kinds hated and disgraceful. 'Do we not see that in the southern states of the American Union, and in Barbados, the white race will submit to almost any extremity of privation rather than have recourse to labour, which is degraded in their estimation by being usually the lot of the despised and miserable negro?' However, he added, since the apprenticeship system had been adopted he felt that it was in the blacks' own interest to keep them for a further period in bondage because they would otherwise sink into an unhappy state of barbarous indolence, and that would do neither them nor the economies of the colonies any good. 'For my part,' he said, 'it has always appeared to me that we are bound to regard the white inhabitants of our slave colonies, not with any feelings of irritation, or of harshness, even when we most have right to complain of their conduct, but, on the contrary, with sentiments of indulgence and compassion as persons hardly less deeply wronged than the slaves themselves.' That the slaves had not broken out in revolt was, in his opinion, a great reason for the legislature to congratulate itself. Then, taking a leaf directly out of the book of Wilberforce, Clarkson and most of the leading abolitionists, he concluded: 'True it is they have been exempt from those physical sufferings which have weighted so heavily upon the unfortunate negroes, but physical sufferings are not the worst that can be inflicted upon men—moral corruption and degradation carry with them misery, less obvious, perhaps, but not less keen, nor less lasting, and the white inhabitants of our slave colonies have been exposed to that moral blight which pervades and corrupts the air wherever slavery is allowed to exist.'[11]

In May 1838 Sir Eardley Wilmot succeeded in getting a resolution passed by the three votes to abolish immediately the apprenticeship system.[12] 'The intelligence was received with such a shout by the Quakers (myself among the number)', wrote Thomas Buxton who was then not in parliament as a Member, 'that we strangers were all turned out for rioting! I am right pleased.'[13] But it all came to nothing. When Wilmot was pressed by Lord John Russell on behalf of the Government to explain how he meant to follow up the resolution, telling him quite plainly that the Government would oppose any measure for abolishing the system, Wilmot backed down. 'It was not my intention to proceed with the matter', he said apologetically. 'The resolution will have more effect than an unsuccessful endeavour to bring in an enactment.'[14]

The whites in the colonies, notwithstanding expressions by the British Government of support and sympathy in their difficult predicament, came to realise that they had at last reached the end of the road, and that to have some blacks apprentices and others completely free would only lead to potential danger. They therefore anticipated London and reluctantly brought in emancipation enactments of their own. The smaller islands had, in fact, started earlier: Antigua two years before, Montserrat in January 1838. Nevis followed in March; Tortola in April; Barbados in May; the Bahamas and Jamaica in June; Dominica in July.[15]

In the end, for all its back-patting and self-applause, the British parliament did not actually give the slaves full and unconditional freedom. It had given them—as it had always done—the name without the substance. It had talked for fifty years about humanity and justice for the blacks. It had prided itself on ending the slave trade and colonial slavery, ending them, it must be added, with considerable reluctance and ill-will. But to what extent did its legislation affect the real situation? During those fifty years the importation to the colonies of blacks from Africa continued. During those fifty years the treatment of the slaves in the West Indies remained as brutal and unjust as it had always been. At the end of those fifty years the emancipation of the slaves from all forms of coercive labour had come as a result, finally and again with great reluctance, of the legislative acts of their former masters, the assemblies of the colonies concerned.

Because resounding speeches with noble sentiments had been made from time to time about the conditions of the slaves by men like Wilberforce, Pitt and Brougham, and because these individuals had from time to time nobly demanded an improvement in the slaves' condition and finally their emancipation, it came to be assumed, once it was all over, that parliament itself had been the powerful, forceful instrument of change. In fact, as we have seen, little had really changed, but successive members of parliament during these fifty long years—and how long they must have seemed to the slaves themselves—had taken the word for the deed. They had blinded themselves to the realities which existed outside the doors of parliament by their reverence for the spoken word and for the supposed glory of parliament to which they were forever paying exaggerated homage.

Following their politicians' lead, the British public indulged itself for nearly one hundred years in paeans of self-praise, with the result that, instead of Britain coming out of this shameful period with some humility which, if it had might have saved Africa much sorrow, it emerged with even greater arrogance. 'A great cause in which a whole people can feel themselves honoured is the prime secret of national unity and vigour', Joyce Cary wrote. Forgetting the massive opposition to emancipation within Britain and by successive British Governments, he considered that it had given to national action 'a moral dignity, very rare in history, but enormously valuable to any people and any Government'.[16]

This may be good politics or morale-boosting mythology, but surely not history. Britain's pockets had been filled by the West Indian slave system it had created. Its pride was puffed up by the erroneous belief that it had destroyed the system; but it was slavery that destroyed slavery. The economics of the system forced it in the end to collapse, as Adam Smith had predicted sixty years before it did. The emotional attitudes against it, which certainly existed in Britain—very strongly at times—and which the emancipationists channelled, helped to bring it down. But parliament and, even more so, the Governments of the time limped behind both the economic and the emotional forces at work, never really catching up with either.

The end of slavery did not mean the end of the plantation system. In the West Indies the 'grateful peasantry' of the ex-slaves which the abolitionists had predicted did not come to pass; instead the workpeople left the plantations to set up wherever they could on their own. The white plantation owners, unable to obtain white workers, looked to India for labour. Between 1833 and 1917 Trinidad imported 145,000 East Indians and British Guiana nearly a quarter of a million. Indians were also brought to other West Indian islands.[17]

The exploitation of the blacks by the whites continued in different forms in different countries. The need of the whites to justify their acts by persuading themselves of the supposed inherent inferiority of the blacks continued throughout the nineteenth and into the twentieth century. The question whether 'they' were 'fit for freedom' became 'fit for equality', and the same circular arguments heard in the emancipation debate were, and still are, applied to this new problem the whites created for themselves. The blacks, it was argued, are not yet ready for equality and have to be prepared for it by the whites; but since, so long as there is inequality they will never be ready for it, the blacks must remain forever unequal. The white man still clings in places to this antiquated logical merry-go-round; most blacks got off in disgust some time ago.

On examining some children who lately came into the school, I found many of them quite ignorant that they had a soul. They had such erroneous and confused ideas of the Deity that it seemed as though, in some cases, such an idea had never been broached to them at home. One boy told me he did not know if he had a part about him that could never die; neither had he heard of such a person as Jesus Christ. . . . These children were from seven to ten years of age.

(Mr ——,
St James, Jamaica)

We have introduced much of the infant school system into the boys' British School; such as singing, repeating the table of weights and measures. . . . This system comes down to their capacity, blends amusement with instruction, and just meets that cheerful, active, playful disposition which is everywhere found in the negro character. The apprentices are but infants in mind; they require the first rudiments of knowledge.

(The Agent for Trinidad,
November, 1837)

Report of the Trustees of Lady Mico's Charity, 31st May 1838

Dame Jane Mico bequeathed in 1670 the sum of £2,000 'to redeem poor slaves'. The Trustees (at present) include:

James Gibson	Stephen Lushington Ll.D.
John Gurney Hoare	James Stephen
Thomas Fowell Buxton	

The Trustees have only, in conclusion, to report their fixed determination . . . to persevere in imparting to the negro race those moral benefits which, under every circumstance of his condition, are best fitted for making him wise and happy.

As political economists—as men devotedly attached to the cause of the long and deeply injured negro—as Christian men desirous of giving him a moral elevation above the beasts that perish, and of placing within his reach a knowledge of his God and Saviour, the Trustees submit that the question as to whether the colonists of Great Britain shall prosper or not depends, not so much upon any act of the Legislature, however benevolent in its purpose, nor upon the administration of that act, however just, as upon the moral influence of Christian education; which, with God's blessing, is calculated to preserve these colonies no less for the aggrandisement of the State, than for the interests of that generous people whose £20,000,000 have redeemed their slave population; they, therefore, earnestly plead for the means of extending Christian education among them.

(Parliamentary Papers, Vol. VII, 1837)

Fair England, False America

Fair islands of the sunny sea! midst all rejoicing things
No more the wailing of the slave a wild discordance brings;
The pride of all fair England shall these ocean-islands be,
Whose peasantry with joyful hearts keep ceaseless jubilee.

Thus did Miss Whittier, the sister of the Quaker 'poet
laureate' of the American abolition movement, John Green-
leaf Whittier, eulogise the success of the British emancipationists after the ending of the apprenticeship system in
1838.[1] Written and dedicated to Joseph Sturge, her poem was
one of joy and sorrow; joy for her friends' achievements and
sorrow for the continuation of slavery in her own country.

The friend of freedom everywhere, how mourns he for
 our land,
The brand of whose hypocrisy burns on her guilty hand,
Republicans, yet scorning the democracy of Right
While planting upon servile necks the tyrant foot of might!

Since the early days of the movement the abolitionists
on both sides of the Atlantic had kept closely in touch with
each other, exchanging views and comparing the progress
of their respective campaigns. One of the first acts of the
Committee for the Abolition of the Slave Trade, after its
formation in 1787, was to write to the President of the
Pennsylvania Society for Promoting the Abolition of
Slavery, and the relief of free negroes unlawfully held in
bondage—to give it its full title. It can be seen from their
respective names that the ambitions of the Americans were
far greater than those of the British Committee, as the latter

pointed out in their letter. In that patronising tone which the British abolitionists occasionally adopted when addressing their American counterparts, the Committee wrote: 'Gentlemen, our satisfaction in hearing of a society established for the purpose of promoting the abolition of slavery etc. induces the committee of an institution formed with a more particular view to the discouragement of the slave trade, to give this early testimony of our hearty approbation of your benevolent plan.'[2]

What went on in America, especially as regards its slave and free black population, was always of great interest to the abolitionists in Britain and also to their West Indian opponents. Six months after its formation the Committee recorded that 'undoubted accounts have been received from North America of the good conduct and capacity of many of the negroes resident there with specimens of their improvement in useful learning at a school established in Philadelphia for their education which satisfactorily proves the absurdity of the notion that their understandings are not equally susceptible of cultivation with those of white people'.[3]

In the same year the *Gentleman's Magazine* reported the information it had received about Jededia Buxton, a slave and a 'prodigy of calculation', whose arithmetical powers were superior not only to his own people, but to most whites also. This, the *Magazine* thought, was extraordinary since 'it is somewhere remarked that few of the race of woolly-headed blacks can go further in the art of enumeration than the number 5'. Buxton was asked how many seconds a man of seventy years, some odd months, weeks and days had lived. In a minute and a half he gave the answer. His questioner, after making the same calculation on paper, said that Buxton was wrong. ' "Stop, Massa", replied the black. "You forget the Leap Years"; and on including them, the gentleman found the black man was precisely right.' The *Gentleman's Magazine* suspected some underlying political or humanitarian motive had prompted their correspondent to report the incident, but that 'by no means lessens their credit'.[4]

Ten years later the same magazine reported the speech

of Noah Webster, speaking to the Connecticut Society for the Promotion of Freedom. 'The zeal which some persons discover to effect a *sudden total abolition* of slavery in the United States appears to be very intemperate', said the celebrated lexicographer. 'It is a zeal which counteracts its own principle; for the sudden emancipation of such a number of slaves instead of bettering their condition would render it worse, and inevitably expose them to perish with cold and famine.'[5]

Most Englishmen, including the leading abolitionists, would have agreed with Mr Webster's sentiments in 1798, though this did not prevent them from criticising the Americans. What upset them most of all was the fact that the slave-owning colonies of America had gone to war with Britain for their independence and, having achieved it, had the effrontery to boast of being the land of the free. The Declaration of Independence, written by Thomas Jefferson, a slave owner, and asserting the inalienable right of every man to liberty and equality was regarded by many Englishmen as a grotesque absurdity.[6] 'As this is the land of liberty and freedom, and as every man has a right to buy a Nigger, what do you want for your Nigger?' was Charles Mathews's ironic comment.[7]

The English poet Thomas Day, who wrote the popular poem 'The Dying Negro', was far more scathing about American pretensions. In a letter in reply to an American, Colonel John Laurens, who died in the War of Independence, Day addressed himself to all Americans 'who have taken up arms against the government . . . rather than pay a tax of threepence'.[8] 'You do not go to Africa to buy or steal your Negroes', he said, referring to the fact that the Americans had not yet established in 1776 as institutionalised a slave trade as had the British; 'perhaps because you are too lazy and luxurious: but you encourage an infamous, pitiless race of men to do it for you, and conscientiously receive the fruits of their crimes. You do not, merciful men, reduce your fellow-creatures to servitude . . . men of liberal minds like yours acknowledge all mankind to be their equals. . . . Your worst actions, therefore, the greatest crimes which even your enemies can object to are only that you are the voluntary causes of all these mischiefs! You, you encourage the English pirate to violate the laws of faith and hospitality, and stimulate him to new excesses by purchasing the fruits of his rapine. Your avarice is the torch of treachery and civil war which desolates the shores of Africa, and shakes destruction on half the majestic species of man.'

Day attacked the argument which the Americans liked to use that the slave trade and slavery had been begun, not by them and their government, but by the British Government which continued to sanction it. 'The continuance of the evil is so far from justifying, that it is an exaggeration of the crime', he declared.

In words which are as relevant now as they were 200 years ago when Day wrote them, he said: 'If men would be consistent they must admit all the consequences of their own principles; and you and your countrymen are reduced to the dilemma of either acknowledging the rights of your negroes, or of surrendering your own. If there be certain natural and universal rights, as the declarations of your Congress so repeatedly affirm, I wonder how the unfortunate Africans have incurred their forfeiture. Is it the antiquity or the virtues, or the great qualities of the English Americans which constitute the difference, and entitle them to rights from which they totally exclude more than a fourth part of the species? Or do you choose to make use of that argument . . . that they are black and you white; that you have lank, long hair, while theirs is short and woolly?'

Criticism had not always been one-sided. Cotton Mather used sharp words in his letter to the Society for the Propagation of the Gospel in 1716 about the quality of their members. 'On the Continent, the Colony of Carolina, was in a fair way to have been filled with a religious people; until your Society for the Propagation of Religion in foreign parts unhappily sent over some of their missionaries thither; and, I am informed, that with them and from that time a mighty torrent of profaneness and wickedness carried all before it; and everything that might be worthy to be called religion is very much lost in that woeful country.'[9]

Edward Long, writing on behalf of all planters in America

and the West Indies in 1774, said bitterly, 'America has long been made the very common sewer and dungyard to Britain. Is it not therefore rather ungenerous and unmanly that the planter should be vilified by British men for the crimes and execrable misdeeds of British refugees.'[10]

After both nations had abolished the slave trade—Britain in 1807 and America in 1808—the British abolitionists began to blame the Americans for continuing the trade illegally. That British citizens were also participating was acknowledged, but it was the Americans and their fast clippers which were seen to be the worst culprits. For the next fifty years the stoppage by British ships of American vessels suspected of carrying slaves was one or the most explosive issues between the two countries. With both Americans and Britons involved in the illegal slave trade and both countries (up till 1833) actively supporting and encouraging the slave system, it was a case of the pretended liberal pot calling the supposed humanitarian kettle black. On the one hand the Americans upheld the principle of 'freedom of the seas'; on the other, the British claimed to act on the principle of 'rights of search'.[11] The Americans were reluctant—and frequently refused—to co-operate by allowing their ships to be searched and this, to the British abolitionists, was a constant source of anger and frustration. The result was that though the slave trade continued, both countries could feel that they were preserving their honour and holding fast to their cherished principles.

With the end of slavery in the West Indies and the continuance of the system in America, the British were able to criticise the Americans without fear of retort or retaliation. Freed of the burden of guilt which had hung over them for so long, the British could indulge themselves in odious comparisons between their own untainted virtue and the patently hypocritical American way of life.

On July 7th, 1838, Daniel O'Connell, who had fought hard for the emancipation of the British West Indian slaves, wrote to his colleague Joseph Sturge, urging him to form a society to aid in the universal abolition of slavery. 'Specify America, if you choose, or leave the name out of your plan. But frame your announcement in such a way as to enable us to begin the work with the vile and sanguinary slaveholders of Republican America. I want to be *directly* at them', he said. 'No more side-wind attacks; firing directly at the hull, as the seamen say, is my plan. . . . Our voices will go over the Atlantic and cheer the worthy abolitionists in America. . . . Raise the white flag of *universal freedom'*, he concluded with a dramatic flourish. 'We will move Britain and all Europe against the vile union of republicanism and slavery . . . and I hope soon to see the day when not a single American will be received in civilised society unless he belong to an anti-slavery union or body.'[12]

It was not only slavery that concerned the British; it was also what the slave system was doing to the white Americans who were upholding it. Now without a guilty conscience to obscure their view, they could see more clearly what until recently had been their own experience. Edward Eliot, the archdeacon of Barbados, in a sermon preached in Cornwall in 1836, referred to attacks on those Americans working for abolition. Typically, Eliot, himself no opponent of slavery while it existed in the West Indies, put aside the fact that only a few years before his brethren were being thrown out of the islands for giving aid to the blacks. These events, he commented airily, 'are now among the records of history'. But not in America.

'If we desire to see this sort of persecution fully developed and carried out into all the details of practical outrage against those who are anxious to raise the slave from his state of brutal ignorance,' he said, 'we have only to turn our eyes towards the slave districts of the United States of America. The fierceness of despotism is there triumphant. It is mournfully evidenced in furious menaces; in deeds of oppression and violence; and even in deliberate murder. If anyone in that land of partial freedom dare to instruct the wretched negro, he will truly encounter the sufferings, and he runs the hazard of experiencing the death of a martyr.'[13]

In March 1841 Joseph Sturge visited America and found to his disappointment that the abolition movement there was racked by dissension. He saw, talked and argued with as many colleagues as possible to help unite the movement.[14]

His success was small; the split was too deep to be healed by one man, but his friend, Whittier, felt that Sturge's visit had done great good for the cause of abolition. 'Prejudices have been softened,' he wrote to Sturge, 'attention aroused, and deep feeling called in many minds.'[15]

Whittier kept Sturge fully informed of the activities of the movement in America. In October 1843 he wrote: 'Heaven bless O'Connell for his noble speech on American slavery. . . . It was the blow of a giant, a well-directed and terrible in its execution.'[16] And the next year he reported; 'We have very cheering accounts of our cause in Virginia and Kentucky.'[17]

When Mrs Harriet Beecher Stowe visited England after the publication of *Uncle Tom's Cabin* in 1852 Sturge's house became one of her homes where she could find respite from the continual round of activities to which she was subjected as the authoress of one of the most successful books of the century. After one brief stay she recorded: 'My Sunday here has always seemed to me a pleasant kind of pastoral, much like the communion of Christian and Faithful on the Delectable Mountains.'[18]

Thomas Clarkson never lost contact with the abolition movement. He gave Sturge useful letters of introduction to friends in America before the latter's visit. A few years before, when he was approaching eighty (he died in 1846 at the age of eighty-six), he also took up his pen to warn America against itself. 'To be familiar with the sound of injustice daily in your ears and to lend no helping hand must produce in time a taint of corruption which must injure the moral character. Has not this corruption already begun?' he asked, and his answer in 1839 has an ominously modern sound to it. 'Has it not proceeded from Blacks to Whites? From a systematic familiarity with oppression have not your Rulers begun to oppress you, their fellow-subjects? You are forbidden to speak, you are forbidden to write on this subject. . . . Surely it could have never been foreseen that this would have been the case in the United States. It becomes you therefore to do all you can to wipe away this stain from your country. . . . to rise up under such circumstances, amidst the growing darkness and immorality spreading over your once happy land, to meet the evil in question.'[19]

Britain and the British Americans before 1776 had been, to use Benezet's phrase, *participes criminis*, since they had both been involved in the creation and expansion of the slave system. At times this partnership caused great anxiety to the Americans. In 1739 the worried inhabitants of Georgia petitioned their Governor, General Oglethorpe, to stop the importation of slaves into the colony. 'It is shocking to human nature that any race of mankind and their posterity should be sentenced to perpetual slavery', they declared self-righteously; but what they were even more concerned about was the future; 'nor in justice can we think otherwise of it than that they are thrown amongst us to be our scourge one day or other for our Sins. And as freedom must be dear to them as to us what a scene of horror must it bring about! And the longer it is unexecuted the bloody scene must be the greater.'[20] The General, of course, did not heed their warning.

The special relationship of partners in crime formally came to an end after American independence was won; the Americans were now, strictly speaking, foreigners with their own slave trade, their own slaves subject to their own laws. Independence removed from British citizenship a large and stubborn body of slave owners and made the abolition movement in Britain a possibility. 'As long as America was our own', Clarkson said in 1788, 'there was no chance that a minister would have attended to the groans of the sons and daughters of Africa, however he might feel for their distress.' But once that impediment was removed 'our affection, by a wonderful concatentation of events, has been taken off and a prospect presented to our view which shows it to be a policy to remove their pain'.[21]

From then on British and American abolitionists worked together for the same object. Regrettably for their cause, so, too did American producers and British merchants. They were selling and making vast profits from the goods the British public was buying which had been produced by slave labour, long after the abolition of the slave trade and long after the abolition of slavery in the West Indies. 'We are partners with the Southern planter', pointed out *The Times* in an editorial in 1857, 'and we take a lion's share in the profits of slavery.' Cotton, it reminded its readers, picked and cleaned by 'Uncle Tom' and his fellow-sufferers, was 'the great staple of British industry'.[22]

Fair England might have castigated false America for maintaining the slave system she had abandoned, but she thrived on it as she had done on her own system. For all the recriminations, therefore, that passed across the Atlantic, the two countries remained what they had been from the start, partners in crime, until finally economics, emotion and a civil war brought the Anglo-American system, which had lasted for practically 300 years, to an end once and for all.

The intermixture of whites, blacks and Indians has generated several different casts which have all their proper denominations invented by the Spaniards who make this a kind of science among them:

Direct lineal ascent of the Negro Venter

White man = Negro woman
|
White man = Mulatta
|
White man = Terceron
|
White man = Quateron
|
White man = Quinteron
|
White

Mediate or Stationary, neither advancing nor receding

Quateron = Terceron
|
Tente-enel-ayre

Retrograde

Mulatta = Terceron
|
Saltatras

Negro = Mulatta
|
Samba de = Negro
Mulatta |
|
Negro

Indian = Mulatta
|
Mestize

Negro = Indian
|
Samba de
Indian = Samba de
| Mulatta
|
Givero

In the Spanish colonies it is accounted most creditable to mend the breed by ascending or growing whiter. . . .

(*The History of Jamaica*—Edward Long, 1774)

To: The Reverend J. Smith, Plantation de Resouvenir.
Dear Sir,

The bearer, Dumfries, informs me he cohabited with Eve, both the property of Mr Gladstone, for some time back, and that he now wishes to marry her; I can only say that their conducts have been such since I have known them as puts it out of my power to say anything to the contrary.

John Stewart (sgd)
Plantation Success, 10 Sept 1820.

(House of Commons—Session Papers, 1824)

From Orang-outangs to Pumpkin Eaters

Anti-black feelings existed before slavery. So, probably, did anti-white feelings. Human strangers have always been suspicious of each other, and when they look different and live in very different cultures, what separates them and makes them unlike seems far more important than their similarities. Where black and white have to live together, the close proximity has in some cases reduced mutual fear and suspicion and replaced these with something approaching tolerance. The similarities have become more obvious, the differences less so. Much depends on the historical background to their coming together.

In the British West Indies and the American South the background to white/black relationships was slavery. As long as the system lasted the physical differences were deliberately exaggerated by the whites in order to justify it while the cultural distinctions were sharpened by the operation of the system itself. The whites were masters and the blacks slaves. The whites controlled all the social and economic power; the blacks none. As slaves the blacks lived in a rigidly confined area of society and their actions and responses to the whites were controlled by severe codes of custom and law, the slightest breach of which would lead to punishment.

Once the slaves were emancipated new codes of behaviour had to be invented, new patterns of response worked out by whites and blacks. To fall more or less into the same poses of superiority and inferiority was the easiest method, particularly when it was reinforced by reality: the whites still owned the land and were in control of government and the courts; the blacks still laboured in the fields and the domestic kitchens. The extreme racial prejudices which were an essential part of the life of the slave colonies became, if possible, even more extreme as former owners confronted the formerly owned.

In the Cape Colony the situation altered with emancipation, because the white slave owners left their homes to trek north. In so doing they came face to face with blacks as enemies in combat. The white man's defeat of the black confirmed his technical superiority, and once he established his villages and towns in the interior, he could again adopt the extreme postures of masterhood in relationship to the conquered blacks around him which he had abandoned when he left the Cape Colony.

Anti-black feelings of the whites outside the slave states of America and the sugar islands tended in the main to be personal, vague, incoherent and variable so long as slavery was acceptable. However, once the system came under scrutiny and had been challenged on moral and religious grounds, these attitudes became more general, more coherent, more concrete and inflexible. The casual interest of the philosopher-scientist of the seventeenth and early eighteenth centuries in such topics as the origin and cause of the black pigmentation of the skin became distorted as the need to defend opinions about slavery and racial differences became more urgent. Curiosity and supposition about racial distinctions gave way to certainty and dogmatism; respect for differences became contempt and even hatred; attempts to reason gave way to racism.

In the journal of his African voyage the botanist, Adanson, observed that 'in general the negroes are very human and hospitable'. He found this the case because, instead of making judgments on the flimsy evidence of other people, he went to see for himself. 'I never departed from this principle that nothing contributes more to gain the confidence and friendship of strangers among whom you reside than to conform to their customs and manner of living.'[1] However, when his book came out in England in the mid-eighteenth century his translator already felt it necessary to point out, in direct contradiction to the sentiments generally expressed by the author, that 'from so exact and judicious a narrative one may therefore form a just idea of this part of Africa; a country overspread with misery, the natural consequence of laziness.'[2]

David Hume, the Scots philosopher, could not have met many Africans, slave or free, yet unlike Adanson he was quite prepared to pass judgment on them in a note to his essay *Of National Characters*. 'I am apt to suspect the negroes ... to be naturally inferior to the whites. There never was a civilised nation of any other complexion than white, nor even any individual eminent either in action or speculation. No ingenious manufactures amongst them, no arts, no science.'[3] A fellow-Scot, James Beattie, whose *Essay on Truth* was written against Hume, said that Hume could not possible generalise about character for the simple reason that 'no man could have sufficient evidence except from a personal acquaintance with all the negroes that are now, or ever were, on the face of the earth'. Beattie went on to make the point which has taken Europeans 200 years to realise, and even now with reluctance: 'That every practice and sentiment is barbarous which is not according to the usages of modern Europe seems to be a fundamental maxim with many of our critics and philosophers.'[4]

Travellers who went to Africa to observe and not to judge almost invariably returned with good things to say about the particular people they met. Other writers who did not travel, but who read the journals, selected from them the points critical of particular individuals or tribes and generalised for all Africans on this basis. The favourable judgments of the travellers were usually lumped together as 'exceptions', and certain features were interpreted in such a way as to appear in the black man as odious which in the white man would be considered praiseworthy.

'The portrait of the negro has seldom been drawn but by the pencil of his oppressor, and he has sat for it in the distorted attitude of slavery', was how the African Institution saw the position. 'If he be accused of brutal stupidity by one of those prejudiced witnesses, another taxes him with the most refined dissimulation and the most ingenious methods of deceit. If the negroes are represented as base and cowardly, they are in the same volume exhibited as braving death in the most hideous forms. . . . Insensibility and excessive passion, apathy and enthusiasm, want of natural affection, and a fond attachment to their friends . . . are all ascribed to them by the same inconsistent pens.'[5]

The Europeans saw Africa as one homogeneous country and the Africans as one people with slight local differences here and there. They, of course, did not see themselves in that way, though, no doubt, the Africans did. It was generally believed by Europeans that most Africans were cannibals. Travellers wrote of being told about such-and-such a king who ate his prisoners of war, though none actually saw it happening. On such flimsy evidence was the belief founded. For Edward Long it was enough. 'The difficulty indeed of believing it to be true is much lessened when we reflect on the sanguinary, cruel temper and filthy practices of these people in other respects', he wrote in *The History of Jamaica*.[6]

What Long was probably not aware of was that Africans were convinced that Europeans were also cannibals. Slaves waiting to be transported had seen with their own eyes their fellows leave the coast in ships; they had never seen them return. This cultural curio even cropped up in a contemporary poem:

> Here de white man beat de black man,
> Till he's sick and cannot stand.
> Sure de black be eat by white man!
> Will not go to white man land.[7]

Long's *History of Jamaica* was an extended attempt to justify slavery by a detailed exposition and explanation of the supposed 'natural inferiority' of the black man. In the obituary notice in the *Gentleman's Magazine* in 1813 it was said that Long's judgeship in Jamaica had given him every opportunity of 'procuring authentic materials which he digested with ingenuity and candour'.[8] What, in fact, it had given him was the opportunity to collect material to support previously held views about the blacks; to support, in other words, his extreme racial prejudices.

The mechanism of racial prejudice works by selecting such information which conforms to previously held opinions about the racial group towards which the prejudice is directed; by distorting the information which does not fit these opinions, and by making exceptions when it is impossible to either ignore or distort certain facts.[9] In Long all these three were at work. Despite the lengthy and detailed analyses of 'the negro character', the actual information—as opposed to opinion—which he imparted was very limited. He would go on for paragraphs about the social and sexual habits of the blacks, selecting and distorting, to produce a picture of them as being no better than beasts—a picture he had in his mind before he started. What then he was describing was not the people as they were, but a mental image he had of them.

'At their meals they tear the meat with their talons and chuck it by handfuls down their throats with all the voracity of wild beasts.' Of the slaves from Guinea: 'Their hearing is remarkably quick; their faculties of smell and taste are truly bestial, nor less their commerce with the other sex; in these acts they a libidinous and shameless as monkeys and baboons.'[10] Where available facts contradicted his prejudices, Long had to make exceptions, and then only partially and reluctantly: 'we have heard but of one or two insignificant tribes who comprehend anything of mechanic arts or manufacture; and even these for the most part are said to perform their work in a very bungling and slovenly manner, perhaps not better than an orang-outang might, with a little pains, be brought to do.'[11]

Colour being the most obvious distinguishing feature between master and slave it was bound to become closely associated with notions of 'superiority' and 'inferiority'. Long devoted much space to the subject. In talking about Africa he advanced the theory that the part of the continent which was 'blackest', i.e. 'negro-land', was the more 'backward', and by backward Long meant—as did most writers—less European. 'As we receded from Negro-land this blackness gradually decreases. . . . We observe the like gradations of the intellectual faculty, from the first rudiments perceived in the monkey kind to the more advanced stages of it in apes, in the orang-outang, that type of man, and the Guinea negro; and ascending from the varieties of this class to the lighter casts, until we mark its utmost limit of perfection in the pure white.'[12] Ironically, Long was writing more than a century before either Rhodesia or South Africa came into existence, but how vigorously would the present white inhabitants of those two countries applaud Long's sentiments.

Regrettably for the relationships between black and white, the kind of nonsense Long wrote was not universally rejected, but instead was considered by his contemporaries as containing 'much just reasoning'.[13] Yet there were writers who had the wit to prick the arrogant bubble of white pretensions. In *The History of the Travels of Scarmentado* Voltaire wrote of the traveller to Africa who was taken captive by the blacks. 'Our captain railed bitterly against the captors, asking them the reason why they thus outrageously violated the laws of nations? They replied, your nose is long, and ours is flat; your hair is straight, and our wool is curled; you are white, and we are black; consequently we ought, according to the sacred and unalterable laws of nature, to be ever enemies. You buy us on the coast of Guinea as if we were not human creatures, then treat us like beasts . . . and therefore when we meet with you and are the strongest we make you our slaves and force you to till our ground, or else we cut off your nose and ears. We had nothing to say against this wise discourse. I was employed to till the ground of an old Negro woman, having no inclination to lose either my nose of my ears.'[14]

The European's image of the innocent savage was used by him as an object of both envy and contempt. On to it the white man could project anything he wished; most of all he was able to project all the secret desires which his own society was trying with increasing determination to suppress. By condemning these desires in the black man he was able to overcome his sense of guilt for experiencing them in himself.

The frequent reference to bestiality and to the sexuality of the blacks in Long's work indicate in him some strongly suppressed desires for the forbidden pleasures of the flesh. Long talked of the large size of the nipples of black women;[15] he said that their men had 'no taste but for women',[16] and that in the wilds of Africa where the thickness of the jungle could hide what went on orang-outangs carried off black women to enjoy them.[17] 'Ludicrous as the opinion may seem I do not think that an orang-outang husband would be any dishonour to an Hottentot female; for what are these Hottentots? . . . They are more like beasts than men.'[18] The people from Guinea were the same. 'The equally hot temperament of their women had given probability to the charge of their admitting these animals frequently to embrace.'[19] Finally, the picture he drew of black cannibals enjoying their feast had the same kind of obscene quality and the same neurotic projection of repressed desires common to all racist literature. 'Why should we doubt but that the same ravenous savage who can feast on the roasted quarters of an ape (that *mock-man*) would not be less delighted with the sight of a loin or buttock of human flesh prepared in the same manner?'[20]

Long's views, though influential, were extreme rather than typical for their time; but most sane, sensible men found it difficult, if not impossible to distinguish between the institution of slavery which their Government condoned and the people who were enslaved. They could condemn the slave system for what it did to slaves, yet still hold the slaves in contempt. They could admire qualities in the blacks, yet condemn them for being slaves. Dr. George Pinckard illustrates the confusion which existed in the minds of liberal thinking men of the period. He was a fellow of the Royal College of Physicians and in 1806 he published an account of a sojourn in the West Indies[21] which the abolitionist, James Stephen, referred to with approval.[22]

Pinckard's book is a mixture of sensitive observation and prejudice. He describes a slave women in a West Indian tavern with skill and sympathy. 'Her whole deportment bespoke a degree of refinement, with a superiority of understanding; and indicated talents capable of high improvement. Probably, if fortune had so placed her life in as to have offered her the acquirements of a chaste and cultivated education, this woman, notwithstanding the colour of her skin, would have made a faithful and virtuous wife; been an ornament of her friends and society, and a blessing to the man who should have made her the partner of his hours.' A few pages back, however, he scorns the black slaves, struggling for room in their cramped holds of the slave ships, for their 'filthy habit of depositing their natural excretions upon the spot where they sleep'.[23]

Pinckard saw slavery at first-hand, 'and while nature animates my breast with even the spark of humanity, I can never forget it! . . . I endeavoured to combat the effect of these impressions by directing my mind to . . . the kind treatment of negroes under humane masters . . . but all in vain! The repugnant influence would not thus be cheated. With such distress before my eyes, all palliatives were un-availing. The whole was wrong, and not to be justified. I felt that I execrated every principle of the traffic. Nature revolted at it; and I condemned the whole system of slavery under all its forms and modifications.'[24]

Yet, in spite of this outright and wholesale condemnation, Pinckard was unable to take the next step and suggest eman-cipation. To do this meant facing the idea of the black man as his equal. This he apparently could not do. He had seen him only as an abject slave, grovelling, beaten and humiliated, and he had identified that state with the man. If slaves were suddenly emancipated they would all be kings, all be planters and not labourers. 'In the gloomy imbecility of their uncultivated faculties they would be jealous of the whites; and suspicious of future chains; hence to give them unbridled liberty would be to let loose an irritated race of beings.' Either the ex-slaves would murder every white or they would 'sink into the torpid states of their darker brethren of the African forests, and relapse into a state of rude and savage nature'. Here, Pinckard was imitating Edward Long, projecting on to the 'savage' every-thing that his own society hankered after but condemned. 'Their wants being few, and their food easily procured, their exertions would only be commensurate to their cravings: disdaining labour, they would repose under the soft shade of the plaintain, equally regardless of the riches of commerce and the honours of industry. The yam, the plaintain, and the pepper-pot, the banjar, the merry dance, and their beloved Wowski would gratify all their wishes and crown their highest ambition.'[25]

Pinckard's solution was to bring 'people of colour', that is, children of mixed parentage, and any blacks 'as might display any peculiar marks of intellect' to England to be educated. The coloured inhabitants and then, presumably, the blacks, having acquired an English education, would be made fellow-citizens with the whites . . . 'and they would aspire to be Englishmen!'[26] With local variations, this was the idea that many 'liberals' in South Africa had, and possibly still have, to solve their racial problems. It is also the cherished ideal of the Portuguese whites in the Portuguese 'provinces' in Africa; by allowing certain blacks to become educated and assimilated, they hope to put a barrier between themselves and the rest of the black population. What happens, of course, is that, having acquired the white man's education, the 'coloured' or black man becomes the leader of the organised resistance to white domination. This the South African rulers realised, and they changed their education policies for the blacks so that, instead of the latter aspiring to be equal to the whites, they would be content to be blacks and, therefore, 'inferior'.

In 1824 James Stephen, who like Pinckard had direct experience of slavery in the West Indies, wrote a two-volume treatise on the subject.[27] In it he examined more objectively than Pinckard the way in which the characteristics of slavery had been grafted on to the character of the black man by the white man. His discussion of racial prejudice is for its time remarkably clear and rational, yet it reveals in the words used some of Stephen's deep-seated prejudices. 'As the African race only can be enslaved, the abject and vicious character known to be commonly produced by the state itself is naturally associated and confounded in the imaginations of the superior class with the disgusting exterior of that enslaved people as if it were generated by blood than by their degraded and brutalised condition; though if we may rely on the best authorities there is not on earth an uncivilised people chargeable with fewer vices or possessed of a larger share of amiable qualities than negroes in their native land. . . . Amiable qualities are proverbially more pleasing when found in a beautiful person . . . so also vice becomes more odious when coupled with bodily deformity. Can it be doubted then that vices inseparable from slavery excite the more disgust from the unsightly exterior under which they are always discovered? That the slave is more hated and despised because he is a negro; and the negro more repulsive because he is a slave?'

In a note to this point Stephen remarked that the term 'slave' was not one of obloquy or reproach, but that 'amidst all the reviling epithets used in anger towards these poor bondmen 'you negro' pronounced with angry or contemptuous emphasis is a word of superlative reproach. . . . In the colonies it is not said by way of depreciating one of slavish extraction that his mother, grandmother, or ancestor was a 'slave' . . . but that he is a *coloured person*, or that he has 'black blood in his veins' . . . nor is there any moral obloquy that bears any proportion to this disgrace.'[28]

Stephen's prejudices are mild in comparison to those expressed by another leading abolitionist, Henry Brougham, when he was a young man. In his early study on the colonial policies of Britain, France and the other European Powers he also showed how the intelligent man could at one moment express firm emancipationist views and at the other reveal attitudes which rivalled those of the most diehard white colonist. 'It cannot be doubted that the total abolition of slavery in any of the sugar colonies and the cultivation of its territories by free subjects whose constitutions are adapted to the climate would be attended with the most beneficial effects.' Brougham maintained.[29] Yet, when speaking of the blacks in relationship to the whites as equals he regarded them as 'the common enemy'. 'The negroes, then, are the enemy most to be dreaded in America by all Europeans; they are the natural foes of those white men who are distinguished from them by indelible marks in body, and by marks almost indelible in mind. . . . The negroes are alike hostile to all who have been masters of Africans; to all who are civilised and white . . . a peace with such men must be chimerical—a mere truce with the wild leaders of savage tribes whose numbers surround and overwhelm the handful of their weak and polished enemies.'

More than anything else Brougham feared the foundation of black republics like Haiti; in other words he feared black men as equals. 'If any power, then, deserves the name of a natural enemy it is the negro commonwealth; a state with which no other power can live in amity or form an alliance.' So great was Brougham's fear and hatred of a state of free and equal blacks that he even recommended that if Britain and France, who were then (1803) at war with each other, valued their colonial possessions 'it becomes them to unite against this tremendous enemy'.[30] Having put these views on record, it is no wonder that Brougham was hounded for them by his West Indian opponents throughout his involvement with the abolitionist cause. Despite his public renunciation of them, Brougham was never allowed to forget that, at heart, he was no different from the men he condemned.

Pinckard and Brougham attacked the system of slavery, but feared and held the black man in contempt. In contrast, Bryan Edwards, a planter, West Indian merchant, and outstanding advocate of colonial interests, considered slavery merely 'a calamity interwoven into the constitution of the world for purposes inscrutable to man'. Yet he was able to write with all sincerity a love poem in celebration of the beauty and intelligence of an African woman and to regard her in every way the equal of the white woman.

> O sable queen! thy mild domain
> I seek, and court thy gentle reign
> So soothing, soft and sweet;
> Where meeting love, sincere delight,
> Fond pleasure, ready joys invite,
> And unbought raptures meet.
>
> The lovliest limbs her form compose,
> Such as her sister Venus chose,
> In Florence where she's seen;
> Both just alike, except the white,
> No difference, no—none at night
> The beauteous dames between.[31]

In the eighteenth and early nineteenth centuries it was still possible to hold such contrasting and variable views on colour and race as Pinckard's, Stephen's and Edwards's. By the mid-nineteenth century, with the West Indian slaves already emancipated and the North American slaves soon to be, attitudes had polarised. The black man, no longer merely a chattel, an object to be bought and sold, had to be forcibly subjected wherever he threatened the security of the whites, or stood in the way of white imperialism.

'Twenty millions, a mere trifle dispatched with a single dash of the pen, are paid, and far over the sea we have a few black persons rendered extremely "free" indeed', complained Thomas Carlyle in his essay, *On the Nigger Question*.[32] 'Sitting yonder with their beautiful muzzles up to their ears in pumpkins, imbibing sweet pulps and juices; the grinder and incisor teeth ready for ever new work, and the pumpkins as cheap as grass in those rich climates; while the sugar crops rot around them uncut because labour cannot be hired so cheap as pumpkins.'

Carlyle, who was years later offered a state pension for his contribution to English language and thought by Disraeli and a burial at Westminster Abbey, expressed in the essay published in 1849 not only his hatred for all the so-called liberal and philanthropic movements, which had, in his opinion, brought about a state of ruin in the colonies, but also his hatred for the black man—a hatred made much more vehement by the fact that the latter represented some kind of threat to his security. 'A true work of the devil' was how John Stuart Mill described the essay, but it was a work with an already established ancestry and, worse still, an ever-reproductive progeny, the end of which is still not in sight.

Not pseudo-scientific (as Edward Long's), but teasingly facetious was the tone adopted by Carlyle to express his tormented image of his stereotypical black man. The white man was the 'enchanter' who brought order to the chaos of the West Indies; he was the hero and he alone could compel. The black man, however, had 'an indisputable and perpetual *right* to be compelled by the real proprietors . . . to do competent work for his living. . . . If your nigger will not be induced? In that case it is full certain he must be compelled; should and must.'

The morbid fear of the black man was revealed in the

contemptuous picture he drew of 'poor Quashee'. 'I decidedly like poor Quashee; and find him a pretty kind of man. With a pennyworth of oil you can make him a handsome glossy thing of Quashee. . . . A swift, supple fellow; a merry-hearted, grinning, dancing, singing, affectionate kind of creature, with a great deal of melody and amenability in his composition.' In this caricature are echoes of the comic 'nigger' of the turn of the century, but the use Carlyle put it to was different from that of Dibdin or Mathews. He was making not jokes, but a political statement as was Edward Long. It was politically necessary for the future of white supremacy that the black man be seen to be inferior so that he could be kept in an inferior social and economic position. 'Not a square inch of soil in those fruitful Isles, purchased by British blood, shall any black man hold to grow pumpkins for him, except on terms that are fair towards Britain.' Carlyle did not want a 'black Ireland' of chaos and poverty, but a West Indies with a black working population in adquate numbers, 'all "happy" if they find it possible'. 'The thing must be done everywhere; *must* is the word. . . . you will have to be servants to those that are born wiser than you, that are born lords of you; servants to the whites if they *are* (and what mortal can doubt they are?) born wiser than you.'

Carlyle died in 1881, long after the original abolitionists had come together to end the slave trade, long after the Clapham Sect had met at the homes of Wilberforce and Thornton. Yet there was a curious family link between them. A close disciple and friend of Carlyle's, and one of his executors, Sir James Fitzjames Stephen, was the grandson of James Stephen. There was another even more important link in the attitudes they held. Though Wilberforce would have dismissed Carlyle's essay as 'imbecile' as he had done another piece of racist literature,[33] he did express similar sentiments to Carlyle's, less crudely and for different reasons. On the one hand he and the members of his group rejected the notion that white was naturally superior to black. 'On the whole our observations are not of that length of time and accuracy of manner on which to build the fond opinion of northern superiority and reason, and revelation forbids the haughty thought', wrote the Reverend James Ramsay.[34] On the other hand the abolitionists were faced with the facts of black technical inferiority which allowed them to be captured and turned into slaves. Their problem, as they saw it, was to explain to the public why the African did not comport himself like a European, why he had different social codes which by European standards were 'immoral', and why, above all, he was not a Christian, did not believe in Christ, and exhibited no great desire to do so. To say that it was his nature was to fall into the racist's trap: since he was inferior, why not use him for inferior slave work? To say that he was the same in all respects as the white man was patently untrue if one judged all blacks —as they did—by the narrow standards of the literate, wealthy European gentleman. Their answer was to say that slavery made the black man what he was, but that by converting him to Christianity—and freeing his soul from barbarous paganism, if not freeing his body—he could be made virtually the same as the white man.

In their view he could never be exactly the same. The abolitionists anticipated Carlyle's picture of the happy peasants of the West Indies, toiling in the sun for the benefit of the white man. Blinkered by their prejudices and inhibited by their lack of imagination, they, too, were unable to conceive of the emancipated slaves as men equal in every respect to their former white masters. Wilberforce, when he referred to emancipation always spoke of the future ex-slaves as the 'grateful peasantry'. 'I own I look forward, and I hope do many others, to the time when the West Indies shall have the full enjoyment of a free, moral, industrious peasantry.'[35] Years later he was still looking forward to the time 'when these unhappy beings might exchange their degraded state of slavery for that of a free and industrious peasantry.'[36] 'Taught by Christianity, they will sustain with patience the sufferings of their actual lot, while the same instructions will rapidly prepare them for a better; and instead of being objects at one time of contempt and at another of terror . . . they will soon be regarded as a grateful peasantry,' was how he put it in his essay on slavery.[37]

Even Joseph Sturge, who quarrelled with Wilberforce on almost everything else, repeated the same idea in a letter to a friend in 1838: 'If they [the negroes] can get fair and equitable wages, and if they are industrious, they will be one of the most prosperous peasantry in the world.'[38]

The abolitionists, by introducing the element of Christianity into their view of the black man, managed to extricate themselves from the difficulty that the logic of their position forced them into. So long as the black man remained a heathen he could never be equal to the white man; once he became a Christian he was on the road to equality, but as it was only the white man who could give him what he lacked, who could bring to him the light of the Gospel, he would always remain to some extent inferior even when he was converted. The relative positions of white and black would therefore in their view always be that of teacher and students, minister and congregation, or, as it turned out, governor and governed.

The extreme racism of Carlyle with its fevered images of the heroic white man, 'the rose-pink cant all peeled away . . . remorseless, fierce as the old Buccaneers . . . worthy to be called old Saxons' wielding absolute command over pumpkin-eating black 'Quashees' in perpetuity[39] never became the respectable white view of the relationships between the races. The abolitionists' apparently more moderate, but, in fact, more dangerous because more subtle, view did.

The presence of these degraded people in a colony, whether they are negro slaves, 'free niggers', convicts in bondage . . . is a public nuisance, a political danger, and a social plague. . . . Africa is the country from which it is proposed that the emigras tion of labour should be attracted: and there are some provision- for causing the civilisation of negroes in the West Indies to have some good effect on the barbarism of Africa. . . . It is a scheme for wounding slavery and the African slave trade at its roots.

(*A View of the Art of Colonisation*—
Edward Gibbon Wakefield, 1849)

Extract from a *Report from the Select Committee* to consider what measures ought to be adopted with regard to the Native Inhabit-ants of Countries where British Settlements are made . . .
T. F. Buxton, in the Chair
Rev. Wm Shaw: (6 years in S. Africa)
Question: Without reference to their kind reception of you, did you find them uncivilised and sunk in ignorance?
Shaw: I found them in an exceedingly ignorant and degraded condition.
Question: How did you acquire influence amongst them?
Shaw: Very gradually, and by taking all opportunities of proving myself their real friend.
Question: And by being so superior in knowledge?
Shaw: Probably that had its influence; no doubt it had.

(House of Commons—Session Papers, Vol. VII, 1836)

We have long laid to our souls the flattering unction that we are a civilised and a Christian people. We talk of all other nations in all other quarters of the world as savages, barbarians, uncivilised. It is high time that we looked a little more rigidly into our pretences. It is high time that we examined, on the evidence of facts, whether we are quite so refined, quite so civilised, quite so Christian as we have assumed to be. It is high time that we look boldly into the real state of the question, and learn actually whether the mighty distance between our goodness and the moral depravity of other people really exists. Whether, in fact, we are Christian at all!

(*Colonisation and Christianity*—William Howitt, 1838)

Philanthropists and Conquerors

'Today Mr Malthus called on me and stated that he is not a favourer of the slave trade, and that he intends to add an appendix to his essay to that effect.'[1] With these words spoken on the occasion of the momentous second reading of the Slave Trade Abolition Bill in 1807, William Wilberforce unwittingly introduced a connection between two subjects—overpopulation and the slave trade—which in time would merge together into a third subject of all-consuming importance to Britain—imperialism.

Thomas Malthus published his *Essay on the Principle of Population* in 1798, in which he suggested that the human population was growing faster than its means of subsistence, and that if it continued to increase it would eventually starve. In 1801 the first census taken in England confirmed what many had been fearing—that the country was becoming overpopulated. After the Napoleonic wars unemployment rose rapidly, and this combined with the threat of starvation resulting from overpopulation started an agitation for emigration. For many thousands for whom starvation was no longer a threat but a fact emigration meant survival. Space had to be found for the poor and destitute of Britain and Ireland in the continents across the sea. The only way in which this space could properly be secured for the emigrants was to colonise it, and to colonise meant to expand Britain's empire.

The old colonial system of America and the West Indies declined after the loss of the American colonies; and the economic instability of the sugar islands had become so endemic by the beginning of the nineteenth century that they could not be regarded as effective colonies able to support large numbers of skilled and unskilled British citizens. If emigration was ever to become a viable alternative to overpopulation and starvation it was necessary to find new land and to found new colonies. 'Colonising can only be looked to as the means of salvation to the kingdom of Great Britain', said the *Anti-Jacobin Review* in November 1816. Reactionary in most of its politics, in this it was ahead of its time because successive British Governments rejected the call to make new colonies, though this did not stop them from acquiring more land for Britain; in Southern Africa, for example, during the nineteenth century, through a series of military campaigns, the so-called Kaffir Wars, large acquisitions were made by white settlers which would later be incorporated by Britain into her African empire.[2]

Through the 1820s and 1830s the urge to emigrate grew. In 1826 the House of Lords received petitions from the poor in the manufacturing districts for aid to emigrate,[3] and in the same year the House of Commons introduced resolutions stating that emigration was a measure necessary to relieve the distressed areas of the country.[4] The 1840s and 1850s saw the start of mass emigration: three and a half million to the United States, one and a half million to Canada, one million to Australia.[5] Africa did not attract the emigrants, nor did it greatly interest the British Government until the latter part of the nineteenth century. The only people interested in Africa up to that time were the missionaries and those closely associated with them in ideas and organisations—the slave trade abolitionists.

From the very early days of the abolition movement, trade with Africa was regarded as a necessary part of their programme. If a legitimate trade between Africa and Britain could be established this would in time supplant the need of both the British merchants and the Africans to deal in slaves. 'It must be acknowledged that the amount of British manufactures exported to the coasts of Africa for the purposes of this commerce is considerable', read a report of the Committee for the Abolition of the Slave Trade in 1788, 'but there is room to apprehend that demand for those would be much greater if in the place of it [the slave trade] was substituted an amicable intercourse which instead of spreading distress and devastation amongst the unoffending inhabitants would introduce the blessings of peace and civilisation.'[6]

In 1792 when William Pitt was still enthusiastic about abolition he conjured up for parliament a picture of the future prospects for Africa. 'We may live to behold the natives of Africa engaged in the calm occupations of industry, in the pursuits of a just and legitimate commerce. We may behold the beams of science and philosophy breaking in upon their land, which, at some happy period in still later times, may blaze with full lustre. . . . Then we may hope that even Africa . . . shall enjoy at length, in the evening of her days, those blessings which have descended so plentifully upon us in a much earlier period of the world. Then also will Europe, participating in her improvement and prosperity, receive an ample recompense for the tardy kindness of no longer hindering that continent from extricating herself out of the darkness.'[7]

In 1807 when the African Institution was founded, the original committee members stated quite clearly in their Rules that it was no part of their plan to purchase territory in Africa, to found a colony, or even to carry on commerce. All they wanted to do was to 'diffuse knowledge and to excite industry in Africa by methods adapted to the peculiar situation and manners of the inhabitants'. Their desire to 'help' Africa was also inspired by a wish to compensate the continent for the depravations caused by the slave traders. 'Let our benevolence interpose to repair the ruin and degradation which we have contributed to bring upon her.'[8]

British benevolence did not mean money; it did not mean ploughs; it did not mean food; it did not mean technical know-how. It meant Christianity. Just as the West Indian slaves on their emancipation were to receive the benefits of conversion as their compensation while their masters got the cash, so the Africans—and, indeed, any other society or tribe upon whom the British settled themselves—were to receive the Gospel for the wrongs committed by their traders. As Archdeacon Broughton of New South Wales said: 'Natural and much more Christian equity points out that, as in the occupation of their soil we are partakers of their worldly things, so in justice should they be of our spiritual. As through the tender mercy of our God the dayspring from on high has visited us, we are solemnly engaged to impart to them the glorious beams of Gospel truth, to guide their feet into the way of peace.'[9]

Broughton was giving evidence to a select committee of the House of Commons and the title of the committee's report accurately reflects the mood of the day (1836): 'Report . . . to consider what measures ought to be adopted with regard to the Native Inhabitants of Countries where British Settlements are made, and to the neighbouring Tribes, in order to secure them the due observance of Justice and the protection of their rights; and to promote the spread of civilisation among them, and to lead them to the peaceful and voluntary reception of the Christian Religion.'[9] It is not surprising that Thomas Fowell Buxton was the chairman of the committee.

The eagerness of the 'saints' to spread the Gospel to the heathen grew with their obsession with the continuance of the slave trade. The British, the Americans and the Swedes were all still at it, the African Institution reported in 1810. 'Vessels under foreign flags have been fitted out in the ports of Liverpool and London for the purpose of carrying slaves from the coast of Africa to the Spanish and Portuguese settlements in America.'[10] The Americans as always were regarded as the worst culprits. 'Instead of the large commodious vessels which it would be to the interest of the slave trader to employ, we have, by our interference forced him to use American clippers,' a British naval captain reported. 'Every quality [has been] sacrificed for speed. In the holds of these vessels the unhappy victims of European cupidity are stowed literally in bulk.'[11]

'Twice as many human beings are now its victims as when William Wilberforce and Thomas Clarkson entered upon their noble task', Thomas Buxton said of the foreign slave trade in his *magnum opus*, *The African Slave Trade and its Remedy*, published in 1840. 150,000 blacks were being imported into Brazil, Cuba, Puerto Rico, Buenos Aires, and the United States. 'Every day which we pass in security and peace at home witnesses many a herd of wretches toiling over the wastes of Africa to slavery or death.' He hoped that all Christian powers would unite to end the trade and to call 'into action the dormant energies of Africa', but if this was not possible, Britain would have to undertake the task alone.

The first step was to increase the naval patrol around the African coast, to make the trade more precarious and less profitable; but this was a negative approach. It was far more important to 'elevate the native mind . . . and to provide a larger source of revenue than that derived from the trade in man'. He objected to the suggestion that Britain's interest in Africa might have been actuated by anything other than humanity. 'We know from the Duke of Wellington's dispatches that the Powers on the continent were absolutely incredulous as to the purity of motives which prompted us . . . to urge beyond everything else the extinction of the slave trade. . . . It should then be made manifest to the world that the moving spring is humanity, that if England makes settlements on the African coast it is only for the more effectual attainment of her great object; and that she is not allured by the hopes of either gain or conquest, or by the advantages, national or individual, political or commercial, which may, I doubt not, will follow the undertaking.'

He disclaimed—as had all the abolitionists before him—any disposition to erect a new empire in Africa, but added that 'granting that the danger to African liberty is as imminent as I consider it to be slight, still the state of the country is such that, change as it may, it cannot change for the worse.' In other words, if Britain was to erect an empire in Africa, it could only be for Africa's good. 'I believe that Great Britain can, if she will, under the favour of the Almighty, confer a blessing on the human race. It may be that at her bidding a thousand nations now steeped in wretchedness, in brutal ignorance, in devouring superstition, possessing but one trade . . . shall under British tuition emerge from their debasement, enjoy a long line of blessings.'

Buxton did not stop at merely outlining his suggestions

in the book. He went further and organised an expedition
to West Africa. It consisted of one frigate and two steamers,
and they were ordered to explore the banks of the Niger
and, if possible, to start commercial relations with the tribes
living there. They were given a great send-off on the Thames
by no less a personage than the Prince Consort; but the
expedition was a complete failure: forty-one out of the 300
men died of fever and nothing was accomplished. Buxton
was severely criticised.[12] His book, however, did lead to
another, longer-lasting result: the establishment of the
Society for the Extinction of the Slave Trade and for the
Civilisation of Africa. Despite its presumptuous title, it only
lasted a few years before being dissolved, but it did revive an
interest in the slave trade and fostered the agitation against
it which has lasted through to the present day.

The coercion policy of maintaining naval patrols which
Buxton had praised in 1840 fell into disfavour. It was costly
in men and equipment, it was dangerous, it increased the
sufferings of the slaves, it excited animosity from foreign
powers who objected to having their ships searched or captured, and it did not work very effectively. This was proved
by the fact that many thousands of slaves in the slave states
of America still could not speak English, or so claimed Mr
William Hutt in a Commons debate on the subject in 1845.[13]
'The Papers before the House constantly refer to slave ships
belonging to American owners, fitted out with American
capital, sailing under American colours.' It was preposterous
to meddle and interfere out of Britain's sphere of action, and
besides it had cost the country about £15 million since the
end of the war with Napoleon. He called on the Government
to stop the cruisers, to encourage commerce with Africa,
and to form simple and inexpensive settlements on both sides
of the African coast. He concluded with a warning to
America that if she persisted in encouraging slavery she
would see her most prosperous provinces going the way of
San Domingo!

Sir George Stephen also criticised the pretended humanity
of Buxton's plan for Africa. 'If we found settlements in
Africa,' he wrote in an open letter to the then Colonial
Secretary, Lord John Russell, 'colonisation must follow. . . .

It is sheer hypocrisy to pretend that this is not the consequence of our civilisation plans . . . and therefore I do
most deeply regret the postponement of a legislative or at
least an official declaration of the principles on which the civil
government of all British possessions in Africa will hereafter
be conducted.'[14]

Side by side with the abolitionists' insistence on bringing
a regular trade and Christianity to Africa was the growing
demand for more countries to emigrate to in safety. Both
these demands later merged and were satisfied—as far as
Africa is concerned—by imperial expansion. The impulse
to colonise was strengthened by the arrogant belief in the
superiority of the white Briton, a belief consistently pro-
moted by the abolitionists.

In 1838 William Howitt, a Quaker's son whose wife,
Mary, was the English translator of Hans Christian Ander-
sen, wrote an influential work entitled *Colonization and
Christianity*. It was a fierce attack on British colonial policies
up until that time and of the treatment by Britain of the
black races. 'They know us chiefly by our crimes and our
cruelty.' Of the Europeans he wrote: 'Never was there a
race at once so egotistical and so terrible!' The criticism,
however, did not extend to Christian missionaries; where they
had been 'permitted to act for any length of time on the
aboriginal tribes, what happy results have followed'.
Howitt welcomed the dawn of a new era. There was no
doubt in his mind 'that by the mere exercise of common
honesty on the part of the whites, the greater part of all
these countries would now be civilised, and a tide of wealth
poured into Europe, such as the strongest imagination
can scarcely grasp; and that, too, purchased, not with the
blood and tears of the miserable, but by the moral elevation
and happiness of countless tribes'. He considered it no less
than 'a libel on the honour and faith of the nation to doubt
for a moment that a new era of colonisation and intercourse
with unlettered nations has commenced'.

Philanthropy, trade, a sense of mission, both religious
and cultural, racial arrogance and imperial aggrandisement
—all these provoked the colonial movement and in turn were
encouraged by it. The early abolitionists could justifiably

claim a major share in starting the movement; their descendants in administering the results.

> Queen of the Seas! enlarge thyself;
> . . . Be thou the hive of nations,
> And send thy swarms abroad!

exclaimed the poet Southey.[15] 'The British race would be heard upon every wind, coming in with mighty hurrahs, full of power and tumult . . . and crying aloud . . . to make ready their paths for them', wrote another Lake poet, De Quincey.[16] Coleridge, not to be outdone by his friends, is recorded in *Table Talk* as saying: 'Colonisation is not only a manifest expedient, but an imperative duty of Great Britain. God seems to hold out his finger to us over the sea.' They all had visions, as did Carlyle and other leading intellectuals of the day, of heroic white Englishmen, browned a mahogany tint, ruling in new climates. Not only did it satisfy a romantic ideal, it also helped to solve the pressing problem of what to do with all the potentially dangerous unemployed who roamed the streets of Britain's cities.

Though people from the upper and middle classes did not emigrate to the extent that the 'labouring poor' did, it was the middle class intellectuals who most encouraged the movement. Henry Fawcett, the blind professor of Political Economy at Cambridge and the Postmaster-General under William Gladstone, published *The Economic Position of the British Labourer* in 1865. In it he exclaimed, 'Emigration has achieved the great result of benefiting those who have left our shores, and at the same time has affected a marked improvement in the condition of our home population.' The reason for this was simple. 'If a man finds his labour is not wanted in one country, he ought not to stagnate there in hopeless poverty; there is placed before him in other lands a great and glorious career; a great career, because he may become the progenitor of mighty nations.' Looking back over the past century, Fawcett came to the conclusion that 'it is peculiarly the destined mission of our own country to become the mother of nations', and, echoing the abolitionists and missionaries, considered that 'the lot of the whole human race might be improved if inferior races were gradually enlightened and elevated by bringing them into contact with ideas and institutions of a high civilisation'.

By the 1880s the British Government had caught up with the demands for African colonisation, the final impetus being given by the realisation of its mineral wealth, and by the interest shown in the continent by other European Powers. The anti-slavery crusade had already secured for Britain a series of footholds along the west coast: Sierra Leone, which had been a colony since 1788 thanks chiefly to the efforts of Granville Sharp in the first instance, and to Zachary Macaulay and others of the philanthropic movement; Gambia in 1816, and the Gold Coast in 1821. But there was the east coast and the whole of the interior still open for exploitation, though it was not on this basis that the Government began diplomatic and other manœuvres to gain more territory. It borrowed from the philanthropists and used the slave trade and the supposed civilising effects of a British influence as its excuse.

Writing from the Berlin Conference in 1885 when West Africa was being divided up between the European Powers, the British Ambassador told the Foreign Secretary that England, 'by her successful efforts to stop the export of slaves beyond the seas, has been the chief benefactress of the natives', and accordingly, with Portugal, the other Power which had old settlements in Africa, she should 'endeavour to effect an arrangement in the interests of all'.[17] Ironically, then, two of the oldest and biggest slave-trading nations in the world were back in the business they knew best of all—exploiting the blacks.

In February 1855 the Ambassador wrote to the Foreign Secretary that the objection had been raised that while the interests of the traders were being carefully studied, the interests of the Africans were not, 'and the fear had been expressed that the welfare of the blacks may have been subordinated to the commercial wants of the whites. . . . If the present condition of the negro in the Congo were his highest happiness, it might be contended that he might not benefit by his contact with civilisation; but the inhabi-

tants of the districts of the Congo Basin can calculate on no
such existence; hanging over their lives is the constant
terror of the slave gang with all its attendant horrors. The
approach of civilising Powers brings them to safety.'

Earl Granville replied to the Ambassador on the achievements of the Berlin Conference in words which swept back
the years to the 1780s, to Clarkson and his Committee, to
Benezet and the Quakers, and to Wilberforce and his
fellow evangelical philanthropists of the Clapham Sect. Now
the words were not of a small though effective pressure
group; they were the words of the sovereign herself, Queen
Victoria. 'Her Majesty cannot doubt that the conclusions
thus arrived at will lead to the permanent advantage of
Africa, and she trusts that, while fresh markets will be
opened to the unrestricted commerce of all nations, the
blessings of Christianity and civilisation will be brought
nearer to the people of that continent.'[18]

The year before, on the 1st of August, a great meeting was
held at the Guildhall, London, under the presidency of
the Prince of Wales, to celebrate the jubilee of the coming
into force in 1834 of the Abolition of Slavery Act. Sons and
grandsons of the Clapham Sect and the leading abolitionsists
were well represented: Edward Lushington, son of Dr
Lushington who sat in parliament with Wilberforce and
Buxton during the crucial years of abolition and emancipation, Canon Wilberforce, William's son, Sir Sydney Buxton,
the grandson of Thomas Buxton, and the man who was later
to become the second Governor-General of South Africa,
following after Viscount Gladstone, the son of the slave
owner William Gladstone. Of Buxton, Field-Marshal
Smuts of South Africa said, 'Self-government in Rhodesia
was largely due to his favourable report, and time has
justified his wise advice.'[19] On the dais behind the Prince
of Wales were two busts, one of Granville Sharp and the
other of Thomas Clarkson. In front of them were placed a
set of slave chains brought back from Zanzibar, one of
Britain's latest colonial acquisitions.

The Prince repeated the hundred-year-old abolitionist
argument that the answer to slavery was civilisation, but it
was after the meeting that the secretary of the Anti-Slavery

Society, in an interview with the press, brought the situation up to date and in line with the realities of Britain's imperial expansion. He accepted the fact that soldiers, not missionaries were then the most important representatives of Britain in Africa. 'We do not seek to extend the sovereignty of England in the hope that the conqueror will prove the emancipator', he said on behalf of the Society. 'We only insist that when the soldier has made his conquests, the legislator shall not forget his responsibilities. In other words, that when England has exerted her power, she shall not neglect her duty. Our Society has been a sort of conscience to the empire, and it will be an evil day for the coloured man when England allows that conscience to be silenced by their neglect.'[20]

As things turned out, he was proved wrong. Notwithstanding the existence of the Society, the people of Africa for whose moral, spiritual and physical welfare it claimed exclusive responsibility were forced to suffer yet another seventy years. To suffer Britain's rapacity, and, in addition, to suffer its ostentatious but close-fisted philanthropy, its illiberal liberalism, its unequal notions of equality, and its unimaginative and insensitive humanitarianism.

In 1895 Mr Joseph Chamberlain, the nonconformist Colonial Secretary under Lord Salisbury, addressed parliament. To rousing cheers he told the House of Commons that a few years before the West African colonies were thought of as almost worthless possessions; but, he added, 'I believe at the present time the trade with those colonies alone is as much as that with some considerable European countries.' How happy Thomas Clarkson and his friends would have been to hear their theories vindicated. Their dreams of a regular trade with Africa had come true. But what would they have made of the rest of Mr Chamberlain's speech? 'No trade is possible as long as native disturbances are taking place, and when hon. Members, animated no doubt by philanthropic intentions, protest against the expeditions, punitive or otherwise, which are now the only way we can establish peace between contending tribes in Africa, they are protesting against the only system of civilising and practically of developing the trade of Africa.'[21]

Would the abolitionists of 1795 have cheered along with the Members of Parliament of 1895, or would they have realised that they had helped history to play on the Africans another cruel trick? They had been instrumental in substituting one kind of slavery for another. Their heirs, by distinguishing themselves in the colonial service, became the managers and the overseers for the new regime, assisting it to plunder the continent. The time had come for someone like Granville Sharp who had stood alone against the former slave masters to recall again the warning of his ancestor, Archbishop Sharp, spoken in parliament in 1679:

'I forsee the vengeance of God falling on this church and nation, this our England, which Jeshurun-like is waxed fat and grown proud, and has kicked against God.'[22]

The winds roared, and the rains fell
The poor white man, faint and weary,
Came and sat under our tree.
He has no mother to bring him milk;
No wife to grind his corn.
Let us pity the white man:
No mother has he.
    (*The African's Pity on the White Man*—
    F. H. Barthelemon and G. G. Ferrari, 1798)

Notes

Introduction
1. Sir Reginald Coupland, *The British Anti-Slavery Movement* (London 1933), 21.
2. Eric Williams, *Capitalism and Slavery* (London 1944, 1964), 98–107.
3. Martin Luther King, *Chaos or Community?* (London 1967), 38.
4. Leroi Jones, *Home* (London 1968), 111.
5. Ibid.
6. Kurt Godel's theorem quoted by Nigel Calder, *The Mind of Man* (London 1970), 263.
7. W. E. Lecky, *A History of England in the Eighteenth Century*, (London 1919).
8. Williams, op. cit.
9. Montesquieu, Charles Baron de, *De l'Esprit des Loix*. Oeuvres (Tome 1) (1758) Livre XV. c. V., 330.
10. Coupland, op. cit., 160–76.

Chapter 1
1. Minute Books of the Committee for the Abolition of the Slave Trade (British Museum); 3 vols.
2. Thomas Clarkson, *The History of the Rise, Progress, and Accomplishment of the Abolition of the African Slave Trade by the British Parliament* (London 1839), 65. See also, *Gentleman's Magazine*, XI (1741), 147.
3. *An Abolitionist, The Negro's Memorial or Abolitionist's Catechism* (London 1824), 3.
4. Ibid., 4.
5. Quoted by Edward Lascelles, *Granville Sharp* (London 1928), 9.
6. Ibid.
7. *State Trials*, XX, 80–2. *English Historical Documents* (London 1957), Vol. 10, 263–4.
8. For a discussion of Somersett's case and other cases involving black slaves in England, e.g. Cay vs. Chrichton, May 1773,

and Rogers vs. James, 1776, see Granville Sharp, *Essays* (London 1776), 72. See also Clarkson, op. cit., 66–72.

9. Anthony Benezet, *Thoughts on the Slavery of the Negroes* (London 1784).
10. Clarkson, op. cit., 138.
11. Ibid., 139.
12. Ibid., 143.
13. Ibid., 145.
14. Ibid., 240.
15. *Cobbett's Parliamentary History* (Referred to hereafter as *Parl. Hist.*) XXIII, 1026–7. June 17, 1783.
16. Minute Books of the Committee. July, August, 1787.
17. Ibid. July 1787.
18. Clarkson, op. cit., 177.
19. Letter to the Society for the Abolition of the Slave Trade (London 1787).
20. Clarkson, *An Essay of the Impolicy of the African Slave Trade* (London 1788), 88.
21. Ibid., 102
22. Lascelles, op. cit., 66–9.
23. J. Steven Watson, *The Reign of George III, 1760–1815. The Oxford University History of England* (Oxford 1960), Vol. 12, 324.
24. William Hunt, *The History of England, 1760–1801*, Vol. 10, 267.
25. Clarkson, *History*, 612.

Chapter 2

1. James Houston, *Some New and Accurate Observations of the Coast of Guinea* (London 1725), 43.
2. Malachy Postlethwayt, *The National and Private Advantages of the African Trade Considered* (London 1746), 1.
3. Ibid., 3.
4. Clarkson, *History*, op cit., 49.
5. Ibid., 48–53.
6. Sir Reginald Coupland, *The British Anti-slavery Movement*, op. cit., 18.
7. David Brion Davis, *The Problem of Slavery in Western Culture* (New York 1966), Chapter 6, 165–96.
8. Lecky, op. cit., Vol. 7, 367.
9. Williams, op. cit., 36. For details of the triangular trade and its effect on British commerce and industry, see Williams, Chapters 3 and 5.
10. *English Historical Documents, 1660–1714*, Vol. 8, 883.

11. Report of the Lords of the Committee of Council Appointed for the Consideration of All Matters Relating to the Trade and Foreign Plantations, 1788. Part 4, No. 14.

12. Basil Davidson, *Africa, History of a Continent* (London 1966), 225.

13. Coupland, op. cit., 21.

14. M. I. Finley, *Slavery in Classical Antiquity* (London 1964).

15. Davidson, op. cit.

16. 13 Geo. III. c. 14.

17. Bryan Edwards, *The History of the British Colonies in the West Indies* (London 1793), Vol. 2, 55–6.

18. Adam Smith, *An Inquiry into the Nature and Causes of The Wealth of Nations*, ed. Edwin Cannan (London 1950), Vol. 1, 364.

19. Ibid., 16

20. Ibid., Vol. 2, 234.

21. Williams, op. cit., 43.

22. John Wesley, *Thoughts Upon Slavery* (London 1774), 36–47.

23. Clarkson, *History*, op. cit., 91.

24. Ibid., 88.

25. Ibid., 101–7, 112–13.

26. Ibid., 90.

27. *The Case of Our Fellow Creatures, the oppressed Africans, respectively recommended to the serious consideration of the legislature of Great Britain by the people called Quakers* (London 1783), 4.

28. Davis, *The Problem of Slavery . . .*, 304–5. See also Williams, op. cit., 43–4.

29. Clarkson, op. cit., 118.

30. Anthony Benezet, *Thoughts on the Slavery of the Negroes*, 23–4.

31. Coupland, op. cit., 64.

32. Clarkson, op. cit., 614.

33. Book XII, lines 64–71.

34. Sharp, *Essays*, 20

Chapter 3

1. *Gentleman's Magazine*, LVIII (1788), 322.

2. *Parl. Hist.*, XXVII, c. 579. May 28, 1788.

3. *Gentleman's Magazine*, LXVIII (1798), 325.

4. *Parl. Hist.*, XXVII, c. 579–581.

5. Ibid., c. 583–4.

6. Ibid., c. 639–41. June 25, 1788.

7. 28 Geo. III. c. 54.

8. *Parl. Hist.*, XXVII, c. 575. Mr Hamilton. May 21, 1788.

9. Report of the Lords of the Committee of Council, op. cit.

10. Ibid., Part I. Government, Religion, Manners and Customs.
11. Ibid., Part II. A View of Evidence concerning the Manner of Carrying Slaves to the West Indies.
12. Ibid., Part III. A View of the Principles of the Slave Laws by Mr Reeves.

Chapter 4

1. Robert Isaac and Samuel Wilberforce, *The Life of William Wilberforce* (London 1863), 77–80.
2. Ibid., 79.
3. Ibid., 82.
4. Ibid., 2–5.
5. Ibid., 6.
6. Ibid., 11.
7. Report of the Lords . . . Part IV, No. 4.
8. See also, C. L. R. James, *The Black Jacobins* (New York 1963).
9. Sir Reginald Coupland, *Wilberforce* (London 1923), 93.
10. R. I. and S. Wilberforce, *Life*, 84–95.
11. *Parl. Hist.*, XXVIII, c. 41–67. May 12, 1789.
12. Minute Books of the Committee, op. cit., July 28, 1789.
13. John Newton, *An Authentic Narrative* (London 1764), 147.
14. Ibid., 174.
15. Ibid., 192.
16. *Dictionary of National Biography* (London 1894), Vol. 40, 398. In 1806, when his friend and biographer, Richard Cecil, entreated the almost blind Newton to give up preaching, Newton replied, 'I cannot stop. What! Shall the old African blasphemer stop while he can speak?'
17. J. S. A., *The Slave and the Preacher* (London 1851).
18. Wilberforce, *Life*, op. cit., 48.
19. John Newton, *Thoughts Upon the Slave Trade* (London 1788).
20. Wilberforce, *Life*, op. cit., 48.
21. Sir Leslie Stephen, *History of English Thought in the Eighteenth Century* (London 1876), Vol. 2, Chapter XII, Secs. 106–12. See also, Elie Halévy, *History of the English People in the Nineteenth Century* (London 1924–49), Vol. I, 389–421.
22. Robert Isaac and Samuel Wilberforce, *The Correspondence of William Wilberforce* (London 1840), Vol. II, 141.
23. Coupland, *The British Anti-Slavery Movement*, 76–81; Coupland, *Wilberforce*, 248–52.
24. N. G. Annan, *The Intellectual Aristocracy; Studies in Social History*, edited by J. H. Plumb (London 1955).
25. Because of the extent of his influence, Stephen was some-

times referred to by the sobriquet of Mr 'Oversecretary' Stephen.

26. In a letter to his sister of October 18, 1793, Wilberforce wrote: 'I don't say it lightly; I believe the contempt into which the sabbath has fallen, bids fair to accelerate the ruin both of church and state more than any other single circumstance whatever.' Wilberforce, *Correspondence*, Vol. 1, 101.

27. Muriel Jaeger, *Before Victoria* (London 1956), 16.

28. Wilberforce, *Correspondence*, 130.

Chapter 5

 1. *Gentleman's Magazine*, LIX (1789), 553.
 2. Clarkson, *History*, 322.
 3. *Parl. Hist.*, XXVIII, c. 713. Lord Penryhn. April 23, 1790.
 4. Ibid., XXVII, c. 643. June 25, 1788.
 5. Clarkson, op. cit., 415.
 6. Ibid., 417.
 7. Ibid., 416.
 8. William Fox, *An Address to the People of Great Britain on the propriety of abstaining from West India Sugar and Rum* (London 1791).
 9. Clarkson, op. cit., 495–6.
10. Wilberforce, *Life*, 151.
11. Clarkson, op. cit., 613.
12. *Parl. Hist.*, XXIX, c. 335–43. April 19, 1791.
13. Ibid., c. 354.
14. Ibid., c. 358.
15. Ibid., c. 250–86.
16. Ibid., c. 358. Mr William Drake.
17. Ibid., c. 1073. April 2, 1792.

Chapter 6

 1. Edward Long, *The History of Jamaica* (London 1774), Vol. 2, 267.
 2. Ibid., 269.
 3. Ibid., 270.
 4. Edwards, op. cit., Vol. 2, 35.
 5. *Thoughts on the Necessity of Improving the Condition of Slaves in the British Colonies, with a view to their ultimate Emancipation; and on the practicability, the safety, and the advantages of the latter measure.*
 6. *Parl. Hist.*, XXVIII, c. 49.
 7. William Wilberforce, *An Appeal to the Religion, Justice and*

Humanity of the Inhabitants of the British Empire in behalf of the Negro Slaves in the West Indies (London 1823).

8. Minute Books of the Committee. June 25, 1795.

9. *Hansard*, Second Series, IX, c. 258. May 15, 1823.

10. Wilberforce, *An Appeal . . .*, 74.

11. Sir Lewis Namier, *Crossroads of Power* (London 1962), 174.

12. Elizabeth Coltman, *Immediate, not Gradual Emancipation* (London 1824), 30.

13. Quoted by James M'Queen in *The West India Colonies, the calumnies and misrepresentations circulated against them by the Edinburgh Review, Mr Clarkson, Mr Cropper etc; examined and refuted* (London 1824), 380.

14. October 1817. Wilberforce, *Correspondence*, 382.

15. *The West Indies. Annual Register*, 1810, 725–30.

16. Lowell Joseph Ragatz, *The Fall of the Planter Class in the British Caribbean, 1763–1833* (New York 1928), 267.

17. Polinus, *Thoughts on the Abolition of the Slave Trade, considered chiefly in a prudential and political view. Gentleman's Magazine*, LVIII (1788), 407.

18. Written anonymously by A Country Gentleman (London 1792).

19. *Parl. Hist.*, XXXII, c. 880. Henry Dundas. March 15, 1796. '. . . if we abandoned our colonies, America could take them under her protection. . . . The Americans could scarcely fail to avail themselves of that occurrence, and incorporate or ally themselves with the colonies.'

20. Quoted by Lady Holland, Viscountess Knutsford in her biography of her grandfather, *Life and Letters of Zachary Macaulay* (London 1900), 258n. Lady Holland, daughter of Sir Charles Trevelyan, was the second wife of Sir Henry Holland, Secretary of State for the Colonies, 1888–92.

Chapter 7

1. In a letter from Fox to Richard Fitzpatrick, his close friend and political ally, July 30, 1789.

2. Clarkson, op. cit., 382.

3. Watson, op. cit. See also, Asa Briggs, *The Age of Improvement, 1783–1867* (London 1969).

4. Briggs, ibid., 133.

5. Clarkson, op. cit., 426.

6. 1801. R. Brimley Johnson (ed.), *The Letters of Hannah More* (London 1925).

7. *A very new Pamphlet indeed! Being the truth addressed to the people at large containing some strictures on the English Jacobins.*

8. *Parl. Hist.*, XXXI, c. 467. May 2, 1794.

9. Ibid., XXXII, c. 292–5. November 10, 1795.

10. *Gentleman's Magazine* LXXIX (1809), 1149.

11. *Annual Register*, 1792, 128–9.

12. For a full and fascinating account of the history of San Domingo, see C. L. R. James, *The Black Jacobins*, op. cit.

13. 'Thomas Clarkson's letter explaining the causes of insurrection in San Domingo printed—1000 copies.' Minutes of the Committee. February 14, 1792.

14. Henry Brougham, *An Inquiry into the Colonial Policy of the European Powers* (Edinburgh and London 1803), Vol. 2, 308–9; Vol. 1, 506: 'Men who have been long accustomed to servitude and dependence are unfit for liberty suddenly acquired.'

15. 1798. Quoted by Knutsford, op. cit., 217.

16. Minute Books of the Committee. January 31, 1792.

17. Ibid., April 10, 1792.

18. Ibid., May 6, 1794.

19. Ibid., March 29, 1797. 'Meeting resolved to repel injurious charges by Bryan Edwards in his History of San Domingo.' April 12, 1797. 'Resolved to publish letter in newspapers refuting Bryan Edwards's charges.'

Chapter 8

1. *Pity for Poor Africans* (1788). One of the shortest and sharpest literary attacks on Britain's hypocrisy over the slave-trade issue. The opening verses read:

I own I am shock'd at the purchase of slaves,
And fear those who buy them and sell them are knaves,
What I hear of their hardships, their tortures and groans,
Is almost enough to draw pity from stones.

I pity them greatly, but I must be mum,
For how could we do without sugar and rum?
Especially sugar, so needful we see?
What? give up our desserts, our coffee and tea?

Besides, if we do, the French, Dutch and Danes,
Will heartily thank us, no doubt, for our pains;
If we do not buy the poor creatures they will,
And tortures and groans will be multiplied still.

2. *Parl. Hist.*, XXIX, c. 1133–58. April 2, 1792. 10,000 copies

of the speech were published by the Abolition Committee in June 1792.

3. Coupland, op. cit., 99–100. See also Lecky, Vol. 5, 341.
4. *Dictionary of National Biography*, Vol. 16, 190.
5. *Parl. Hist.*, XXIX, c. 1104–10. April 2, 1792.
6. Ibid., c. 1114.
7. Ibid., c. 1110. Mr Henry Addington (The Speaker; later Viscount Sidmouth).
8. Williams, op. cit., 147.
9. Ibid., 148. See also, Lecky, op. cit., 342.
10. December 23, 1823. Knutsford, op. cit., 414.
11. Wilberforce, *Life*, 178.
12. *Parl. Hist.*, XXXVI, c. 882. May 27, 1802.
13. Knutsford, op. cit., 218.
14. J. W. Fortescue, *A History of the British Army* (London 1906), Vol. 4, 546. The cost of San Domingo had risen steadily from £300,000 in 1794 to close upon £800,000 in 1795, to more than two millions in 1796, and to £700,000 for the month of January 1797 alone.
15. *Parl. Hist.*, XXXII, c. 752. February 18, 1796.
16. Ibid., XXXIII, c. 581. The hon. Andrew St. John. May 18, 1797.
17. Ibid., c. 581–7.
18. Ibid., c. 586–7.
19. 39 Geo. III. c. 80
20. *Parl. Hist.*, XXXIV, c. 1092–1105. July 5, 1799.
21. Ibid., c. 526. March 1, 1799.
22. Ibid., c. 530. Mr John Dent.
23. Ibid., XXXII, 949. Mr. Philip Francis. April 11, 1796.
24. Lecky, op. cit., 344.
25. Wilberforce, *Correspondence*, Vol. 1, 266.
26. Minute Books of the Committee. June 25, 1795.

Chapter 9
1. Michel Adanson, *A Voyage to Senegal, the Isle of Goree, and the River Gambia.*
2. Ibid., Introduction, vii.
3. Ibid., 53.
4. James Montgomery in his poem, *The West Indies, Annual Register*, 1810, 726 on.
5. Adanson, op. cit., 42.
6. Mungo Park, *Travels in the Interior Districts of Africa in the Years 1795, 1796 and 1797* (London 1799), Vol. 1, 280.
7. Ibid., 311.

8. Houston, *Some Observations* . . ., 27.

9. Long, *The History of Jamaica*, Vol. 2, 353.

10. Ibid., 383.

11. James Montgomery, op. cit., *Description of Africa and the Negro*, 726.

12. Ibid., 730.

13. *The Anti-Slavery Album* (London 1828).

14. *Gentleman's Magazine* LXI (1791), 1046.

15. Thomas Day and John Bicknell, *The Dying Negro* (London 1793).

16. *Oroonoko: or the History of the Royal Slave* (London 1688).

17. The play first appeared at the Drury Lane Theatre in 1695, and thereafter almost continually in one theatre or another throughout the eighteenth century. In 1795 David Garrick played the role of Oroonoko for the first time. Alterations were made later to the text by Dr Hawksworth and Francis Gentleman. See *The London Stage* (Southern Illinois University Press, 1965) Part 1, 454–5.

18. *Gentleman's Magazine* LXVIII (1788), 598.

Chapter 10

1. Minute Books of the Committee. May 23, 1804.

2. Knutsford, op. cit., 312.

3. Ibid., 14 on.

4. Sir George Stephen, *Antislavery Recollections* (London 1854), 50. The book was in the form of a series of letters addressed to Mrs Harriet Beecher Stowe, author of *Uncle Tom's Cabin*, in response to her request for a history of the abolition of slavery in Britain.

5. *Cobbett's Parliamentary Debates* (Referred to hereafter as *Parl. Deb.*) II, c. 440–459. May 30, 1804.

6. Ibid., 463. Mr J. F. Barham.

7. Watson, op. cit., 332–6, 504–16, for a summary of the industrial and technological advances made in the last two decades of the eighteenth century and the early part of the nineteenth century. As it affected Britain's relationship with the West Indies, see also Williams, op. cit., Chapter 7, 126–134.

8. Sir Llewellyn Woodward, *The Age of Reform, 1815–70. The Oxford University History of England* (Oxford 1962), Vol. 13, 44.

9. *Parl. Deb.* II, c. 780. June 20, 1804.

10. Ibid., c. 926–33. July 3, 1804.

11. Ibid., III, c. 521. February 15, 1805.

12. Ibid., c. 673. February 28, 1805.
13. Minute Books of the Committee. July 9, 1805.
14. Wilberforce, *Life*, 332. See also, Lecky, op. cit., Vol. 5, 341.
15. Wilberforce, *Correspondence*, Vol. 2, 74. The letter was written to the Reverend Thomas Gisborne in February 1806. Gisborne was one of the founder members of the Clapham Sect and was married to Thomas Babington's sister.
16. 46 Geo. III. c. 52.
17. *Parl. Deb.*, VIII, c. 431. January 12, 1807.
18. Ibid., c. 672.
19. Ibid., c. 717.
20. Wilberforce, *Correspondence*, Vol. 2, 114.
21. *Parl. Deb.*, VIII, c. 994. February 23, 1807.
22. Ibid., c. 995.
23. 47 Geo. III. c. 36.
24. George Stephen, op. cit., 3.
25. *Parl. Deb.*, VIII, c. 977. Sir John Doyle. February 23, 1807.
26. Ibid., c. 692. February 6, 1807.
27. Knutsford, op. cit., 297. April 5, 1813.
28. Wilberforce, *Correspondence*, Vol, 2, 115. February 24, 1807.
29. Clarkson, *History*, 614.
30. Knutsford, op. cit., 269.
31. *Parl. Deb.*, IX, c. 142. March 17, 1807.
32. Both the slaves and the planters in the West Indies used this nickname for Wilberforce, the former with affection, the latter with contempt. See *Parl. Deb.*, c. 780. 'Mr John Fuller said the blacks thought that "Massa King Wilbee" meant to free them.' June 20, 1804.
33. *Parl. Deb.*, IX, c. 146. March 17, 1807.

Chapter 11

1. *Hansard*, New Series, VIII, c. 729–32. March 26, 1823. See also, Jaeger, op. cit., 102.
2. Coupland, *Wilberforce*, 284.
3. *The Spirit of the Age* (London 1825), 330.
4. Wilberforce, *Life*, 379. 'He now became involved with a multitude of other useful efforts or benevolent designs.'
5. Coupland, op. cit., 385.
6. April 22, 1921. Wilberforce, *Correspondence*, Vol, 2, 447.
7. *Hansard*, New Series, XXVI, c. 831–72. June 22, 1813.
8. Wilberforce, *Correspondence*, Vol. 1. 353–95.
9. Knutsford, op. cit., 368.
10. Clarkson, *History*, 3–6.

11. Henry Russell and Angus B. Reach, *Negro Life*. Musical Bouquet No. 34 (London 1835).
12. William Law Mathieson, *British Slavery and its Abolition, 1823-38* (London 1926), 21-6.
13. *The Edinburgh Review* (1811), XVIII, 308.
14. *Parl. Deb.*, XVII, c. 658-75. June 15, 1810.
15. Ibid., c. 681.
16. Ibid., c. 676.
17. 5 Geo. IV. c. 13.
18. 51 Geo. III. c. 23.
19. Report of the Committee of the African Institution, Rules and Regulations, July 1807.
20. *The Edinburgh Review and the West Indies* (Glasgow 1816), Letter 39.
21. Wilberforce, *Life*, 388.

Chapter 12

1. Davis, *The Problem of Slavery* . . . op. cit., Chapter 3. Slavery and Sin: The Ancient Legacy, 62-90.
2. *Scriptural Researches on the Licitness of the Slave Trade, showing its conformity with the principles of natural and revealed religion, delineated in the Sacred Writings of the Word of God. To which are added Scriptural Directions for the Proper Treatment of Slaves* (Liverpool 1788).
3. *Essays* (London 1776).
4. Ibid., 33.
5. Ibid., 66.
6. In a number of statements Sharp was ahead of his time. In a letter to a 'gentleman at Philadelphia' quoted in the Essays, he outlined his scheme for the abolition of slavery which incorporated a form of apprenticeship not unlike that which was eventually passed by the British parliament in 1833,
7. *Gentleman's Magazine*, XI (1741), 147.
8. *The Bishop of London's Letter to the Masters and Mistresses of Families in English Plantations Abroad* (London 1727).
9. William Warburton, *A Sermon before the Society for the Propagation of the Gospel*, February 21, 1766.
10. Mathieson, op. cit., 216n. In 1829, six years after its abolition was recommended by parliament, the Codrington estate admitted to the use of whips to drive the slaves to work.
11. Wesley, *Thoughts* . . ., 30.
12. Benezet, op. cit., 27.
13. Privy Council Report, op. cit., Part III.

14. Quoted by Sir George Rose, *Letter on the Means and Importance of Converting Slaves to Christianity* (London 1823).
15. Ibid.
16. Long, op. cit., Vol. 2, 238.
17. James M'Queen, *The West India Colonies*, 275.
18. Gilbert Mathison, *A Short Review of the Reports of the African Institution* (1816).
19. Robert Young, *A View of Slavery* (Jamaica 1824, London 1825), 18.
20. Ibid., 22–32.
21. E. P. Thompson, *The Making of the English Working Class* (London 1963), Chapter XI. The Transforming Power of the Cross, 250–375.
22. Ibid., 353.
23. Edward Eliot, *Christianity and Slavery: a course of lectures preached at the Cathedral and Parish Church of St Michael, Barbados* (London 1833), 87.

Chapter 13

1. Clarkson, op. cit., 3. 'Mr Stephen and others, at first deemed the certainty of the Act passed in 1807 being evaded under the stimulus and the insurance against capture afforded by the enormous profits of the traffic so clear that they expected the law to become, almost from the time of its being enacted, a dead letter. There soon appeared the strongest reasons to concur in this opinion.'
2. James Ramsay, *An Essay on the Treatment and Conversion of African Slaves in the British Sugar Colonies* (London 1784), 69 on.
3. Ragatz, op. cit., 399–402. Stephen, op. cit., 11–17.
4. Stephen, op. cit., 20–38.
5. *Hansard*, XXVII, c. 637. May 2, 1814.
6. *Annual Register*, 1815, 358–60; Ibid., 1816, 356.
7. *Hansard*, XXXIII, c. 526. March 22, 1816.
8. Ibid., c. 528.
9. Ibid., XXXIV, c. 1170. Mr C. N. Pallmer. June 19, 1816.
10. Ibid., c. 1190–1210. Mr J. F. Barham.
11. Ibid., c. 1210–18.
12. Ibid., c. 1224. Mr William Manning.
13. Ibid., XL, c. 977. Mr H. Goulbourn. June 8, 1819.
14. Ibid., XXXVIII, c. 310. April 22, 1818.
15. 59 Geo. III. c. 120.
16. *Hansard*, op. cit., XXXVIII, c. 298.

17. Stephen, op. cit., 21.
18. Clarkson, op. cit., 73.
19. *Hansard*, New Series, VII, c. 1785. July 25, 1822.
20. M'Queen, op. cit., 244.
21. *Hansard*, New Series, VII, c. 624–30. March 18, 1823.
22. Stephen, op. cit., 224–5.
23. Coupland, *Wilberforce*, 471.
24. Jaeger, op. cit., 139.
25. *Hansard*, New Series, IX, c. 258–87. May 15, 1823.
26. Ibid., c. 347. Mr A. Baring.
27. Ibid., c. 298.
28. Ibid., c. 275–87.
29. Stephen, op. cit., 64.
30. Knutsford, op. cit., 445. 1827.

Chapter 14

1. December 6, 1823.
2. February 10, 1824.
3. For a report of Smith's trial, etc., see House of Commons, Session Papers, Vol. 23, 1824, 373–601.
4. *The Times*. March 20, 1824.
5. James Montgomery, *The West Indies*, op. cit., 726.
6. *The Times*. March 16, 1824.
7. Session Papers, op. cit., 525.
8. The report of the meeting appears as an appendix to Robert Young's, *A View of Slavery*, op. cit.
9. Ragatz, op. cit., 431–3. See also *Hansard*, New Series, XIII, c. 1285–1311. Thomas Fowell Buxton. June 23, 1825.
10. Session Papers, op. cit., 403–417.
11. Hansard, New Series, XIII, c. 1302.
12. Knutsford, op. cit., 332. September 1816.
13. July 1816.
14. An Examination of the Report of the Berbice Commissioners (London 1817).
15. The circular from the Colonial Office dated May 24, 1823 and signed by Earl Bathurst reads: 'I am aware that a necessity may exist for retaining the punishment of flogging with respect to males, though, at the same time, it should be subject to defined regulations and restrictions; but as an immediate measure I cannot too strongly recommend that the whip should no longer be carried into the field, and there displayed by the driver as the emblem of his authority, or employed as the ready instrument of his displeasure.
16. *Annual Register*, 1824, 166.

17. Wilberforce, *Life*, 511.
18. In a letter to T. F. Buxton, November 1823. Knutsford, op. cit., 394.
19. Clarkson, *History*, op. cit., 14.
20. *Hansard*, New Series, XI, c. 961–99. June 1, 1824.
21. *Hansard*, New Series, XIII, c. 1285. March 1825.
22. History may not repeat itself, but it certainly has a curious way of appearing to do so. Parallels can be drawn between the events in the colonies during the 1820s and events in southern Africa today. The persecution of Smith and Shrewsbury is not very different in quality from the recent attacks by South African and Rhodesian authorities on Anglican and Roman Catholic churches; nor is the reaction in Britain to those attacks very different from the reaction of the British press to the colonial persecutions in the 1820s. Just as slaves were executed in the colonies for rebelling against their white masters without much fuss being made of the fact in the British press, so, too, have many Africans been dealt with in a similar fashion for their struggle for freedom without any noticeable reaction in Britain. However, when a white man in South Africa, like the Dean of Johannesburg, is giving a gaol sentence of five years for aiding families who have fallen foul of the police, the press express the same horror and indignation as they did 150 years ago. 'The Dean [of Johannesburg] is a man of the church in a country where the acts of government run directly counter to the doctrines his church teaches', said an editorial in *The Times* of November 2, 1971. 'The trial has been an attempt to portray the Dean as a very different kind of man, as an advocate of sabotage and violent revolution.' *The Times* also saw a 'resurgence of the old struggle between a conscientious liberalism that springs from British humanitarianism and Krugerism as the essence of Afrikanerdom'. (November 20, 1971).

Chapter 15

1. Prompt edition by Thomas Dibdin, prompter of Theatre Royal, Drury Lane (London 1815).
2. *Songs of Charles Dibdin* (London 1842). Despite a huge fortune made during his lifetime, Dibdin died a bankrupt.
3. Songs, ibid.
4. *Gentleman's Magazine*, LXIII (1793), 749.
5. *The London Mathews* (London 1823), 18–26.
6. In 1791 Blake provided sixteen plates for J. G. Steadman's,

A Narrative of a Five Year's Expedition against the Revolted Negroes of Surinam, in Guiana, on the Wild Coast of South America; from the years 1772–1777 (London 1796), showing the cruelties of the slave owners and the contrasting dignity of the suffering slaves.
7. Act 1. Scene 1.

Chapter 16

1. Coupland, *Wilberforce*, 423.
2. *The Times.* May 2, 1825.
3. The motion of thanks was proposed by William Smith and seconded by Thomas Fowell Buxton.
4. *Immediate, not Gradual Abolition* (London 1824), 15–25.
5. Wilberforce, *Correspondence*, Vol. 2, 501.
6. The Calne Society. Quoted by the anonymous author of *Letters to the More Influential Classes*; see below.
7. The full title is *Letters to the More Influential Classes on the Necessity of a prompt extinction of British Colonial Slavery.* I have not been able to trace the author of this important pamphlet.
8. Stephen, op. cit., 227–8.
9. Ibid., 223.
10. Lascelles, op. cit., 79.
11. Coupland, *Wilberforce*, 421.
12. *The Spirit of the Age* (London 1825), 324–30.
13. Coupland, op. cit., 176.
14. Stephen, op. cit., 790n.
15. Briggs, op. cit., quotes a children's poem of 1855 that expressed this view so well:

> I thank the goodness and the grace
> Which on my birth have smiled,
> And made me in these Christian days,
> A happy English child.

16. Stephen, op. cit., 98.
17. Woodward, op. cit., 69–77.
18. *Hansard*, New Series, XVIII, c. 979. March 5, 1828.
19. Ibid., XIX, c. 1779. July 25, 1818.
20. Ibid., XXI, c. 1774. June 5, 1829.
21. Ibid., c. 1746.
22. Stephen, op. cit., 77–8.

Chapter 17

1. *Hansard*, New Series, XI, c. 998. June 1, 1824.

2. T. S. Winn, *Emancipation, or practical advice to British Slave-Holders, with suggestions for the General Improvement of West India Affairs* (London 1824), 107.

3. *Hansard*, New Series, XII, c. 1111. March 21, 1825.

4. Smith, op. cit., Vol. 2, 93.

5. Ibid., 159.

6. Klause E. Knorr, *British Colonial Theories, 1570–1850* (Toronto 1944, London 1963), 317–25.

7. Ragatz, op. cit., 411.

8. Ibid., 434.

9. V. T. Harlow, *The New Imperial System, 1783–1815. The Cambridge History of the British Empire* (1940), Vol. 2, 163.

10. *Parl. Deb.*, XXI, c. 278. January 22, 1812.

11. For a summary of the complex battle between the West Indian monopolists and the English sugar refiners who were fighting for cheaper sugar, see Williams, op. cit., 163–6.

12. *Hansard*, New Series, XXII, c. 849. Mr Keith Douglas. February 23, 1830.

13. Ibid., c. 853. Mr Ralph Bernal.

14. *Hansard*, Third Series, II, c. 787. February 21, 1830.

15. *An Impartial Review of the question pending between Great Britain and her West Indian Colonies respecting the abolition of Negro Slavery, by a Resident and Proprietor in the West Indies* (1824).

16. Winn, op. cit., 106–7.

17. A West-India Fortune (London 1950), 265.

18. *Hansard*, New Series, XV, c. 203. April 14, 1826.

19. *Hansard*, Third Series, III, c. 1135. March 29, 1831.

20. Ibid, VIII, c. 176. October 6, 1831.

21. 2 & 3 Will. IV. c. 125.

22. *The Times*, April 6, 1832.

23. *Hansard*, Third Series, XVIII, c. 551. June 10, 1833.

24. Ibid., c. 548. Edward Stanley.

Chapter 18

1. *The Times*. May 17, 1830.

2. Stephen, op. cit., 127.

3. Ibid., 129.

4. *Hansard*, Third Series, XXV, c. 1126–1230. Mr. Otway Cave. July 13, 1830.

5. Stephen, op. cit., 130–58.

6. Ibid., 75.

7. Ibid., 148.

8. Ibid., 162.

9. Ibid., 154.
10. Ibid., 156–7. July 16, 1832.
11. Ragatz, op. cit., 444.
12. *Narrative of Certain events connected with the late disturbances in Jamaica and the charges preferred against the Baptist Missionaries in that Island* (London 1832).
13. Knutsford, op. cit., 470.
14. London 1833.
15. Mathieson, op. cit., 230.
16. Ibid.
17. Stephen, op. cit., 167.
18. Ibid., 168. 'I looked back to those days as providing some of the "finest fun" that I ever enjoyed.' But Macaulay's grand-daughter writes: 'Macaulay's patience was a good deal exercised by the vagaries of the Agency Committee, but although he was occasionally the object of most unwarrantable and ungrateful attacks from some of their number, yet most of these ardent younger spirits regarded him with respect, amounting to veneration.' Knutsford, op. cit., 467.
19. Knutsford, ibid., 469. August 26, 1832.
20. Stephen. op. cit., 168.
21. Mathieson, op. cit., 227.
22. Henry Richard, *Memoirs of Joseph Sturge* (London 1864), 101–2.

Chapter 19

1. Richard, op. cit., 104–5.
2. Winn, op. cit., 108.
3. Stephen, op. cit., 198.
4. *Hansard*, Third Series, XVI, c. 826. March 19, 1833.
5. Ibid., XVII, c. 1193 on.
6. Ibid., c. 1231 on.
7. Ibid., XVIII, c. 238.
8. Ibid., c. 527.
9. Ibid., c. 531. June 10, 1833.
10. Ibid., c. 541.
11. Ibid., c. 552. Mr Gisborne.
12. Ibid., XIX, c. 1186. July 24, 1833.
13. Ibid., c. 1218.
14. Ibid., c. 1066–9.
15. Ibid., XVIII, c. 339–57. June 3, 1833.
16. Ibid., c. 531. Mr Slaney. June 10, 1833.
17. *Parl. Hist.*, XXIX, c. 274 on. April 18, 1791.

18. *Hansard,* Third Series, XIX, c. 1208. July 24, 1833.
19. Ibid., c. 1231 on. July 25, 1833.
20. Ibid., XVIII, c. 472–85. June 7, 1933.
21. Ibid., c. 308–18. June 3, 1833.
22. Stephen, op. cit., 204.
23. Coupland, *Wilberforce,* op. cit., 493.
24. Wilberforce, *Life,* 562.
25. 3 & 4 Will. IV. c. 73.
26. Richard, op. cit., 119.

Chapter 20

1. *Christian Responsibilities arising out of the recent change in our West India Colonies* (London 1836) Discourses 1 and 3
2. Pares, op. cit., 318.
3. Williams, op. cit., 43.
4. House of Commons. Session Papers, 1837–8, Vol. 48, 329–695, for full details of compensation payments in all the relevant British colonies.
5. Report of the Select Committee appointed to Inquire into the working of the Apprenticeship System in the Colonies. Parliamentary Papers, 1837, Vol. 7, 745.
6. Richard, op. cit., 121.
7. *The West Indies in 1837, being the Journal of a Visit by Joseph Sturge and Thomas Harvey* (London 1837), 187–91.
8. Mathieson, op. cit., 283–5.
9. *Hansard,* Third Series, XLII, c.1. March 29, 1838.
10. Ibid., c. 5.
11. Ibid., c. 190–208. March 30, 1838.
12. Ibid., XLIII, c. 87.
13. Richard, op. cit., 171.
14. *Hansard,* op. cit., XLIII, c. 149. May 24, 1838.
15. Mathieson, op. cit., 300.
16. *Britain and West Africa* (London 1946. New Edition, Texas 1962).
17. Williams, op. cit., 28–9.

Chapter 21

1. Richard, op. cit., 186.
2. Minutes of the Committee. July 5, 1787. After his victory in the Somersett case in 1772, Granville Sharp began a correspondence with Anthony Benezet which continued for many years.
3. Minutes, ibid. January 15, 1788.

4. *Gentleman's Magazine*, LVIII (1788), 112.
5. Ibid., LXVII (1798), 41.
6. Lecky, op. cit., Vol. 7, 362 on.
7. See above. *The London Mathews*, 20.
8. Thomas Day, *Fragments of a Letter on the Slavery of Negroes* (1776), published as an appendix to the 1793 edition of *The Dying Negro*.
9. *Diary of Cotton Mather, 1709–1724. Massachusetts Historical Society Collections*, Seventh Series (1912). Vol. VIII, 412.
10. Long, op. cit., Vol. 2, 270.
11. Coupland, op. cit., 167 on.
12. Richard, op. cit., 176.
13. Edward Eliot, *Christian Responsibilities . . .*, Discourse 5.
14. Richard, op. cit., 227.
15. Ibid., 245.
16. Ibid., 362.
17. Ibid.
18. Ibid., 391.
19. Clarkson, *Letters on the Slave Trade*. To William Dawes, October 1839.
20. *Gentleman's Magazine*, XXV (1775), 30.
21. Clarkson, *Essay on the Impolicy . . .*, 34.
22. January 30, 1857. Williams, op. cit., 176.

Chapter 22
1. Adanson, op. cit., 55.
2. Ibid., 42.
3. *Essays, Moral, Political and Literary*, 1748 (1875 edition), Vol. 1, 252 n.
4. Quoted in *Gentleman's Magazine*, XLI (1771), 595.
5. Report of the Committee of the African Institution. July, 1807.
6. Long, op. cit., Vol. 2, 381.
7. An anonymous poem entitled 'The African's Complaint on Board a Slave Ship'. *Gentleman's Magazine*, LXIII (1793), 749.
8. Ibid., LXXXIII (1813), 490.
9. See Otto Klineberg, *Social Psychology* (New York 1962); *Race and Psychology* (UNESCO 1951): Ruth Benedict, *Race and Racism* (London 1942), etc.
10. Long, op. cit., 383.
11. Ibid., 354.
12. Ibid., 374.
13. *Gentleman's Magazine*, LXXXIII (1813), 659.

14. Ibid., XXVIII (1758), 221.
15. Long, op. cit., 352.
16. Ibid., 353.
17. Ibid., 360.
18. Ibid., 364.
19. Ibid., 383.
20. Ibid., 381.
21. George Pinckard, *Notes on the West Indies* (London 1806, 1816).
22. James Stephen, see below
23. Pinckard, op. cit., 117.
24. Ibid., 358.
25. Ibid., 528.
26. Ibid., 531.
27. James Stephen, *The Slavery of the West India Colonies Delineated* (London 1824). The book was sponsored by the London Society for Mitigating and Gradually Abolishing Slavery throughout the British Dominions.
28. Ibid., Vol. 1, 30–1.
29. *Colonial Policy*, op. cit., Vol. 2, 120.
30. Ibid., 301–2.
31. Edwards, *History*, op. cit., Vol. 2, 27–33.
32. First published in *Fraser's Magazine*; the extracts are from the 1858 Chapman and Hall edition of *Critical Essays*, Vol. 14.
33. Coupland, *Wilberforce*, 115.
34. Ramsay, op. cit., 218.
35. *Parl. Deb.*, III, c. 673. February 28, 1805.
36. *Hansard*, New Series, VII, c. 1785. July 25, 1822.
37. Wilberforce, *An Appeal . . .*, 73.
38. Richard, op. cit., 202.
39. *On the Nigger Question*, op. cit.

Chapter 23
1. *Parl. Deb.*, VII, c. 993. February 23, 1807.
2. *The Cambridge History of the British Empire*, Vol. VIII, 301–23.
3. *Hansard*, New Series, XVI, c. 317. December 7, 1826.
4. Ibid., c. 298.
5. Woodward, *The Age of Reform*, op. cit., 601. The number of people born in the United Kingdom and resident in the U.S. was 1,364,986 in 1850; in 1860 it was 2,224,743.
6. Minute Books of the Committee. January 15, 1788.
7. *Parl. Hist.*, XXIX, c. 1157. April 2, 1792.
8. Report of the Committee of the African Institution.
9. Parliamentary Papers, Vol. VII, 1836.

10. *Gentleman's Magazine,* LXXX (1810), 562–3.

11. *The African Slave Trade and its Remedy* (London 1840).

12. Coupland, op. cit., 160–80.

13. *Hansard,* Third Series, LXXXI, c. 1156–74. June 24, 1845.

14. Stephen, *A Letter to Lord John Russell* (London 1840).

15. Quoted in Knorr, op. cit., 398.

16. Ibid., 400.

17. *British Parliamentary Papers Relating to Africa, 1802–1899* (Irish University Press Series), Vol. 8, 258.

18. Ibid., 259.

19. *Dictionary of National Biography, 1931–40* (London 1949), 132.

20. *Report of the Anti-Slavery Jubilee* (1884).

21. *Hansard,* Fourth Series, XXXVI, c. 642. August 22, 1895.

22. Sharp, *Essays,* op. cit., 41.

Index

Compiled by the author